Archaeological Approaches to the Present

Models for Reconstructing the Past

STUDIES IN ARCHEOLOGY

Consulting Editor: Stuart Struever

Department of Anthropology
Northwestern University
Evanston, Illinois

Archaeological Approaches to the Present
Models for Reconstructing the Past

JOHN E. YELLEN

National Museum of Natural History
Smithsonian Institution
Washington, D.C.

Academic Press   NEW YORK   SAN FRANCISCO   LONDON
A Subsidiary of Harcourt Brace Jovanovich, Publishers

ACADEMIC PRESS, INC.
111 Fifth Avenue, New York, New York 10003

United Kingdom Edition published by
ACADEMIC PRESS, INC. (LONDON) LTD.
24/28 Oval Road, London NW1

Library of Congress Cataloging in Publication Data

Yellen, John,   Date
    Archaeological approaches to the present.

    (Studies in archeology series)
    Bibliography: p.
    1.   Kung (African people)   2.   Archeology—Method-
ology.   3.   Ethnology—Methodology.   I.   Title.
DT797.Y44   930'.1   77-4886
ISBN 0–12–770350–0

PRINTED IN THE UNITED STATES OF AMERICA

To Dr. Julius Yellen

CONTENTS

PREFACE

Within the past decade, a small but growing number of archaeologists have shifted their glance upward and have assumed what has traditionally been considered the ethnographer's role. While prehistorians have mined the ethnographic literature, and presumably will continue to do so, actual extended fieldwork among modern-day peoples is a relatively recent phenomenon. In part, this change reflects a swing of the archaeological pendulum away from description and typology aimed at cultural historical reconstruction and toward elucidation of the same underlying processes and regularities that shape both present and prehistoric ways of life. Coupled with this search for broader explanatory patterns is a concern with methodology itself, and it has become increasingly clear that grab-bag analogy from the ethnographic present can not walk hand in hand with the logical or "scientific" study of man's past.

With this new awareness has come the realization that the archaeologist can not rely solely on the ethnographer but, rather, must collect such information himself. It is unreasonable to ask even the most sympathetic ethnographer to produce a meticulous map of an abandoned village, including in it the location of each scrap of bone and each small cluster of debris. But for the archaeologist, attention to such fine detail is crucial. Thus, increasing numbers of archaeologists have taken to the field.

For the Palaeolithic archaeologist interested in man's hunting and gathering past, Africa and Australia, for obvious reasons, have served as focal points for such ethnographic work. Desmond Clark has long emphasized the need for such studies (Clark 1960), and Gould's (1969, etc.) pioneering work with stone tool using aborigines in Australia provides a concrete example of just how valuable such an approach may be. In Africa, one may point to Brain's (1967, 1969) pioneering work among the Namib Desert Khoi (Hottentot) and Isaac's (1967) East African studies. I believe that my own work follows in this tradition.

As the title indicates, my immediate goal in this book is to examine several aspects of the relationship between archaeology and ethnography. For the most part, I try to show how archaeologists may fruitfully employ ethnographic data, but I also indicate how the archaeologist's long-range view can cast a slightly different perspective on the ethnographic present. My underlying aim is to suggest approaches to the study and understanding of man's history and evolution in a hunting and gathering milieu. The tacit assumption is made that data recovered through archaeological means provide the basic building blocks for any such reconstruction of the past, and may also serve as the source of speculative hypotheses. In the final analysis, any formulation or theory must be tested against evidence recovered from the ground. Although I propose one broad-scale model, it is more toward archaeological methodology that this book is directed. I suggest analytic frameworks that may prove of value, critically evaluate assumptions archaeologists often make, and offer specific techniques that may aid in the interpretation of individual sites.

Finally, I provide a unique body of data which, I believe, constitute my major contribution. My own analysis of it is far from complete, and my hope is that others will use it to test their own techniques and achieve their own ends.

In 1963, Richard Lee and Irven DeVore began long-range and intensive studies of !Kung groups in northwestern Ngamiland, Botswana. The total number of !Kung, a San (Bushman) people, is estimated at 13,000 by Lee (1965:19), and speakers of this language inhabit adjacent regions in western Botswana, northeastern Namibia (South West Africa) and southern Angola (see Map 1). Lee estimated that, during the early 1960s, perhaps 4000 !Kung still followed an almost exclusive hunting and gathering way of life, whereas the remainder had established close economic ties with either Bantu or European pastoralists and farmers. Today the number of free-ranging !Kung approaches zero. Ethnographic coverage for the !Kung is excellent and I include many of the key references in the bibliography. The most recent and comprehensive of these is *Kalahari hunter gatherers* (1976) edited by Lee and DeVore.

Well aware that information derived from the !Kung could be of value to archaeologists, Lee early on in his work in the early 1960s mapped in a rough-and-ready way a series of !Kung campsites. After his return from Botswana, he and DeVore invited me to expand this project as a member of the Harvard Kalahari expedition. I arrived in Botswana in early 1968, spending over 2 years there. This book represents a continuation of that work. Although I never gained great fluency in the language, after the first year or so in the field I was able to dispense with an interpreter and conduct direct interviews in !Kung. In essence, my goal was to obtain plans of a large enough series of campsites to permit statistical analysis, and to obtain relevant information about how long each site was occupied, who lived at each, and what activities occurred there. The latter data I collected primarily by after-the-fact interview, although in some instances I was present or nearby throughout an occupation. Only after my return to the United States did I realize that my data raised as many questions as they answered and could be put to uses that I had not originally envisaged. In retrospect, it also became clear that I had allowed my own presence to affect !Kung informants more than I might have wished. In the text that follows, I take pains to point out just where such transgressions have occurred.

By the Spring of 1975 I completed the manuscript for this book and that summer returned to Botswana for another year's work with the !Kung. Observation quickly showed that the statistically derived conclusions presented in Chapter 6 were correct. It also pointed out quite graphically how great are the changes that have taken place between 1970 when I completed my original stint in the field and 1975. Acculturation has proceeded much more rapidly in some areas than I would have expected, and the kind of relatively "pure" hunter-gatherer data presented in Chapter 4 can never again be obtained. The political situation has also changed; in Map 1, read "Namibia" for South West Africa and "Zimbabwe" for Rhodesia.

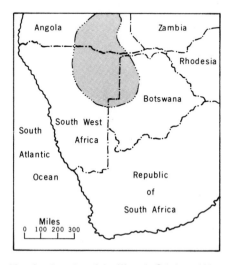

Map 1.   Location of the !Kung in Southern Africa.

ACKNOWLEDGMENTS

I wish to acknowledge my gratitude to a number of institutions and individuals. To the people and the government of Botswana I offer special thanks, both for the hospitable climate for scientific endeavor that they have created and for the personal kindness and assistance extended to me. I conducted my fieldwork as a member of the Harvard University Bushman Studies Project, directed by Irven DeVore and Richard B. Lee. Much of this research was first suggested by them, and I give my thanks for their support, so willingly extended. In the course of my work, I have received indirect financial aid from the National Institutes of Mental Health (MH 13611) and direct grants from the Wenner Gren Foundation (Grant No. 2476), the National Geographic Society and the Smithsonian Institution.

My work in Southern Africa was facilitated by a number of individuals. Irven DeVore guided me through the earlier stages of this research, working closely with me. I wish to express my gratitude to my field companions: Pat Draper, Henry Harpending, and Nancy DeVore. I would also thank Alex Campbell, Director of the Botswana National Museum and Art Gallery, Mr. Letsolatebe, Paramount Batwana Chief, and Isak Utuhile, headman of the area in which my research was conducted. The Dobe !Kung willingly gave information, guidance, friendship, and sound advice during my 2-year stay, and my debt to them is both deep and heartfelt.[1] I would also like to thank Harakwe Chibane and Simon Mpho for their valuable field assistance.

---

[1] Throughout this book I use pseudonyms to preserve the anonymity of my informants and I regret that I can not name them here.

I also acknowledge my intellectual debt to a number of individuals kind enough to share their thoughts and doubts with me. Among others, they include Lewis Binford, C. K. Brain, Desmond Clark, Irven DeVore, Clifford Evans, Brian Fagan, William Fitzhugh, Richard Gould, Glyn Isaac, C. C. Lamberg-Karlovsky, Richard B. Lee, Betty Meggers, Hallam L. Movius, Jr., Ruth Tringham, and Edwin Wilmsen.

The camp plans, presented in Appendix B, were first drafted by Polly Wiessner and then redrawn for publication by Robert Lewis. Katherine Condliffe drafted the figures that accompany Appendix C and organized most of the other data presented in that section. The remaining figures were drafted by Robert Lewis of the Smithsonian Institution. Rosemary DeRosa and Susan Brown typed much of the original manuscript. Susan Cook helped me revise the final version. H. Daniel Roth and my sister, Janet L. Yellen, were kind enough to lend their mathematical and statistical assistance, and Beryl Simpson permitted me to work in her office and use the calculator there. Lynne Fitzhugh volunteered, and subsequently proceeded to proofread the entire manuscript.

I would also like to express my appreciation to my family: to my parents and to my wife, Alison S. Brooks.

A final word of explanation is necessary. In 1972, Henry Harpending and I published an article (Harpending, H. and Yellen, J. E., Hunter–gatherer populations and archaeological inference, *World Archaeology* 1972, *4*) which considered the relevance of modern hunter and gatherer demographic patterns to archaeological interpretation. This article provides one of the interwoven themes presented in Chapter 3, and parts of that article have been incorporated, with minimal changes. I wish to acknowledge the very direct contribution that Harpending has made. In a similar way, Chapter 2, which deals with environment, is based on a joint article with Richard B. Lee (Yellen, J. E. and Lee, R., The Dobe– /du/da environment: Considerations for a hunting and gathering way of life. In *Kalahari hunter-gatherers,* edited by R. B. Lee and I. DeVore. Cambridge, Mass.: Harvard University Press, pp. 27–46). Map 1 originally appeared in Kolata, G. B., Kung hunter–gatherers: Teminism diet and birth control, *Science* 1974, *185:*993. Figures 1, 2, and 3 are reprinted from Harpending, H. and Yellen, J. E., Hunter–gatherer populations and archaeological inference, *World Archaeology* 1972, *4:*246; 247; 248.

As tradition requires, I assume sole responsibility for all and sundry errors.

1

ARCHAEOLOGICAL THEORY AND ETHNOGRAPHIC FACT

MY AIM IN this book is to examine the relevance of the present to our understanding of the past. For the most part, I focus on ethnographic data because these constitute my own area of expertise and because archaeologists have traditionally relied so heavily on them. But I would emphasize at the outset that ethnographic material comprises a single class within a broader realm of observable phenomena where both cause and effect can be directly determined and should be considered in the same light as replicative studies of stone tool production and function (i.e., Semenov 1964) or research by Brain (1967) and others, who use controlled experiments to examine the deposition, dispersal, and differential preservation of faunal remains. In all such studies the crucial question is this: In what ways, if any, is it valid to apply controlled observational data, and conclusions derived from them, to explicate a past revealed only in the archaeological record?

The arguments I present in this first chapter may be summarized as follows: First, from the mid-1800s to the present time, archaeologists have relied heavily on ethnographic data; second, this relationship is both a close and an unavoidable one. Thus, it is superfluous to ask whether or not ethnographic data *should* be employed. I offer the arguments of both Sabloff, Beale, and Kurland (1973) and Chang (1967a) to support this point of view. Next, I briefly summarize the major criticisms leveled against this

1

approach and agree that some are both valid and nontrivial. But I propose that the ethnographic present may be used in four different ways to explicate the archaeological past: These are given the convenient titles of *general model, buckshot, spoiler,* and *laboratory* approaches, and each is described in turn. Finally, I briefly consider the overall and final goals of archaeology and argue against methodological arrogance.

Orme (1973) has shown that from the 1800s to the present time archaeologists have not only relied heavily on ethnographic information but also have used it in basically the same ways throughout this entire span of time. Orme singles out Wilson (1851), Evans (1860), and Christy and Lartet (1865) as archaeological pioneers who relied heavily on the use of ethnographic analogy, and he shows how that thread is maintained over time. Discussing papers presented to the 1970 Research Seminar on Settlement and Urbanization in which she took part, Orme notes that "It is interesting to see that the majority of the contributors . . . do make use of ethnography, some scarcely without realizing it [1971:2]." And, on this side of the Atlantic, one need only look at *New Perspectives in Archeology* (Binford and Binford 1968), the outgrowth of a 1965 American Anthropological Association meeting, to see the numerous, clearly articulated, and very specific ways in which similar types of information have been used. Among the contributors, for example, Deetz (1968a), Longacre (1968), Hill (1968), Binford (1968), and Flannery and Coe (1968) clearly stand with their feet in the ethnographic present and their eyes on the past.

Like religious devotion, archaeological interpretations require a "leap of faith." The observable phenomena, such as pottery designs or site locations, which form the basic material of archaeological investigation may be described, enumerated, and analyzed. Often, statistically or intuitively significant patterns can then be demonstrated, but one can only guess at the causes of the variables which interact to give the observed configuration, and it is this step that requires the leap of faith. Deductive approaches, on the other hand, start with a preexisting belief in a set of relationships, and theoretically, one need only determine how closely a specific body of data conforms to an already established criterion. This should considerably simplify the problem of understanding the past, but, unfortunately, relatively few archaeological problems have been successfully couched within this framework, and as a rule it is easier to laud the methodological advantages of deductivism than to devise nontrivial models relevant to specific situations. Sabloff *et al.* (1973), in their analysis of Binford's (1967), Longacre's (1968), and Hill's (1968) use of ethnographic analogy within a deductive framework, demonstrate deductive proof—in the strictest sense of the term—is difficult to obtain. The archaeologist's problems arise not only from the limited and fragmentary nature of the data with which he works but also from the more fundamental difficulty of discerning laws applicable to the material remains of human culture. And these limitations become all the more frustrating because, on the one hand, the number of sophisticated techniques for data collection and statistical manipulation are constantly increasing and, on the other, allied fields such as population biology and animal ethology provide models theoretically applicable but practically difficult to apply.

For a priori hypothesis formation as well as the after-the-fact cultural interpretation of observed patterns, one needs some feeling or idea of what may constitute a reasonable explanation. In some subjective way, one must be able to ask how "reasonable" the results appear. To meet these ends, recourse to analogy—whether ethnographic or other—provides a most expedient and perhaps unavoidable approach. Chang sets forth an extreme defense for this line of reasoning when he writes:

> Indeed, in a broad sense, archaeological reconstruction *is* analogy, with or without explicit ethnological recourse. To claim any information at all, other than the stone or the potsherd that is actually discovered, is necessarily to presume knowledge of man and culture in general and to assume the existence of cultural regularities, however broadly conceived. Since each archaeological object and situation is unique, every archaeological reconstruction is analogy based on a number of such presumptions and assumptions. The ethnological recourse does not make analogy possible; it only renders its results probable or even scientifically true [1967a:230].

In a similar vein, Sabloff *et al.* state:

> What does emerge is the possibility of extracting lawlike generalizations from the analysis of existing cultures and, in the context of the premise of uniformitariansm, applying them to cultures that are fragmentary. Moreover, it should be emphasized that the possibilities of analogy are not limited to ethnography, but may emerge from such fields as human geography [1973:112f].

At this very general level, Freeman has provided what is perhaps the strongest criticism of this approach when he argues that

> The use of analogy has demanded that prehistorians adopt the frames of reference of anthropologists who study modern populations and attempt to force their data into those frames, a process which will eventually cause serious errors in prehistoric analysis, if it has not done so already [1968:262].

While I agree, and believe that alternative techniques for reconstruction should be encouraged, I would also note that, at our present state of expertise, it would be difficult to make any statements about prehistoric ways of life without recourse to such analogy.

To conclude this consideration of why ethnographic data—in the form of ethnographic analogy—have played and will continue to play such an important role in archaeological interpretation, I would stop short of Chang's position and emphasize the lack of such readily available alternatives and the all too often direct applicability of ethnographic information. One can also note the educational and historical biases in this same direction among North American anthropologists. But I would not let the matter stand at that. The difficulties archaeologists face when they turn to ethnographic data are real, and, because of them, such material should be labeled, "Handle with extreme care."

I examine three separate aspects of what is in fact a single problem. First comes the realization that the life-styles of prehistoric hunting and gathering groups are not necessarily or even likely replicated by recent surviving counterparts. This has cast considerable doubt on the value of modern ethnographic data as an aid in archaeological interpretation. Howell (1968), for example, rightly emphasizes early Pleistocene site diversity evident in the archaeological record which indicates that even at that time no single "simple pattern" existed. From this he concludes that the present provides too shaky a base upon which to generalize about the past, and that

> In secondary sources and in many texts relating to early man, there is a lot of generalization about stages in the Pleistocene. I think, however, that we may safely disregard *everything* that has been said about Pleistocene stage, because all the new evidence provides exceptions to the existing generalizations. Many sites show a great diversity in local ecological and regional settings. All that one can now say about the earlier range of Pleistocene times is that the sites are immensely diversified; there is no single pattern [1968:287f].

When one extends Howell's scope to include the entire span of time and space encompassed by Paleolithic archaeology, the problem is magnified a hundredfold, since both the Bed 1 hominids at Olduvai Gorge and the Upper Paleolithic hunters of southwestern France then fall in the same bag. Thus, the first of three problems concerns variability in the past.

The second revolves around a noticeable absence of a corresponding variability among modern hunters and gatherers. Since hunting and gathering societies have survived into the twentieth century only in the most marginal and unhospitable areas, the majority of detailed ethnographic studies deal with adaptations to desert, tropical rainforest, and arctic tundra environments. Thus, one cannot look at the available ethnographic sample to find a near approximation to life 15,000 years ago in Southwestern France, and, because of systematic bias, conclusions may easily prove misleading. Archaeological evidence indicates that hominid occupation of the Australian and Kalahari deserts, the Central African rain forests, and the

Arctic tundra and seacoast is relatively recent, since these areas require specialized techniques for survival. Consider, for example, the problems involved just in the reconstruction of the recent past in Southern Africa, where one may assume that the present day San (Bushman) inhabitants are direct descendents of Late Stone Age hunters and gatherers. Data from physical anthropology and from archaeology lend strong support to this belief (Clark 1970, Sampson 1974). Evidence from rock paintings in Rhodesia and in South Africa reveal aspects of prehistoric San culture—communal game drives and the use of masks and animal disguises, for example—that have no modern counterparts. In fact, this style of painting is unknown today. Most of these rock painting areas are located in well-watered, game-rich uplands, while San populations that retain a measure of their traditional hunting and gathering economy are now confined to the arid and semiarid lowlands. Thus, one should not be surprised to learn that many prehistoric San activities can no longer be observed.

The third problem goes beyond this lack of variability and strikes at a more basic fact: Since relatively few hunting and gathering societies have been carefully studied, cross-cultural analysis of a statistically adequate sample is rarely possible and many kinds of quantitative questions cannot be posed. This difficulty is heightened by the rapid continued assimilation of the few remaining groups. Thus, studies that deal with population density, rates of birth and death, or long-term relationships between group size and environmental variation, for example, are no longer possible, and cross-cultural data can at best serve only a suggestive role. This means that archaeologists, unfortunately, are forced to turn more and more to individual societies—San, Hadza, Australian Aborigines, Pigmies, Eskimos, and Great Basin hunters, to name the most important ones—which, in most instances, have been studied neither by archaeologists nor by sympathetic social anthropologists. The archaeologist is lucky if he can find the kind of information he wants for even one of these groups. Thus, all pretence to random sampling techniques, adequate sample size, and consideration of known alternatives must be dropped, and in truth there is often little if any alternative to the grab-bag kind of ethnographic analogy that Ascher (1961) among others has so roundly condemned.

For the archaeologist, such as myself, who has studied a single hunting and gathering society, this last problem is extremely acute, since sample size is limited to one. On the one hand, he must strive to avoid the anthropologist's own brand of "ethnocentricity"—which views the world through the blinders not of his own society but of the culture he studies—and, on the other hand, he must attempt to find ways in which the specific may be related to the more general whole. This problem is central to my own work, which is based on study of a limited area within a single tribal range.

Granted such difficulties, one possible justification for research of this kind lies simply in recording for the anthropological record kinds of data that are fast disappearing, and I believe that over the long run herein lies a major contribution of this book. But I would also argue that one can use such specific material—either alone or in conjunction with other sources— to increase our understanding of past events and processes. One may isolate four distinct approaches to this end, and I consider each in some detail. The first two, which I call the *general model* and *buckshot* approaches, are well entrenched in the archaeological literature. The latter two I term the *spoiler* and *laboratory* techniques.

General models include all concepts with broad applicability. They include general analogies and deductive hypotheses as well as the "lawlike generalizations" discussed by Sabloff *et al.* (1973). I devote the whole of Chapter 3 to constructing a model of this type. To use one, the ar-chaeologist must assume that particular past processes fall within a much broader realm, or spectrum, portions of which are observable today. From these latter, one can draw generalizations, or general models, that may be applied across the entire range. In recent years, many American ar-chaeologists have concentrated on this approach and emphasized the importance of stating such general models in the form of hypotheses theoretically susceptible to actual testing. The need for this explicitly "scientific" approach is, I believe, important—if only to separate proven fact from speculation; more realistically perhaps, it forces one to assign at least a subjective "reliability factor" to his conclusions. But to remain solely within the strictures of such "scientific methodology" is overly restrictive, given the incomplete nature of most archaeological data and the difficulty of "proof." Thus, I prefer to define a general model more loosely: If it does no more than provide a foundation for imaginative speculation that may never be susceptible to proof, the effort may still be worthwhile. Of course the unproven status must be recognized as such and treated accordingly. "Lawlike generalizations" can be drawn from existing cultures. The use of language, existence of the nuclear family, sharing, and division of labor are universal, and it makes an intriguing problem to consider how such basic aspects of human culture might be discerned in the archaeological record and how great their antiquity may be.

On a less grand level, Lee (1968), for example, adopts a cross-cultural approach, he looks at basic elements of hunting and gathering cultures and draws conclusions about the relative importance of vegetable foods in rela-tion to meat. He also suggests that a hunting and gathering way of life both past and present is less rigorous than is usually believed. And all such state-ments and generalizations count, in my book, as general models. I believe they are worthwhile, even though difficult to prove because of limited sample size and bias.

One can, however, avoid some of these difficulties by enlarging sample size through a redefinition of the sample itself. I would ignore the standard division between hunting and gathering, herding, agricultural, and mixed agricultural societies and place them all on a single scale. Deetz (1968b), among others, has made this point, and it is commonplace to note that Northwest Coast Indians utilizing rich and relatively stable maritime resources have more in common with agriculturalists than with tropical hunters and gatherers. In tracing the development of a settled Neolithic way of life in the Deh Luran Valley, Hole (1968) proceeds from a historical point of view but emphasizes a similar blurred dividing line. Thus, one can examine a group's resource base, rate it on the basis of richness, variety, and predictability, and ignore the question of whether or not food resources are hunted, gathered, herded, or planted. In Chapter 3 I provide an example of such an approach. I would expand sample size yet further, and I believe it is often advantageous to view the species *man* as one of many specialized biological types within the animal kingdom. In closing this discussion of general models, I would note approaches that deal not with human activity itself but with those byproducts that form the major part of the archaeological record. Through controlled study of modern rates of bone destruction under differing physical conditions for example, one can construct general models of a slightly different sort which are still directly relevant to our understanding of the past. Studies by Ortner, VonEndt, and Robinson (1972), Isaac (1967), and others may serve as examples, and, like their counterparts discussed above, they evince an underlying faith in the laws of uniformitarianism. Such work may proceed in the laboratory as well as in the field.

The goal of anthropology, it is often argued, is to elucidate underlying regularities in human behavior, and, in this context, one role of archaeology is to examine the development of such regularities and processes through time. It is within such an overall framework that I set the preceding discussion on general models. On a more mundane, less earth-shaking level, however, the archaeologist is constantly faced with minor problems relevant only to a particular site or technique: problems that are specific in nature, vexing, and often of minor import. Recourse to an individual ethnographic analogy, while rarely provable, may suggest an answer, and I would term this kind of hit-or-miss use of ethnographic data a *buckshot approach*. It is a form of specific analogy, usually of limited applicability, difficult or impossible to substantiate, and very difficult to avoid. If realized and clearly stated as such, it should not be ignored. The term "grab-bag analogy" has been applied in a pejorative sense to this approach. But one may counter that a probabilistic statement where probabilities are difficult or impossible to determine is better than no statement at all. Only when one presents speculation as fact does a difficulty arise.

To give one example, Jarman, Vita-Finzi, and Higgs (1972) find it necessary to estimate how far a person is likely to walk in a day's gathering trip. In what is admittedly a subjective guess, they settle on a figure of 10 km based in part on Lee's !Kung data. An estimate must be derived from somewhere, and this source is as good as any other, as long as its limitations are realized. One can only take issue when a bit of buckshot is falsely dressed up as a general model. I offer two other examples of how !Kung data may be employed in a buckshot fashion. At some Mousterian sites, a curious fact has been noted: The mandibles of larger animals are split along their entire length, while those of smaller species are left intact. The same phenomenon is found among the !Kung, because inside the jawbones of larger animals one finds a rich, fatty edible marrow which is highly valued as food. Those of smaller species do not contain enough of this to make cracking worth the effort. Also, one might note that the !Kung generally locate their camps at least .5 km from their water source, even though this entails a round trip usually twice a day for water. They do this so as not to frighten away the game which also drink there. I observed an identical pattern in the placement of Late Stone Age sites in this same region, and, while I cannot prove it, I believe it reasonable to offer the same explanation.

Both Chang (1967a,b) and Ascher (1961) have discussed the problems of analogies that can be evaluated only by a combination of the thorough consideration of possible alternatives and the use of common sense. I would make two additions. First, that one explicitly states it when using analogy in this way, and, second, that whenever possible such analogies be cast in the form of hypotheses which may ultimately, if not immediately, be susceptible to testing.

With very few exceptions, archaeologists have used ethnographic data in one of the two ways I have described (general model and buckshot), and I make no attempt to underestimate the theoretical and practical difficulties attendant on these approaches. There are, however, two additional ways in which such data may be employed. Both permit the avoidance of major methodological difficulties, and both permit the utilization of data from a single ethnographic source. The first of these I term the *spoiler approach,* and, as its name implies, it is essentially negative in outlook. But it does serve as a valuable check on archaeological speculation based on either unsound or uncertain premises. There are two parts to this spoiler approach and I discuss each in turn.

First, it is useful to judge an archaeologist's conclusions against two criteria: (1) Are there other important variables that have not been taken into account? (2) Are there other equally reasonable, perhaps more reasonable, models that demand attention? Here, single ethnographic cases may play a valuable role. I illustrate just how this may be done by drawing on published faunal analyses by Dart (1957a,b), Kitching (1963), Sadek-Kooros (1972), and Perkins and Daly (1968)—all of which may be evaluated against ethnographic data (also see Yellen in press a).

Faunal material naturally comes in bits and pieces which can be fit into the predetermined categories of *species* and *anatomical portion,* and this predisposes one to an inductive approach. First comes classification, then manipulation of the numerical results, to establish either patterns or glaring irregularities, and, finally (most often), attempts to explain observed results in cultural terms. Dart, in his study of faunal remains from Makapansgat Cave (1957 a,b) for example, noted that 336 distal ends of antelope humerus were recovered, while only 33 proximal ends of the same bone were found; this gives a ratio of approximately 10:1. Similar irregularities were present for other long bones as well, and, given these obvious discrepancies, Dart postulates that the australopithecine occupants used bone tools. Bones that would make good tools were brough back to the site and thus found in large numbers; those less frequently represented were either discarded away from the cave or used as tools elsewhere. To propose such an explanation one must guess the cause of the observed pattern—there is no real way around this—and also assume that a single factor is responsible for it.

Kitching (1963), in a largely subjective analysis of faunal remains from Paleolithic levels in Pin Hole Cave, Derbyshire, confronts a similar situation when he observes that certain bones are consistently modified in the same way. Because of this, he concludes that these bone fragments are tools, purposely shaped to perform specific tasks. Sadek-Kooros (1972) employs sophisticated statistical analysis for much the same ends and attempts to isolate formal fragment categories. She states:

> Bone broken through natural agencies or through random human breaking does not accidentally result in formal categories: such categories reflect purposeful fracturing of bone with the object of producing specific shapes [1972:370].

She then implies that the resulting formal categories are, in fact, tools. To take one final example: Perkins and Daly (1968) do basically the same thing in their analysis of faunal remains from Suberde. For the ox, *Bos primigenius,* foot bones occur more frequently than do bones from the upper leg, and Perkins and Daly argue that the upper leg bones were discarded away from camp while the foot bones were left attached to the skin when the latter was carried home. Again, there is the assumption that a single factor is responsible for the observed pattern.

Both Brain (1967, 1969) and I (Yellen in press a) have used a spoiler approach to examine such conclusions in light of ethnographic data. Brain's controlled study of goat bones collected from modern Namib Desert Khoi

(Hottentot) camps, for example, throws considerable doubt on Dart's conclusions. He found that bones from Khoi refuse heaps quite nearly duplicated the Makapansgat pattern. Brain also recovered individual pieces which in form and workmanship approximate Dart's so-called tools. Since Khoi do not make tools from goat bones, one must seek other explanations. Brain has suggested that some parts of a bone are (for a number of reasons) stronger than others and thus more likely to survive; this leads to the striking disproportions observed by Dart. I have followed in Brain's footsteps and studied !Kung butchering techniques. The !Kung break animal bones with considerable care and expertise, to permit the removal of marrow uncontaminated by bone chips. There is nothing random or haphazard about their technique, and this observation throws serious doubt on Kitching's and Sadek-Kooros's conclusions, since it shows that patterns of shape and treatment do not necessarily imply tool use. And, because preservation depends on the way a bone is broken, its structural properties, and the species from which it comes, one can suggest reasonable alternative explanations to Perkins and Daly's hypothesis.

Thus, in an admittedly negative way, one can employ ethnographic data to evaluate specific studies, and this constitutes my first application of the spoiler approach. But this same kind of specific data can also serve a greater end. The archaeological literature abounds in statements that are basically deductive in nature; they are *underlying principles,* sometimes explicitly stated, often unconsciously accepted, and applied to all hunting and gathering societies. Since statements of this type are meant to be all-encompassing, a first step in either validation or challenge lies in examination of known and documented societies. It takes only one pin to prick the balloon. Given the emphasis in recent years on explicit deductive models, the use of ethnographic data in this manner deserves serious consideration because of its great potential. Binford, in a slightly different way, employs this same argument to justify his own studies among the Nunamiut Eskimo. He states "If archaeology is to achieve the status of a science it must seek to establish law-like propositions. If law-like, such propositions should cover contemporary as well as past organizational situations [n.d.:1]." By implication, if such propositions do not cover the contemporary, they cannot be viewed as laws.

I offer a few examples of archaeological "lawlike propositions." One kind is the *explicit proposition,* which is definitely stated as such. Wilmsen states:

> [A] band most effectively exploits stable food resources by dividing into smaller groups each of which is centered among a set of resource locations which it alone exploits. A single location centered in the band's region and from which members cooperatively hunt mobile animals is most effective for this type of resource [1972:22].

One can take such a statement, in this case primarily to determine its usefulness, and actually evaluate it against ethnographic data. More often, one finds that assumptions are either tacitly taken for granted or at best only partially examined. Whallon, for example, looks at a number of studies dealing with the analysis of artifacts from living floors, and states:

> The aim of such analyses is generally to define "tool kits," or clusters of artifacts and other items which occur together on occupation floors as a consequence of having been used together in certain activities. It is hoped that inferences concerning patterns of prehistoric human activity can be made by interpreting these "tool kits" in terms of their contents and their position on the occupation floors [1973:266].

In many of the studies to which Whallon refers, the concept of the "tool kit," and all this implies about the spatial arrangement of human activities, is either taken for granted or given cursory examination at best. But the concept of a tool kit is nothing more than an assumption; the analysis based on it, and subsequent conclusions, become doubtful when the basic premises are called into question. And the original assumptions may also be evaluated through reference to specific ethnographic data. In Chapter 5 I examine the tool kit concept in just this way.

In all its guises, the spoiler approach is negative in outlook, even though it serves an essential function. But there is another more satisfying way in which the archaeologist may employ ethnographic information. I term it the *laboratory approach;* Flannery (1967) mentions it in passing, but its value is little realized and it is rarely employed.

The ethnographic present, in a loosely defined way, provides the archaeologist with a set of controlled or "laboratory" conditions within which he can evaluate and sharpen his own analytic techniques. Archaeological interpretation is anything but an exact science, and the value and correctness of any particular analytic method can be evaluated only in a most subjective fashion. Because the requisite control is lacking, one cannot refine technique through recourse to archaeological data alone—and it is here that carefully collected ethnographic data can prove of great value. Direct observation of an ongoing society permits one to correlate activities, and even patterns of thought or social organization, with material byproducts that may be preserved in the archaeological record. One then has a starting point, at which the "answers" are known, and this provides a degree of control that is impossible in a strictly archaeological situation. In such a controlled context, analytic methods themselves may be put to the test. The pitfall of circular reasoning is avoided, since no pretence of objectively deriving living patterns from their material remains need be made. What one examines and critically evaluates are alternative techniques for moving from one point to the other. What is the highest degree of accuracy possible? What are the pitfalls along the way? This is, of course, a kind of game, but a valuable one because it is possible to abstract a particular technique, which is the end product of such an exercise, and apply it in real archaeological situations. There is no reason why a pattern that may then emerge need not prove "unique"—that is to say, different from any observed among living peoples.

From this point of view, data, per se, have a great and practical value, and it is the responsibility of the ethnoarchaeologist to assume the mantle of the archaeologist and not limit his publications to conclusions alone. I think the archaeological *site report* approach, which presents the data clearly segregated from interpretation and conclusion, provides an admirable working model, and the three lengthy appendixes to this book reflect this belief.

The personal and often deeply rooted views that most archaeologists hold on the overall goals and methods of their discipline are often lost in their highly formalized public statements; informally expressed verbal reservations all too often do not find their way into print. In that latter forum, necks become stiffer and speculation more often is apt to be cast in absolute terms. I would argue that this is unfortunate, because formal statements often assume a greater relevance and comprehensibility when viewed against a more personal background. Although I think its aims are noble, I myself do not espouse an explicitly *scientific approach* to archaeology. I believe that the various proponents of the scientific approach share three underlying assumptions: first, that the proper goals of archaeology may be explicitly defined and limited; second, that statements not verified or ultimately capable of verification are not worth making; and, finally, that almost all questions are susceptible to explication if only the archaeologist is clever and patient enough. In conjunction with these beliefs, I often find an unfounded optimism and undeniable arrogance. My own outlook is quite different; it accepts as probable that many aspects of past hominid behavior will never be fully understood, that some may be guessed at but never proven, and that the actual materials with which the archaeologist works are scanty and highly biased at best. In this light, I believe that all possible avenues of approach should be opened and explored, that speculation—if it is realized and stated to be such—should be encouraged, and that methodological straitjackets should be avoided. Ethnographic data, and what has been termed the *ethnoarchaeolocal approach,* provide one of many ways to move in this direction. In this chapter I have tried to show just how this may be done, but underlying these arguments is my own belief that the main requirement for its use is an acute awareness of the difficulties and the necessary absence of arrogance which this awareness implies.

2

ENVIRONMENT:
THE DOBE–/DU/DA REGION

AN UNDERSTANDING OF both short- and long-term group movement for any hunting and gathering society must rest on the knowledge of how a particular environment varies over time and space. This most essential information is presented here, and it provides the basis on which my analysis of social and settlement patterns—the subject of following chapters—depends. Unfortunately, we lack the information to make a proper job of it, since our knowledge is spotty and most published studies are purely qualitative in nature. The major sources include Lee (1965), on whom I rely quite heavily, and Yellen and Lee (1976). The only quantitative estimate of any resource—the mongongo or mangetti nut—is extremely tentative in nature (Lee 1973). The lack of even geographical coverage sets up a second stumbling block, since knowledge is confined to an extremely limited portion of the total !Kung range, as one moves outward from this sharply circumscribed region, even general descriptive statements become more difficult to make. In this semiarid region, however, rainfall is the single most important environmental factor, and one can, in theory, determine how precipitation varies over the entire area and extrapolate, in a general way, from the observable present to an unknown past.

This unevenness of data accounts for the basic form of organization of this chapter. I start with the most solid core and work outward, expanding in both space and time. First comes an examination of the !kangwa–/du/da region, with a decided emphasis on aspects of the environment that most directly affect the !Kung who live there.[1] Next, the question of small-scale variation within this region is considered, and, finally, I broaden the focus to include a wider geographic expanse. When this latter shift occurs, statements become more general and substantive evidence decreases.

What I try to do in this chapter is sketch the limits of environmental variation and show that this variability may be examined along more than one axis. From a geographical and a year-to-year (and likely century-to-century) chronological point of view, one may consider resources in terms of regularity. But of greater importance from the !Kung vantage point is the question of predictability. Some kinds of changes are basically predictable, while others are not, and the consequences of this are profound.

GEOGRAPHICAL FEATURES

The area between Dobe and /du/da lies on the northern fringe of the Kalahari desert and straddles the international border between Botswana and Namilia (South West Africa). It falls between 19°20′ and 20°30′ south latitude and between 20°45′ and 21°20′ east longitude, and includes an area of approximately 10,700 km². I use "Dobe" and "/du/da"—waterholes located in the northern and southern reaches of this area, respectively—to designate the entire region, and I would add that the focus on this circumscribed area reflects the spatial limits and emphases of our own research, rather than any geographical or cultural reality. I emphasize this point because in the following chapter I step back and forth across these boundaries with ease. The broader, more relevant physiographic area is approximately 84,100 km² in size, bounded by the Okavango River on the north and east, the Ghanzi Farms on the south, and the edge of the South West African Escarpment to the west. It is characterized by longitudinal (i.e., "alab") dunes and dry river beds (Grove 1969) and covered by Tree Savanna (Northern Kalahari Tree and Bush Savanna, and North-Western Tree Savanna) (Weare and Yalala 1971). Because standing water is scarce, endemic larger fauna include such species as eland and gemsbuck, which can derive moisture from other sources.

[1] In mid-1972, I wrote the first draft of an article on the Dobe–/du/da environment (Yellen and Lee 1976) which was designed to serve as an introductory chapter for a volume on Kalahari hunters and gatherers. Because it was jointly authored by Lee, I drew heavily on Lee (1965) and much of the material from that article is incorporated into this present chapter. I gladly give credit to Lee (1965) for it.

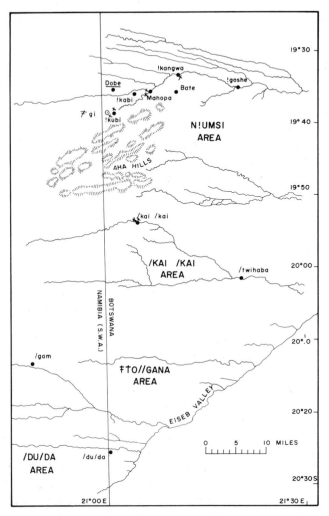

Map 2.   The !kangwa–/du/da region (adapted from a map by Lee in Yellen and Lee 1976:29)

Three dry river valleys run roughly parallel transecting the Dobe–/du/da area from west to east (see Map 2). The !kangwa valley, furthest to the north, crosses the Dobe region. Between it and the /kai/kai valley, approximately 35 km to the south, rise the Aha Hills, the only large formation of exposed underlying rock in the region. South of the /kai/kai, tributaries of the Eiseb valley transect ≠to//gana, /gam, and /du/da. A 60-km strip of land, waterless for most of the year, serves to insulate this region from the Okavango swamps to the east, but both to the north and to the south other dry river valleys conform to the east–west pattern, and they support !Kung populations. !Kung also live at the Nyae Nyae pans about 60 km southwest of Dobe.

Since this area lies on the northern fringe of the Kalahari, it forms part of a transititional zone between the drier shrub savanna (marked on most maps as the "Kalahari Desert") to the south of it and the more lush regions near the Okavango River to the north of it. And, as one moves southward from Dobe toward /du/da, these changes may be noted on a smaller scale: The dunes become higher but are spaced further apart, and the country assumes a more open character with fewer stands of large trees and more grassland. Although I have no figures to prove it, mean annual rainfall is probably slightly lower at /du/da than at Dobe, and the /du/da ungulates probably have a slightly larger range than their northern counterparts.

CLIMATE

At 1100 m above sea level, the Kalahari has a hot summer with 3 to 4 months of rains and a dry, moderate to cool winter. The sun is directly overhead in early December and again in early January, and the highest mean temperatures are recorded in October. In June and July, the coldest months of the year, night temperatures fall to freezing or near freezing, with mean daytime highs of 25°C (see Yellen and Lee 1976). Annual variation in day length is just under 2 hr and the midwinter sun, which rises at about 7:00 A.M., sets by 6:00 P.M. In midsummer, the comparable times are 6:00 A.M. and 7:00 P.M., respectively.

The relationship between two major air masses determines weather patterns in the Kalahari. A region of low pressure created by a warming summer sun draws the rain-bearing equatorial air southward. The position of the southern and westernmost extension of this system, termed the intertropical front (ITF) depends on the relationship between this equatorial air and the cool dry air flowing northward and eastward from the Atlantic. The front, which may be 80 km or more wide, brings cloud and heavy rainfall, and it is followed by lighter, convectional rains in its wake. Its southward movement brings the first rain to the Kalahari, and its northward return may account for later precipitation (Wellington 1955:216–218). The extreme western edge of this front, which passes over the Dobe–du/da region, and even slight yearly variations in its position, can have a dramatic effect. During the 1963–1964, 1967–1968, and 1968–1969 rainy seasons, which are included in Lee's rainfall records, the earliest recorded precipitation fell in October and the latest in April or May. But in 1963–1964 total rainfall equaled only 239 mm (9.5 inches), while the corresponding figures for the following two seasons are 597 mm (23.5 inches) and 378 mm (14.7 inches), respectively. During the first rainy season, December marks the period of highest precipitation, while in the rainy season the peak falls in March. In 1968–1969, February and March shared that honor about equally.

Seasons result from the interplay of changing temperature and rainfall, and most !Kung recognize five of them. With the first scattered and unpredictable *!huma,* spring rains, in October, plants put forth their new leaves and the landscape changes from parched brown to rich green. Then, during the *bara,* main summer rains, which may last from December to March, the most important summer plant foods appear. The approach of winter is marked by a brief */obe,* autumn, with no rain and falling nighttime temperatures. Then comes *!gum,* winter, itself, which lasts from May through August. Days are cool, dry, and windy, and the temperature at night often drops below freezing. Finally, in late August, *!ga,* early spring, begins, with a rapid and continued rise in temperature and a decline in available food and water for the !Kung. This is the harshest time of year for them.

LAND AND WATER

The Kalahari basin, which extends from the Orange River to the South Equatorial Watershed, and from the South West African highlands to the highlands of Rhodesia, formed during the Tertiary. While surrounding areas were elevated as much as several thousand feet, the lack of a corresponding rise in the central part of the subcontinent produced this gigantic basin, which has served to catch detritus from the surrounding highlands. The Aha Hills is one of the few underlying rock formations exposed today. Its dolomite is riddled with sinkholes and caves; it acts as an underground reservoir, and it is likely that much if not all of the subsurface water now in the /kai/kai and !kangwa river beds derives from this source.

Broad sheets of calcrete and silcrete, characteristic of arid and semiarid environments, underlie much of the Kalahari and are widely exposed both in the dry river beds and in the area between Dobe and the Aha Hills. This hardpan is up to .5 m thick in places. The age of the oldest deposits is not known, but in some areas south of Dobe it is in the process of active formation. This exposed hardpan has had a major effect on both past and present inhabitants of the Dobe area, for the silcrete nodules, which form *in situ* in these layers, provided a source of raw material for Late Stone Age tool-

makers, who were probably ancestors of the modern day !Kung. Also, these
rocklike layers of hardpan hold rainwater near the surface but at the same
time effectively prevent !Kung (using only wooden digging sticks) from
sinking wells to tap the underground water supplies that are often not far
below.

A mantle of sand, generally between 3 m and 30 m in depth, covers much
of the Kalahari. It varies in color from brownish-red to greyish-white and
probably was originally derived and accumulated in pre-Quaternary times.
It is probable that they have been redistributed more than once and that the
most recent redistribution has occurred in the last several thousand years.

In the Dobe–/du/da region these sands form parallel longitudinal dunes
from 8 km to 80 km in length that are oriented roughly east–west and give a
unique character to the country. The crests are situated from 1.5 km to 8
km apart. Grove (1969) calls them "alab dunes," adopting a term first used
by Monod (1958) to describe similar formations in areas bordering the
southern Sahara. Following Lee, I use the Sechuana term *molapo* to
describe depressions or small valleys between the dunes. (The Herero counterpart, *omaramba,* is used by J. Marshall (1957), Story (1958), and others.)
Formed by prevailing easterly winds at a time when annual precipitation
was less than 250 mm, the dunes are presently stabilized by fixed vegetation,
and similar formations in Senegal are believed to be younger than 20,000
B.P. (Michel 1967).

Soils are vertically differentiated because rain water removes most of the
finer constituents from the dune crests and flanks, and concentrates them in
adjacent *molapo* beds. On the lower flats and in the *molapos,* this water
reduces the ferric oxide component of the soil to soluble ferrous oxide,
which is then leached out. The result is a gradual and regular verticle shift
from loose sand, relatively high concentrations of iron, and correspondingly
few silt particles on the crests, to a more compact soil, lacking in iron but
richer in silt in the molapos. Lee notes that the consequences of this variation are great because dramatic changes in plant associations correspond
closely to differences in soil. In our article (Yellen and Lee 1976), we
describe these soil changes in greater detail.

Of the three types of standing water sources in the Dobe–/du/da region—
permanent sources in dry river channels, smaller *molapo* pans, and holes in
large trees—the first are obviously the most important because they hold
water throughout the year. No one knows when the three main river valleys
and tributaries were formed but it seems likely that they carried surface
water more than once because the Eiseb and the !kangwa transect some
alab dunes. Thus, the rivers were active at least once after the dunes were
formed. All three carried water eastward, toward the Okavango swamps,
and after exceptionally heavy rains, water still flows down the !kangwa for

brief periods. I also think that such *molapos* as !guasha and /du/da served as small feeders during periods of higher rainfall and represent tributaries channeled along the prevailing *molapo* pattern.

Today, these three main rivers carry underground water throughout the year. At various points along their course, large, roughly circular pans transect this flow and provide the only permanent water sources in the region. By far the largest concentration of them lie in the !kangwa valley, which has six permanent (!goshe, !kangwa, Bate, !kabi, and !kubi) and one semipermanent (Dobe) waterhole. But the Dobe well is a *makondo,* a narrow cleft approximately 8 m deep which cuts through the hardpan to reach the water table. Root action, by which the pressure of the root stems as well as their humic acids mechanically break up and dissolve the hardpan, is the agent responsible, and it is probable that over the years a number of large trees succeeded one another on this spot. The Dobe well lies on the northern extreme of the !kangwa drainage, and it dried up completely during the winter and spring of 1970. The /kai/kai valley has one permanent (/kai/kai) and some semipermanent (/twihaba) source of water, while one permanent (/gam) and two semipermanent (≠to//gana and /du/da) sources are located in the Eiseb valley tributaries.

Temporary pan during rainy season.

Same temporary pan during dry season.

Small seasonal pans in the bases of *molapos* and other low-lying places may range in size from several meters to over 100 m across and are fed by limited areas of internal drainage. Such pans fill during the rains; they are numerous and widely scattered. Depending on their size and catchment area, they may hold water for periods ranging from a couple of days to several months; in years of good rainfall, the largest may retain water until early winter.

Hollows in the trunks and root systems of large trees, which may hold up to several gallons, provide a third source of water. While such supplies are continually replenished during the rainy season, they are quickly exhausted when the rains cease; their location makes them important because they lie on the food-rich dune crests and provide the only source of water in these areas.

VEGETATION

Weare and Yalala (1971) in their revised vegetation map of Botswana, class the entire Dobe–/du/da region as Tree Savanna, but they call the northern and central regions of the area "North-West Tree Savanna," while the extreme eastern and southern fringes are considered to be "Northern Kalahari Tree and Bush Savanna."[2] Their classification does serve to emphasize the shift in association from north to south, but it is not strictly correct; smaller numbers of the mongongo (mangetti) tree (*Ricinodendron rautanenii*), supposedly limited to the northern region, do occur in the south, and the Sour plum (*Ximenia caffra*), supposedly a southern species, is present north of the Aha Hills. What this division does serve to emphasize is that the Dobe–/du/da area may best be regarded as a transitional zone.

Floral Associations

Lee and others have noted the close tie between *molapo* dune typography and plant associations. Following Lee (1965), he and I define four distinct associations (Yellen and Lee 1976): dune (1), flats (2), *molapo* (3), and river valleys and areas of exposed hardpan (4); we further subdivide the flats and *molapo* associations into subassociations: 2a and 2b, and 3a and 3b, respectively, and briefly define each as follows:

1. *The dune association*: The dunes support forests of *Ricinodendron*, and open woodlands of *Burkea*, *Pterocarpus*, and *Terminalia*. The major trees include *Ricinodendron rautanenii*, *Burkea africana*, *Pterocarpus angelensis*, *Baikiaea plurijuga*, and *Terminalia sericea*. Other important constituents are *Combretum mechowianum*, *Bauhinia macrantha*, *Ximenia caffra*, *Strychnos pugens*, *S. spinosa*, and *Guibourtia coleosperma*.

2. *The flats association*: The flats, which lie between the dunes and the *molapos* support a vegetation with affinities to both. The upper flats (2a) contain species that extend into the dune association and also several other diagnostic species, while the lower flats (2b) have some forms in common with the *molapo* association as well as diagnostic types of their own.

---

[2] According to Weare and Yalala (1971) the following characteristic species are found in both regions: trees: *Burkea africana*, *Terminalia sericea*, scattered *Colophospermum mopane*, and *Lonchocarpus nelsii*, shrubs: *Grewia flava*, *Croton megalobotrys*, and *Acacia fleckii*, grasses: *Aristida uniplumis* and *A. meridionalis*. Unique to the North-Western Tree Savanna are the trees *Ochna pulchra*, *Pterocarpus angolensis*, *Combretum transvaalense*, *Ricinodendron rautanenii*, *Adansonia digitata* and *Sclerocarya caffra*, and the shrub *Terminalia prunioides*. Primarily limited to the Northern Kalahari Tree and Bush Savanna are the trees *Peltphorum africanum*, *Croton zambesicus*, *Rhus tenuinervis*, *Combretum zeyheri*, *Acacia luederitzii*, and *Boscia albitrunca*. Characteristic shrubs in this latter area include *Croton subgratissimus*, *Grewia flavescens*, *Acacia mellifera* subsp. *detinens*, *Bauhinia macrantha*, *Ximenia caffra* and *Commiphora pyracanthoides*, along with the grasses *Eragrostis pallens*, *E. superba*, *Antephora pubescens*, *Triraphis schlechteri*, *Heteropogon contortus*, *Cymbopogon excavatus*, and *Perotis patens*.

a. *Upper flats*: Limited to this area are *Lonchocarpus nelsii, Acacia giraffae, A. giletiae,* and *A. fleckii. Terminalia sericea* and *Sclerocarya caffra* are also present.

b. *Lower flats*: Characteristic of this association are *Acacia stolonifera* var., *A. hebeclada, A. dulcis, Ziziphus mucronata, Hyphaene ventricosa, Terminalia prunioides, Combretum imberbe,* and *Grewia flava.*

3a. *Well-defined molapos*: Characteristic of this type of *molapo* are *Acacia mellifera* subsp. *detinens, A. herteracantha, Dichrostachys glomerata, D. cinerea, Croton gratissimus, Boscia albitrunca,* and *Grewia flava.*

3b. *Smaller molapos*: These *molapos* contain dense thickets of *Terminalia prunioides* interspersed with stands of *Sclerocarya caffra* as well as additional species which are also present in (3a). These latter include *Combretum imberbe, Hyphaene ventricosa, Dichrostachys glomerata, Grewia flava,* and *Citrullus lanatus* var. *vulgaris.*

4. *River valleys and areas of exposed hardpan*: The highly basic soils support such species as *Commiphora africana, C. pyracanthoides, Combretum imberbe, Hyphaene ventricosa, Adansonia digitata,* and *Sclerocarya caffra.*

!Kung Plant Foods

Shifting focus, let us now examine these associations from a !Kung's perspective and then continue this approach to consider faunal composition and distribution in the section that follows.

The !Kung recognize and have specific names for over 200 species of plants. They class 85 of them as edible, and these together provide well over 50% of total food intake. Although their relative importance varies from season to season and from area to area, the 9 major and 14 minor species I discuss here provide the staff of life for all !Kung groups. Lee (1965) lists the 9 most important as the *Ricinodendron rautanenii* (mongongo tree),[3] *Grewia flava* (morethlwa berry), *Ximenia caffra* (sour plum), *Citrullus*

---

[3] The terms "mongongo" and "mangetti" mean different things to different people. Most often, mongongo (or mungongo) is used as vernacular for the several species of the genus *Sclerocarya*; less frequently it is equated with the *Ricinodendron* "Mangetti" is the more proper common name for the *Ricinodendron,* but because the *Ricinodendron*-mongongo equation is now so well established in the American literature, I too, for simplicity, follow that rather dubious practice.

lanatus (tsama melon), *Adansonia digitata* (baobab tree), *Hyphaene ventricosa* (vegetable ivory palm), *Sclerocarya caffra* (morula tree), *Bauhinea esculenta* (the tsin bean), and *Fockea monroi* (water root). He classes 14 species as minor foods, including 7 species of edible roots and bulbs (*Coccinia* spp., *Eulophia* spp., *Lapeirousia* spp., *Vigna* spp., and *Walleria* spp.), edible gum from the trees *Terminalia sericea* and *Acacia mellifera,* three species of berries of the genus *Grewia,* and the edible leaves of the species *Dipcadi glaucum* and *Talinum crispatulatum.*   I briefly discuss the more important of these to give some idea of their distribution in time and space.

RICINODENDRON RAUTANENII

Found on dune crests only, the mongongo (or mangetti) tree produces a medium-sized nut which falls in May and June. Although the surrounding fruit rots rapidly, the nut itself can survive on the ground for an entire year. The nuts are easy to collect and highly nutritious (see Yellen and Lee 1976). The trees themselves are important because the hollows in their trunks and root systems hold several gallons of water during the rains (Lee 1973).

A mongongo tree, leafless in winter.

GREWIA FLAVA

These shrubs are located in and along the edges of *molapos* and bear berries during the summer rains. They are abundant, but only for a relatively brief period of time.

XIMENIA CAFFRA

The sour plum tree, located on dunes and upper flats also fruits during the summer rains. The plum, approximately 4 cm in diameter, has a bitter skin, which is discarded, but both the tart, tasty meat and the pit are eaten.

CITRULLUS LANATUS

This is the tsama melon. It appears in great abundance in *molapos* and adjacent flats during the rains. Approximately 15–20 cm wide, the tsama has a whitish, watery meat which can, if necessary, serve as an alternative source of water.

ADANSONIA DIGITATA

The baobab tree, which occurs near large pans with associated areas of exposed hardpan, has an extremely limited and spotty distribution. A large tree will bear over 100 pods, each up to 40 cm in length, which ripen and fall to the ground during the winter months. !Kung break open the pods and eat the whitish meat within. These fruits do rot however, and are not available for most months of the year.

HYPHAENE VENTRICOSA

The vegetable ivory palm is a *molapo* tree. During the rains, a mature form yields an abundant fruit that has very little food value. A dwarf form lacks fruit, but the heart of its stalk is an important food item which is edible in any season.

A baobob tree: a "point resource."

Sclerocarya Caffra

The morula tree is most often found in low areas with exposed hardpan. During the rains, it bears a small edible fruit with an equally edible nut within.

Bauhinia Esculenta

Large patches of the tsin bean are concentrated in the Aha Hills and in the flats to the south. The pods on the tsin shrub contain beans that are like, but slightly larger than, the fava, and are eaten during the summer rains and early winter. In the Nyae Nyae pan area to the west, the beans and roots are both eaten and together provide the primary food source (L. Marshall 1965).

FOCKEA MONROI

The water root is available year round and occurs in most *molapo* bottoms. Important only as a source of water—a large root may contain up to 1 pint—it is utilized only near the end of the dry season when people may move away from permanent water sources to the waterless hinterlands where food is still plentiful. The root may either be sliced and eaten, so that the water is ingested along with the fibrous meat, or the water may be squeezed from it.

COCCINIA SPP., EULOPHIA SPP., LAPEIOUSIA SPP., VIGNA SPP., AND WALLERIA SPP.

Although seven species of edible roots and bulbs from these five genera are eaten year round, they become particularly important during the winter dry season. Found in *molapos* and adjacent flats, they generally lie about 30–40 cm below the surface. The largest species reach 25 cm in length.

TERMINALIA SERICEA AND ACACIA MELLIFERA

These trees exude a sap during the winter that adheres to the tree trunk in the form of small balls. The gum is picked and eaten with no further preparation. *Terminalia sericea* is associated with dune formations while *Acacia mellifera* is localized in the *molapos* and lower flats.

GREWIA BICOLOR, GREWIA FLAVESCENS, AND GREWIA SP.

These three additional species of the genus *Grewia* are associated primarily with *molapos* and yield berries during the summer months.

DIPCADI GLAUCUM AND TALINUM CRISPATULATUM

These small leafy plants are found both in *molapos* and in areas of exposed hardpan, they have edible green leaves which are eaten during the summer rains.

A variety of common vegetable foods.

FAUNA

While our faunal lists are probably accurate for the larger mammals, they are admittedly incomplete, and the definitive study remains to be done. But one fact is certain: Game have diminished in the northwestern Kalahari over the last 50 years. Rhino and springbok have disappeared completely, while zebra are rarely seen. Buffalo and elephant formerly numerous, are now only occasional summer visitors. In the following discussion I deal primarily with the ungulates because of their prime importance to the !Kung (see Table 1).

Prey Species

The absence of available standing water and the scarcity of good feed for most of the year restricts the density and distribution of large ungulates. I would draw two useful distinctions: first, between seasonal migrants and species resident year round; and, second, between animals with relatively small ranges and those less restricted in their movements.

Four of the ungulates are seasonal migrants and enter the region during and just after the rains. All of them—the zebra, roan antelope, impala, and

TABLE 1.   Mammals of the Dobe-/du/da Region

Ungulates

Buffalo	*Syncerus caffer*
Duiker	*Sylvicapra grimmia*
Eland	*Taurotragus oryx*
Gemsbok	*Oryx gazella*
Giraffe	*Giraffa camelopardalis*
Red hartebeest	*Alcelaphus buselaphus*
Impala	*Aepyceros melampus*
Kudu	*Tragelaphus strepsiceros*
Roan antelope	*Hippotragus equinus*
Steenbok	*Raphicerus campestris*
Warthog	*Phacochoerus aethiopicus*
Blue wildebeest	*Connochaetes taurinus*
Zebra	*Equus burchelli*

Carnivores

Aardwolf	*Proteles cristatus*
Bat-eared fox	*Otocyon megalotis*
Caracul	*Felis caracal*
Cheetah	*Acinonyx jubatus*
Genet	*Genetta genetta*
Brown hyena	*Hyaena brunnea*
Spotted hyena	*Crocuta crocuta*
Black-backed jackal	*Canis mesomelas*
Leopard	*Panthera pardus*
Lion	*Panthera leo*
Banded mongoose	*Mungos mungo*
Slender mongoose	*Herpestes sanguineus*
Mongoose	2 additional spp.
Ratel (honey badger)	*Mellivora capensis*
Serval	*Felis serval*
Wild cat	*Felis lybica*
Wild dog	*Lycaon pictus*
Striped polecat	*Ictonyx striatus*

Other

Antbear	*Orycteropus afer*
Baboon	*Papio ursinus*
Bat	3 spp.
Elephant	*Loxodonta africana*
Galago	*Galago senegalensis*
Scrub hare	*Lepus saxatilis*
Pangolin (scaly anteater)	*Manis temmincki*
Porcupine	*Hystrix africaeaustralis*
Rats and mice	11 spp.
Shrew	sp. uncertain
Springhare	*Pedetes capensis*
Bush squirrel	*Paraxerus cepapi*
Ground squirrel	*Xerus inauris*

buffalo—are rare at the best of times and occur either alone or in small groups. Individual elephants are also infrequent visitors at this time, and unconfirmed reports have also placed baboons in this region. Compared to "richer" areas in the north and east, where herds may number well over a hundred individuals, one is struck by the low concentrations of these seasonal migrants.

The larger, more mobile ungulates present throughout the year include kudu, gemsbok, eland, blue wildebeest, red hartebeest, and giraffe; of these, the first four are the most common. We still have no idea of average species density or of changes in number and distribution by season. My impression is that kudu are more abundant during the rains, but perhaps it is based only on the tendency of these species to concentrate in areas with more lush food, salt pans, or other watering places during this period. I have on rare occasion seen herds of up to 15 individuals during the rains, but even then most sightings consisted of lone individuals or groups of 2 or 3. Their numbers are limited, their ranges relatively large, and their distribution uneven. Frequent movement raises obvious difficulties for the !Kung—hunters cannot reliably predict on a day-to-day basis where game will be located.

Smaller ungulates—the steenbok, duiker, and warthog—are all more common than their larger counterparts and have more limited ranges. Steenbok and duiker occur either singly or in pairs, most often in the flats. When I saw warthog they were generally lone individuals on the flats or in areas with exposed hardpan.

Porcupine, springhare, and antbear are all relatively abundant—especially the first two—and make their burrows in *molapos,* flats, and areas with exposed hardpan. Because of these conspicuous holes, hunters have relatively little difficulty finding them. The hare is primarily associated with river valleys and areas of exposed hardpan. Finally, all of the major southern African carnivores are represented, although none are common.

Of the birds most commonly eaten by the !Kung, the crowned guinea fowl (*Numida meleagris*) occurs in scattered flocks of up to 20. The ostrich (*Struthio camelus*), although not so abundant, also has a wide distribution; hunters are more interested in the eggs than in the flesh. The red-billed francolin (*Francolinus adspersus*), and the Swainson's francolin (*Pternistis swainsonii*) are found only in areas with exposed hardpan. Very few of the local insects and other invertebrates have been identified, and I would mention only the two species of beetle—*Diamphidia nigro-ornata* and *Polycada flexuosa*—which are used as arrow poison. Lee (1965) notes that one species of antlion (determination pending) has an annual outbreak in late November and early December, when !Kung eat them by the hundreds. Beehives are found in most heavily wooded areas, and the honey in them ripens in late May and June.

A hunter digs larvae for arrow poison.

RESOURCE VARIATION AND PREDICTABILITY

Against this background, I would now return to the question of resource variability and predictability, and first examine just the area north of the Aha Hills. Both space and time must be considered.

Thus far I have emphasized the regular aspects of spatial variation—the widespread system of alab dunes with regular progressions of dune crest, upper and lower flanks, and shallow and deeper *molapos,* each with characteristic soil and floral associations. This variation is extremely important to the gatherer because it increases the number of plant foods available for exploitation, and, compared with flatter areas in the Kalahari that receive a similar amount of rainfall, the number of plant species is large. Because these associations are arranged in contiguous, parallel, and relatively narrow bands, an individual hunter or collector can exploit each of these during a single day's trip.

But minor breaks in this pattern make for a certain amount of uneven distribution as well. !goshe, for example, has extensive mongongo groves located within an 18 km radius of its waterhole, while the nearest nut grove to Dobe is some 8 km away, and its yield of nuts is small. Numerous local "unique" spots or point resources dot the region and provide a second kind of break. The distinctive Aha Hills vegetation, for example, includes abundant stands of tsin bean, which are rare or absent to the north. The !kubi waterhole supports the only baobob trees found anywhere in the area, while Dobe, which lacks baobobs and tsin beans, is noted for its concentration of nut ivory palms. Let me give one final example: One finds a number of *hwanasi,* salt pans, located in an extinct river bed 32 km north of Dobe. During the rains this otherwise inhospitable area attracts relatively large numbers of gemsbok, kudu, eland, and giraffe, and becomes a rich hunting ground. During the rains, game tend to concentrate near the *hwanasi;* then in early winter, eland move for short periods of time into the area of hardpan just north of the Aha hills, and herds of kudu females and young return to browse on the leafy shrubs in this same region.

Added to this geographical variation is the element of time. First comes the regular and predictable passing of the seasons with precipitation the crucial factor. With the early rains, smaller seasonal pans fill and provide a widespread network of watering points. During the main rains, leafy greens, fruits, and berries ripen. Mongongo nuts that fell the previous year still remain on the ground in edible condition. Seasonal game migrate in, and the numbers of local animals also increase (I think). Toward the end of the rains, the new crop of mongongo nuts fall and beehives are heavy with honey. Autumn and early winter herald a time of drying: Small pans give out one after the other; and the selection of edible plants diminishes, although the last of the summer berries and mongongo nuts near permanent water are still plentiful. Ungulates become more difficult to find as distribution patterns shift. Winter and early summer follow and the country increasingly assumes a dry, parched aspect. Resources that lie within an easy round trip from the waterholes are gradually depleted. With the start of the next rains, the pattern repeats itself—and all !Kung know this will happen.

But superimposed on this annual chronological pattern is a less orderly and less predictable one. Because of its position in relation to both the intertropical front and the cool winds from the Atlantic, the northern fringe of the Kalahari may experience extreme fluctuations in rainfall from year to year. The nearest meteorological station where rainfall records extend over any length of time is at Maun, 250 km east of Dobe. The same factors that control rainfall at Dobe also hold at Maun, and Lee's analysis of these data (1972a) seems to underline the variability of the rainfall. He uses Wellington's definitions (1964:40–43) to show that 29 of the years between 1922 and 1968, or 63%, had "normal" rainfall, while in the remainder drought ranged from "mild" to "severe." Other than this, no patterns are evident, and information about the past has no predictive value. Our own records are widely spaced. Lee maintained observations in 1963–1964 and in a later trip in 1967–1968. The difference in rainfall between the two years is about 50%, and, as Lee points out, spatial variation in rainfall must be considered as well. In an analysis of 1966–1967 rainfall figures from five stations in the Ghanzi district he notes: "In November, Kalkfontein received only 3.5 mm while Scarborough, 50 km away, received 34.0. As a result, the desert may be blooming in one area while a few hours' walk away it will still be parched [1972:132]." The comparable figures for that entire rainy season are Scarborough: 614.6 mm, Kalkfontein: 382.5 mm. And because the absolute amounts are so low, even relatively slight seasonal variations may have significant ecological consequences.

Let me broaden my focus and examine this same kind of variation within an expanded framework of time and space. Relevant information is unfortunately scarce, but I would make several generalizations. Consider

A man checks nest for honey.

Gathering honey from nest in mongongo tree.

geographic variation first. The most important point is that rainfall varies
from north to south because of the direction in which the intertropical front
moves. Average annual precipitation is higher in Southern Angola (which
marks the northern boundary of the !Kung range) than it is in Ghanzi
(which roughly demarcates the southern extremity of that range and abuts
on the central Kalahari). This clinal variation affects flora and topography
as well. The system of well-formed alab dunes is limited to the northern part
of this area, and as one moves southward one notes that the dunes are
spaced farther and farther apart and finally just peter out (Grove 1969).
Vegetation also changes. Weare and Yalala (1971) set the dividing line
between North-West Tree Savanna and Northern Kalahari Tree and Bush
Savanna, just south of the Aha Hills, and this absolute separation reflects
what is really a gradual change. As one moves southward from the Aha

Hills, the country appears to open out: Grassy areas, characteristic of *molapo* bottoms, expand at the expense of larger shrubs and trees. The southern limit of the mongongo tree actually lies about 20 km south of /du/ da (Lee 1973:3). As one travels northward from the Aha Hills, stands of large trees become more widespread and more densely packed. This difference between north and south proved so striking to Harpending that he wrote: "In contrast to the rest of Zu/wa (!Kung) land the north looked like paradise. It had thick forests with great large trees on the ridges and tall lush grass in the valleys [n.d.:5–6]."

Fauna are also affected because water-dependent species, such as zebra and buffalo, live in the north the entire year, while eland are relatively uncommon. As one moves south, numbers of desert-adapted species, such as eland and gemsbok, increase. My own subjective impression is that herd size also decreases and range becomes correspondingly larger. Populations of disease-causing organisms most likely show a geographic patterning as well. Bronte-Steward, Budtz-Olsen, Hickley, and Brock (1960) found that as one went north toward the Caprivi Strip, the prevalence of splenomegaly, a good indicator of malaria, increased directly in relation to proximity to the Okavango River. Similarly, in populations near the Okavango swamps, the variety of antibodies to arboviruses is much higher than in more desert-like areas (Kokernot, Szlamp, Levill, and McIntosh 1965).

What happens to this area over an extended period of time? Again, data are scant, and the question of climatic successions remains an intriguing and largely unanswered one. Grove (1969) postulates at least one wetter period before the alab dunes were formed and a second that postdates the dune formation. Since small shifts in the southern and westernmost extension of the intertropical front can cause extremely marked changes in rainfall, I feel fairly sure that the northern Kalahari has experienced numerous and very pronounced climatic changes that will prove extremely difficult to disentangle by geological means. A final cause of long-term variation may be !Kung actions themselves, since the !Kung set fires in late summer to encourage the growth of new grass. How long this practice has been followed is the unknown and possibly crucial variable. Burning in semidesert environments can, as Tinley (1966) points out, have marked and unfortunate consequences, since, if misused, it can destroy the relatively productive grassland.

In conclusion, I would consider environmental variation along two axes: regularity and predictability. Regular patterns include the topographical, floral, and faunal changes associated with the alab dune system. A broader regular shift may also be discerned along a north–south axis. And, finally, seasons follow one after the other from year to year. Irregularities are caused by minor but important variations in the positioning of alab dunes in relation to water, in the scattered numerous point resources, and in the day-by-day, small-scale movements of larger game. Distribution of rainfall in time or place (or both) can change greatly both from year to year and over the longer run too. From the !Kung point of view, vegetation patterns and location of point resources are predictable and known. Small-scale game movement can be predicted in a general sort of way and so can the changes that each season brings. But, for rainfall, this does not hold, and a !Kung is in the same boat as the statistician when it comes to looking ahead; and all species, both animal and vegetable, must find ways to cope with this uncertainty.

3

THE !KUNG SETTLEMENT PATTERN: BROAD-SCALE GROUPINGS IN TIME AND SPACE

THE NORTHERN KALAHARI, as I have described it, is characterized by both regular, recurrent patterns and sporadic highly unpredictable events. Against this background I now examine how the !Kung arrange themselves on the ground, and I use a frame of reference that extends across the entire !Kung range and expands time well back beyond the ethnographic present. Archaeologists rarely define *settlement pattern* in such an unrestricted way, but I believe that such broad-scale considerations have direct and immediate consequences that definitely fall within the strictest limits of the term and merit careful examination by the archaeologist.

I divide this chapter into two parts: the first deals with !Kung and the second with archaeological interpretation. In the first part, two quite distinct, yet complementary models of !Kung spatial organization are presented. Following one model, group or band distribution and territoriality are considered with minimal regard for the individual or the nuclear family of which he forms a part. For simplicity's sake I term this the *band model*; it usually matches the mental picture of an individual !Kung, can be elicited through interview, and generally corresponds to the settlement picture presented by L. Marshall (1960) or Lee (1972a). I call the second formulation the *individual model*; it has been derived, after the fact, from specific observational and interview data collected by Harpending and from more general observations of my own. Here, the focus is on the individual or nuclear family per se, and larger social and territorial groupings are of secondary importance. I take this approach not through a perverse joy in complicating a simple situation, but because the !Kung in fact seem to say one thing and then do something else. One cannot discount the outstanding and painstaking work and syntheses of Lee and Marshall which point in one direction; yet at the same time one must also come to grips with a contradictory pattern—which Harpending and I have discerned. I try to show how the puzzle fits together, but, whether one buys this or not, the pieces cannot be ignored. The second part of this chapter, then, considers the relevance of this group–individual dichotomy to archaeological speculation.

The central point on which the chapter hinges is that a *group* or *band* may be defined in terms of areal exploitation, but not on the basis of individual members. Bands have a certain stability, and predictions dealing with band size and general movement are likely to fall close to the mark. The movement of individuals or single nuclear families, on the other hand, is difficult to predict, and in the long run may best be conceived as random. Social anthropologists have often made the unwarranted assumption that the one can be defined in terms of the other, and the problem has rarely received archaeological consideration. This raises serious problems both in the archaeologist's use of ethnographic data and in the attempted application of locational and network analysis to prehistoric hunter–gatherers.

THE BAND APPROACH AND THE INDIVIDUAL APPROACH

The Band Model

Take a geographer with an extremely good eye for natural features and a terrible memory for names and faces. Let him drive through the Dobe–/du/da area in August, toward the end of winter. As he travels from waterhole to waterhole, he will find groups of families clustered in camps located near each—the pattern being repeated throughout the region. If the geographer were then asked if the !Kung group themselves into territorial bands, he would have no way to refute this hypothesis. Next, let this same geographer return the following August and repeat his trip. Although he cannot remember the individual faces, he can count, and as he travels he will see that people are clustered in the same general places and that the number of individuals in each place is about the same as before. Probably he will then be even more likely to subscribe to some kind of *band* or *territory* view.

To continue this hypothetical line of reasoning, consider a situation where every adult !Kung in the Dobe–/du/da area might be persuaded to wear a bracelet that could be pinpointed from the air. And imagine that a satellite passed overhead once each week, plotted bracelet locations on an aerial photograph and transmitted the results back to earth. At the end of the year, 52 photographs could be set side by side and patterns in dot position discerned. During the winter and dry season, dots would be grouped in tight and relatively large clusters near sources of permanent water. During and just after the rains, when standing water was available elsewhere, the concentrations would break down and the numerous smaller groups would be more widely spread across the landscape. By examining consecutive photographs, one might rightly conclude that the dots observed at point A one week were the same seen at point B the following one, and a series of arrows could be drawn indicating week-to-week movement across the rainy-season terrain.

The grouping and movements of these dots would in no way contradict our hypothetical geographer's observations and could easily be used to describe the !Kung settlement pattern. The aggregation of dots at the height of the dry season would represent the complete band or social group and the term *band* itself could well be defined in this manner. Similarly, if one followed the movement of this group from photograph to photograph, kept track of the smaller clusters during the rainy-season dispersal, and finally drew a line around the entire area, the circumscribed region could easily be called a *territory*. Some territories would overlap and more than one band might seem to occupy a single territory. Still, it would be possible to delimit territories, to define them as areas utilized by one or more groups over the course of a year, and to conclude that a territory must have a sufficient amount and balance of resources to support a group in its annual rounds.

The !Kung settlement pattern described by L. Marshall (1965), J. Marshall (1957) and Lee (1965, 1972a) conforms in all basic aspects to the hypothetical pattern discussed above. Lee (1965) defined territorial areas for groups in the !kangwa region, and his map is reproduced here (Map 3); in a subsequent publication, he delineated similar traditional areas south of the Aha Hills (Lee 1972a:134–38). In Chapter 4 I present a detailed description of how the Dobe group moved from place to place in 1968, and these data provide a concrete example both of how useful a band–territory model can be and of how well certain kinds of information support it. Each territory, Lee states, contains a permanent water source, and during the dry season, the band or group is forced to camp near it. For the most part they then confine their hunting gathering activities to areas reachable within a

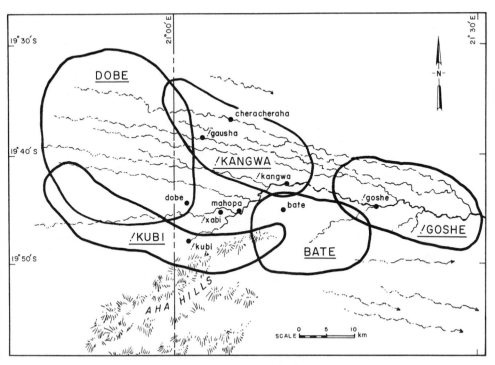

MAP 3.   Territories in the !kangwa valley region (adapted from Lee 1965:134).

day's round trip; as the dry season progresses, gathering becomes more difficult and the group turns to less desirable food sources normally overlooked during better times. Then with the first rains, the band breaks into
smaller groups which move out into the relatively underexploited "hinterland." By frequent movement these units can then adjust to minor changes
in resources, game distribution, and varying food preferences. As the
country dries up in early winter, the larger groups again coalesce around
permanent water sources.

This pattern, as I have described it, would come as no surprise to any
student of hunter–gatherer organization. In its most extreme form,
Radcliffe Brown (1930) argued for a band model in which groups are
associated with individual territories, and band membership is controlled by
patrilocal postmarital residence and band exogamy. Service (1962, 1966)
and Williams (1968, 1974) among others have supported this patrilocal
model and argued that it is applicable to all hunter–gatherer societies. A
scheme of this kind has two main components: first, a band or social grouping which is defined on the basis of designated individuals who claim

membership through kinship ties; second, a territory within which the band moves and which may or may not be defended.

The models for !Kung group organization separately proposed by Lee (1972a,b) and by L. Marshall (1960, 1965) can, with several important modifications, be set in a standard band framework. Lee effectively destroys the notion that the !Kung organize themselves into patrilineal bands. He shows that the !Kung bands are composite in nature, not patrilineal; that exclusive territorial rights are not recognized, boundaries not defended; and that some "core" areas around permanent water points are shared by more than one group. Finally, he points out that the !Kung land arrangement has enough flexibility built into it to permit additional population concentration in especially bad years when some supposedly "permanent" waterholes do run dry.

Lee compares his findings to those of Marshall, decides they are in basic agreement, and presents a picture of !Kung band organization as follows:

> The basic local grouping is a camp (Marshall's band), which is a noncorporate, bilaterally organized group of people who live in a single settlement and who move together for at least a part of the year. At the core of each of these camps are two, three, or more siblings and/or cousins, both male and female, who are generally acknowledged to be the owners (K"ausi) of the waterhole. Around each waterhole is a bloc of land or n!ore. This contains food resources and other water points and is the basic subsistence area for that resident group. Lorna Marshall (1960:344ff) has argued that the ownership of each waterhole resides in the person of a band headman who is always male and who inherits his position patrilineally, but my own research indicates that no headman existed among either the Dobe or Nyae Nyae !Kung Bushmen. Instead the sibling–cousin group of K"ausi collectively held the waterhole (1972a:129).

Lee presents convincing data to show that a *n!ore* may be inherited from the father or the mother or both parents or neither of them, and that the postmarital residence pattern is clearly not patrilocal. On one point, however, Lee and Radcliffe Brown agree: A band is composed of specific individuals tied over a period of years to a particular area or territory.

I personally believe that much may be said in favor of the "Lee model." In the first place, it corresponds quite well with observed group movements, which I discuss hypothetically in the introductory part of this section and examine in more concrete detail in the chapter that follows. Groups are associated with specific areas, and yearly group movement repeatedly conforms to this pattern. Given this framework, one can also see how populations can adapt to the extremes of environmental variation and concomitant stress. The loosely defined territories, which may overlap both at their ill-defined boundaries and at their central permanent water points, allow for a certain "give" or leeway. Population can shift in the face of severe environmental change. Lee himself discusses environmental unpredictability, and he argues that his model permits human responses to drastic changes in resource distribution.

Finally, !Kung see themselves as organized in this way. Lee speaks of taking an elderly !Kung to a hilltop in the southern Aha Hills, looking out toward the horizon and listening as the informant pointed out the areas occupied by different bands in the 1920s and 1930s—before the influx of Bantu with their goats and their cattle altered the pattern. My own experience with !Kung supports this story. Individuals speak of ownership: of who has rights in certain areas, who the band leaders are, and what "hinterland" areas are associated with specific waterholes. Thus observation of group movement, responses elicited through interview, and more theoretical kinds of environmental considerations all tend to support formulation of this kind.

The Individual Model[1]

Let us return for a moment to the hypothetical satellite and consider a different research design. Rather than tagging all adult members of the population, imagine that a limited number of people are given bracelets each of which emits a different radio signal that can be recognized as such by the tracking satellite. And imagine that the satellite takes only one picture each year—during the dry season—and presents it with the position of each subject marked by a unique symbol. What pattern would emerge if a series of consecutive photographs were laid side by side? On the basis of the band model, one would expect little or no change from year to year; however, these photographs would *not* fulfill this expectation.

Data from the Dobe waterhole support this statement. In Figure 1, Harpending and I plot the areas covered by four adult men associated with the Dobe group while we were in the field, and one can see that in no two cases do they coincide. kã//ka n!a, for example, maintains a hut at Dobe; but he sometimes goes west to the chum!kwe settlement in Namibia to visit relatives there, and northeast to the !gausha and cheracheraha pans to camp with one or other of his married children. kã//ka (2), on the other hand, goes to neither of these places, but he has another hut at /kai/kai, where he spends a good part of the year. During our study, tsau visited neither chum!kwe nor kai/kai; he ranged further north and west than any of the others. And finally /"xashe n!a[2] restricted his movements to Dobe and its hinterland to the northwest, without passing beyond the Dobe *n!ore*.

---

[1] The argument developed in this section is based on an article written by Harpending and myself (Yellen and Harpending 1972).

[2] In the figures, /"xashe n!a's name is correctly transcribed as "/"xəshe n!a." For the printer's convenience, I simplified it in the text.

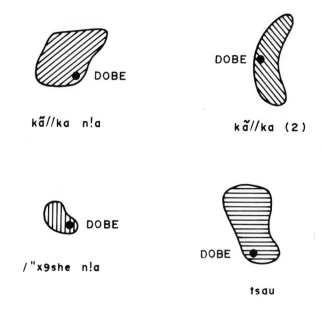

kã//ka n!a

kã//ka (2)

/"x9she n!a

tsau

⊢─────┤

64 Km.

FIGURE 1.   Areas exploited by four adult male members of the Dobe group (from Yellen and Harpending 1972:246).

In Figure 2 we make the same general point in a more striking way. It shows the birthplaces of all the adults in the families of these four men. Almost none were born within the Dobe *n!ore,* yet all would be considered part of the Dobe band. Similarly, compare the Dobe census data for the dry seasons of 1964, 1968, and 1969. (We have no data for the period 1965–1967.) An adult with a hut at Dobe was included even if he was away most of the time. The actual turnover in individuals between 1964 and 1968 was 80%, and between 1968 and 1969 it was 50%.

On a broader scale, one may approach this same question by comparing where such specific milestones as birth and marriage occur in an adult's lifetime and by calculating the distance between spouses' birthplaces. On the basis of such demographic data, Harpending states:

> The point of importance is the vary large distances over which mating takes place and the knowledge of and familiarity with vast areas of terrain and large numbers of people implied by such distances. Incidentally, when distances between birthplace and

current residence are tabulated there are no differences between the sexes; women are fully as mobile as men in this society. When distances between birthplaces of parents and their offspring are plotted, they are almost as large as the parental distances [n.d.:8].

Harpending analyzed 358 pairs and found the average distance between spouses' birthplaces to be 41.3 miles.

I would argue that this large-scale, long-term, almost random movement of individuals and families provides an extremely effective way to adapt to an unpredictable and highly variable environment. The mechanism involved is quite different from the group merger–sharing approach set out by Lee, and may best be understood by comparison to it. Lee describes groups defined by territory and individual; he argues that shared permanent waterholes, overlapping territorial boundaries, and mutual accommodation in extremely dry years provide flexibility in times of great stress and hardship. But given the high probability in this marginal desert area of longer-term quite drastic changes, I doubt that such a mechanism would permit the necessary realignments to take place. When a single "permanent" waterhole dries up, Lee's groups can move in with their neighbors; but what happens when all the !kangwa valley waterholes, which draw from a single limited area, run dry? Probably groups affected cannot concentrate on the

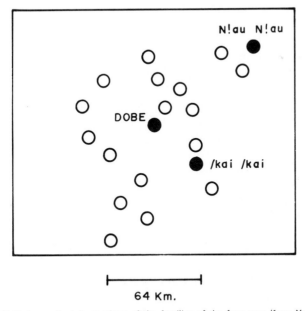

FIGURE 2. Birthplaces of adult members of the families of the four men (from Yellen and Harpending 1972:247).

remaining regional sources because under these circumstances the /kai/kai well would likely run dry as well. By what mechanism can one postulate a broad-scale and more far reaching movement from south to north or vice versa?

I think that the very type of individual and family movement which we have just described provides the basic clue. If family movement is not constrained and one can claim membership rights in a number of territories (and this is the case), then it does not matter if two groups can consolidate or not. If bands are conceived as temporary aggregations of families or individuals, and these families in turn have rights in more than one place, band size can then change very rapidly or melt into nothingness if the need arises. Such a mechanism would permit small seasonal or yearly demographic adjustments as well as much larger and longer-term movements.

Earlier, I singled out several cultural practices, such as possible headmanship, inheritance of property, ownership, and a !Kung's own conceptual model, that accord well with a *group model*. Let me now consider others that facilitate speed and freedom of movement and thus may be understood in terms of the *individual* approach—and a number of such mechanisms do exist.

I would argue that the arrangement described by Lee, whereby married sibs form a core group, facilitates this end because, at any moment in time, more than one residence alternative is open. Consider the common case of a married man whose sibs are married as well. Quite often his spouse will also have married brothers and sisters. Based on these ties alone, the residence alternatives open to this married pair will permit them to move with ease in more than one direction. Bilateral inheritance of *n!ores* extends and multiplies residence possibilities by extending them across generational lines. Tied to these are the criteria for mate selection: Although my information is far from systematic, it seems that in arranging first marriages, parents prefer to pick prospective sons- and daughters-in-law from distant, rather than close, areas, and that two marriages between the same sib groups are discouraged. This works, in effect to widen residence possibilities as well as to increase the bands' mutual responsibilities and obligations between individuals. Binford (personal communication) has argued that an initiation ceremony that draws individuals from a very wide area may work to promote this same goal; although none of us has observed the ritual, the !Kung initiation rite seems to fit that pattern.

Finally, in a similar light, one may consider the !Kung naming relationship first described by L. Marshall (1957). She noted that individuals sharing the same name have certain rights and obligations to one another and that they may establish fictive kin relationships. In a small-scale society such as the !Kung, kinship between individuals can be directly traced. As an observer, I found it largely superfluous and often, to the delight of informants, confusing. At that time it struck me as useful only because it allowed people to emphasize a personal closeness or distance that could not be established by the more straightforward method. But now, in retrospect, I would suggest a different purpose for it. In times of great stress requiring quick and widespread movement, the name relationship can function as a mechanism that extends territorial rights and obligations well beyond those established through marriage and inheritance ties.

Harpending and I have constructed a more general formulation, which in my own mind at least derives from this !Kung *individual model,* and I discuss it here because I believe it can provide an important insight into the evolution of human social organization. We use the concept of nucleation to describe the relative openness of social units—which may be villages, families, individuals, or any other category and may be measured in terms of the network of relations existing between any pair of them. These ties may consist of acquaintance relations, kinship relations, trading relations, or any of a number of alternatives. If these units are condensed into discrete clusters with few ties between the different aggregations, then we call the network *nucleated.* If, on the other hand, such clusters are absent, then the network is *anucleate.* We illustrate the two extreme examples and an intermediate case in Figure 3. In the first instance, links extend evenly in all directions, and no segregation is evident. At the nucleated end of the scale, however, clear-cut clustering may be seen. But we would emphasize that an anucleate condition need not imply an even spread of individuals on the ground.

If the units under consideration are groups of 50 to 200 people, that is, bands or villages, and if this underlying social parameter of nucleation is high, there will be endogamy within the groups and little movement of individuals or goods among them. The result will be high inbreeding levels (measurable by population genetic techniques), increased dialect differentia-

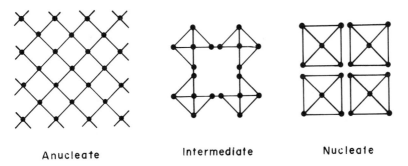

Anucleate   Intermediate   Nucleate

FIGURE 3.   Degrees of nucleation among units (from Yellen and Harpending 1972:248).

tion between units, and quite possibly differentiation of tool traditions in an archaeological context. Thus genes, language, or artifacts may reflect this underlying social parameter.

Where should the !Kung fall along this continuum? Ecological considerations indicate that they should be near the nonnucleated end of the scale. Harpending brought his genetic guns to bear on this hypothesis; he collected information on endogamy, breeding distance, and genetic variation over a large part of the !Kung range (Harpending and Jenkins 1971). He then subdivided this region into nine smaller areas and calculated the proportion of parents in one of these areas who were also born there; this proportion measures group endogamy. For the nine areas (with populations of approximately 200–300 people each), this averages 0.57, which may be compared to 0.97 for a series of Maya villages (Cavalli-Sforza and Bodmer 1971) and 0.83 for a series of Oxfordshire villages (Smith 1969). Harpending also used the Wahlund inbreeding coefficient (F), a standard measure of gene frequency variance, to assess endogamy. Low values indicate relative uniformity, and the figure of 0.14 for the !Kung may serve as a rough basis for comparison with other societies (see Table 2). Because of varying total size and local population size, these figures should not be taken too seriously, but their relative ordering is probably significant.

As Table 2 shows, those hunting and gathering societies for whom data are available do fall toward the anucleate extreme, and this makes sense in the light of the environmental argument I have outlined. One may suggest that nucleation corresponds directly with resource stability and predictability. Conservation of property rights—rich resources on ocean or

TABLE 2.   Wahlund F Inbreeding Coefficient Values for Various Groups[a]

	F estimate
Settled agricultural peoples	
Parma Valley	0.036
New Guinea tribes	0.045
South American tribes	0.082
African groups	0.042
Papago	0.023
Hunter–gatherers	
Pigmies	0.020
Australian tribes	0.040
!Kung	0.014
Greenland Eskimo	0.005

[a] Derived from Harpending and Jenkins (1971).

river shores, cultivated fields and crops, or domestic animals—may best take place in a nucleated society, while rapid flow of information and individuals favors anucleation. Thus, one would predict a considerable variability among hunting–gathering societies, with desert or high arctic adapted groups at one extreme and perhaps some Northwest Coast Indian groups at the other extreme. And societies on this latter end of the scale probably overlap with some primitive agricultural and pastoral groups. While no claim of proof can be made, the data presented in Table 2 support such a view.

If my line of reasoning is correct, the implications are considerable. Our early hominid ancestors who evolved in sub-Saharan Africa and possibly other tropical parts of the Old World almost certainly lived in regions richer in both plant and animal foods than the Kalahari is today. Yet environments can only be understood in terms of a group's ability to utilize them, and early hominid technology was undoubtedly less efficient than the modern !Kung counterpart. Also, early Pleistocene sediments from both eastern and southern Africa reveal evidence of marked environmental fluctuation. The ability, then, to be flexible, to maintain and choose between a number of alternatives would have a strong positive selective value. The !Kung have a term for those who excel at this; they call them *t'xudi kaus,* masters of cleverness. And I would suggest that over the course of human evolution it is the *t'xudi kaus* who have seen a larger proportion of their offspring reach reproductive age. To focus on aggressiveness as the key human adaptive strategy is, I would argue, a serious mistake.

A Comparison of the Band and the Individual Approaches

Any model or generalization can be evaluated against two standards. The first involves validity; How easily does it encompass existing facts? And what, if any, is its predictive value? The second involves its usefulness as a framework for future research: What kinds of interesting questions may be posed within it? Given these criteria, one is not faced with an either–or choice when comparing the band model and the individual model. I have tried to show that both can order certain sets of observations and both may have predictive value. But their utility does vary according to the context in which they are used; the crucial variable is time.

Let me first evaluate the group model from this point of view. If the individual is ignored, the concepts of a territory and a band have great explanatory value and can prove useful over both the short and the long run, as long as a certain amount of flexibility is built into the system. Within such a framework, one can fruitfully discuss such questions as the relationship between carrying capacity, territory size, group size, safety margins, and so on. At Dobe, for example, evidence indicates that some such relationship does exist. In 1964 the camp included 25 adults, in 1968, 22 adults, and in the following year, 28 adults. Within the band–territory model one may try to explain such regularities in terms of optimum group size for information sharing, scouting, hunting and carrying parties, meat sharing and preservation, and so on. Only when the *specific individual* is added to the equation and groups are defined in this way, do difficulties arise. Even with the individual added in, the model is useful if the time frame is kept short. It may serve to explain the particular residence pattern at one moment in time, but it will break down over the long run. To be fair, Lee himself realizes this when he states that "a first approximation of the 'half-life' of a group's tenure at a waterhole can be estimated at 30 to 50 years [1972a:129]."

A model based on almost random long-term individual or family movement realizes its greatest potential when long time spans and either directional or nondirectional change is involved. However, this approach suffers from several serious drawbacks. It is difficult to evaluate, given the short-run data usually collected during anthropological fieldwork; and even a 20-year run may be too brief to give the necessary information. Also, one cannot consider such questions as carrying capacity or group size in this framework. The individual model works only on a microlevel, since it cannot explain cultural boundaries—tribal and linguistic differences—which of course do exist. However, in its more formal exposition, it is well adapted to cross-cultural studies and can best be used in an expanded time frame such as that most often employed by archaeologists and geneticists.

To conclude this section, I would ask the question: Why do the !Kung say one thing and do something else? I will suggest that the two models complement each other. For a society to function effectively, some consistent mapping between people and available resources must exist. Over the short run some balance must be struck so that an individual can predict with some degree of accuracy where other people will be and what options may be open and advantageous for him. A very short-term model, which includes the elements of the territory, the band, and individuals who are at least partly associated with a territory, can accomplish this. To complement this, the individual model allows for long-term demographic changes within the context of bands and territories by emphasizing the different network of kinship ties or inherited rights.

One may suggest that two alternate approaches exist for establishing, justifying, and maintaining complex patterns on a societal level. The first requires strict adherence to an extremely detailed set of rules which take account of all foreseeable problems and alternatives. Of necessity, this involves bookkeeping, either mental or written, and some authority capable of interpreting or adjudicating ambiguous cases when more than one course of action seems permissible. The United States income tax system provides a good example of such a regulatory approach, and I suggest that such systems are most applicable to literate societies that have a centralized power structure. The alternative is to employ an extremely simple set of rules which are ambiguous enough to permit difference in interpretation and loose enough to require only minimal compliance. As such, they may provide a convenient mental framework for deciding on and justifying varying courses of individual action, as well as a means for predicting in a loose way what other people will do. At the same time such a system is flexible enough to permit adaptation to conditions which may shift in rapid and unpredictable ways. Given such an arrangement, one should expect that rules would be simple and specific, that compliance—objectively assessed—would be slight, and that analysis of such a situation would require two levels of examination—one formal, the other empirical.

While a situation of this kind need create no logical problems for an individual !Kung, it can raise major difficulties for the anthropologist who does not distinguish the way people act from the way they say—or even believe—they act. The problem is magnified for the model-building archaeologist who relies directly or indirectly on ethnographic material.

THE GROUP VERSUS THE INDIVIDUAL:
SOME ARCHAEOLOGICAL IMPLICATIONS

In his analysis of excavated materials and application of models that attempt to order past human behavior, the archaeologist must clearly separate the group or band, on the one hand, from the individual and such objects as stone tools or potsherds, which are given form by human hands, on the other. In his use of ethnographic data, he must again be aware of this division and realize that statements that supposedly describe actual behavior patterns may in fact refer only to hypothetical rules that may or may not be followed. Unless specific evidence to the contrary is present—longitudinal census data for example—I think one must assume that statements which summarize marriage patterns, systems of residence, and the like must be placed in the "normative" category. This raises serious problems for the archaeologist.

For studies that employ environmental, geographical, or locational models, difficulties need not arise since the individual need not necessarily be considered. Even though the model builder may assume that groups are composed of specific people, the individual, per se, is irrelevant. For example, if one tries to calculate an ideal band size based on hypothetical utilization of a particular environment or if one tries to define group parameters based on the number of male hunters, amounts of available meat for sharing, and so on, the individual is again irrelevant, and theoretical difficulty need not arise.

A second class of archaeological studies, however, does focus on actual people. For example, attempts are sometimes made to reconstruct cultural rules through analysis of the artifacts made by an individual and thus reflecting the thought process of his mind. Analyses of this type are beset by two procedural problems: First, the proposed hypotheses are not subject to proof—one can only show whether or not the data tend to support them; second, the archaeological models that deal with individual behavior are rarely based on empirical "census-type" ethnographic observation, but on "old !Kung on the hilltop" idealized descriptions. And in these situations formal rules will not suffice. Allen and Richardson (1971) make this point quite well.

Both Deetz (1965) and Longacre (1964) in their reconstruction of prehistoric, postmarital residence patterns run up against difficulties of this kind. Both work from historic, ethnographic, postcontact data to determine a supposed pattern, and then attempt to analyze archaeological data in light of it. Given that both Longacre and Deetz accept absolute statements made by the social anthropologist, what types of problems arise in fitting data to models based on such normative statements? Assume, for simplicity's sake, that the prehistoric societies did follow the supposed pattern of their more recent counterparts and that statements which a prehistoric informant might make coincide with those culled from the ethnographic literature. Grave difficulties still arise, because absolute compliance to a residence rule is unlikely.

I have argued that to deal with complex situations a society may adopt simple rules and then allow great leeway in their application. Thus, when rules are applied to specific individuals (and the archaeologically visible byproducts of their hands), normative rules must be converted into probabilistic ones. A !Kung informant may say that individuals are assigned to specific bands and territories, but the question really is, what percentage of individuals violate such a rule or reinterpret their own rights during a single year. How many Hopi or Arikara over a given period of time follow the postmarital residence rules set out? How many find an exonerating circumstance to avoid compliance, yet still pay lip service to the rule?

With the added element of time, a second problem emerges. Precise control is difficult in the best of cases, and the further back in time one goes, the broader the archaeological "instant" becomes. The crucial point is that time magnifies discrepancies, so that even principles which may be empirically derived over the short run become lost as the period lengthens. Assume the hypothetical case where an archaeologically definable movement includes 100 years or five generations. Also, assume that structures—earth lodges or rooms in a pueblo—are occupied by family groups and their descendents for that length of time and that informants correctly stated that a matrilocal postmarital residence rule applied. Then make one last assumption: four out of five females act as the system says they should. Thus, in the first generation, four out of five women, or 80% end up where they are supposed to. For second generation women, only 64% of them will be living where one would have originally guessed, and by generation five, only 33% would still be living in accordance with the predicted pattern. When the total sample for five generations is combined, one can see that only 54% of the women will have lived where, according to the rule, they should have. And when byproducts of their handiwork are examined, it can be seen why a clear-cut pattern will not emerge. Thus, archaeological models that recognize the individual but assume that people adhere strictly to cognitive rules over an extended period are beset by difficulties likely to be unsurmountable.

In a similar vein, consider hunter and gatherer band models based on the same assumption. When they pass beyond general demographic statements and attempt to deal with between-group interaction, their validity becomes open to serious question. Wilmsen (1972), for example, first considers how bands and territories may be best arranged to utilize differently distributed resources. Realizing the need for some integrating mechanism between bands, he turns, as others do, to the trade of finished goods, mates, raw materials, or information. He describes the composition and distribution of such hypothetical bands and then states:

> Demographic requirements cannot be satisfied by units as small as individual bands. Consequently, each band extends social links to other similar bands by means of affinal and fictive kinship, ritual sanction and prestation. Exchange has a major role in maintaining these ties.

> Sahlins has pointed out that, at the band level, reciprocal exchange between kinsmen serves a social more than an economic function. Bandsmen exchange in order to reassert and maintain the bond between them. And the things which they exchange, whether objects or vows, have attached symbolic meaning [1972:32].

Such a formulation is valid, only if most individuals stay put within their own territory. But for hunting and gathering societies, which tend to be anucleate, such a formulation, along with such associated questions as defense of territories by individuals, may become meaningless.

4

THE !KUNG SETTLEMENT PATTERN:
THE DOBE BAND

THE TERM *SETTLEMENT pattern,* when applied to the
Paleolithic, generally refers to the movement of a band or group within a
territory during the course of an average year.[1] Higgs, Vita-Finzi, Harris,
and Fagg (1967), and White (1971), to choose two from many possible
examples, use such a frame of reference in their attempts to reconstruct prehistoric settlement patterns in Upper Paleolithic Greece and post-Pleistocene Northern Arnemland. In this chapter, I examine the !Kung in a
comparable way, narrowing my focus from the broad demographic patterns
discussed in Chapter 3, and at the same time avoiding the level of greatest
specificity—arrangement of people and activities within a single camp—
since this forms the subject of chapters 5 and 6.

For the ethnographer, concern with settlement patterns is often
peripheral at best, but for the archaeologist, this class of data is usually of
central importance. The spatial organization of individual group activities
within a single camp and examination of the variability between camps
provide the basis for archaeological reconstruction; yet these are questions
often overlooked by the ethnographer, and it is worthwhile to consider why.
The main reason, I believe, is that for archaeologists and social anthropologists alike, explanation rather than description itself is the goal; since

[1] This chapter represents a revised and expanded version of Yellen (1976).

the form of a particular settlement pattern reflects more basic relations between individuals as well as between an entire group and the environment in which it functions, settlement pattern studies in and of themselves can become irrelevant. In an ongoing society, one may seek to understand these relationships through direct observation and interview. A settlement pattern can then be seen as a byproduct of these more basic kinds of interactions, and for this reason it is not termed a "system." One may speak of religious systems, political, economic, or kinship systems, ecological or social systems—and many anthropological "classics" have this word in their title. But for settlements, "pattern" is the more appropriate word.

Two brief comparisons between the !Kung and Western Desert of Australia Aborigines serve to illustrate this point. During the rainy season, the !Kung establish small, widely scattered camps which are only briefly occupied. They build larger, more permanent ones during the drier part of the year. On the other hand, Gould (1969) notes that Western Desert Aborigines congregate in large camps just when standing water is most plentiful and disperse into smaller groups during drier times. Why do these two desert societies, which are in many ways quite similar, exhibit such strikingly opposite patterns in this respect? The answer lies in the different resource distributions and rainfall patterns: The Western Desert lacks permanent water sources and only after a good rain is sufficient water available for population to concentrate at one place. As I have shown, this is not the situation in the northern Kalahari. Thus, to understand the different strategies that a settlement pattern directly reflects, one must first consider the environment. Let me give a second example. In !Kung campsites, most manufacturing activities take place near the family hearth; while comparable observations for Western Desert groups are not available, Gould notes that "The trimming of stone adze flakes is done mainly in the habitation area (*ngura*) of the campsite, with each man performing the work around his own hearth [1971:152]." The problem here is to explain specific similarities, and one reasonable answer is based in the shared !Kung–Aborigine view of the nuclear family as the basic subsistence unit. Activities that relate primarily to the family are carried out in the family area. Here, the underlying explanatory variable is social rather than environmental, and one can begin to understand why ethnographers have given settlement studies such short shrift.

Archaeologists and ethnographers may, and perhaps should, share identical goals. But while goals may be the same, sources of information clearly are not, and the archaeologist has no choice but to rely heavily on settlement pattern reconstructions. Much relevant data can be directly observed, and even badly disturbed sites with poor preservation provide information about location. Expediency often requires the use of this starting point before inferences about seasonal movement, group size, composition, and so on can be attempted. In this context, the basic archaeological unit is the site itself, which, on an ethnographic level, most often, though not invariably, corresponds to a camp. Given the material within a camp, one may try to reconstruct activities, and given a series of camps, more general speculations become possible.

This chapter is organized to reflect the dichotomy between what the ethnographer may observe directly and what the prehistorian must attempt to reconstruct by archaeological means. First, I summarize the data on which my subsequent analysis is based, describe how I collected it, and evaluate its strengths and weaknesses. The second part of the chapter focuses on patterns of environmental utilization, social grouping, and activity arrangement. I describe the seasonal round of the Dobe group and try to isolate the major factors that determine when and where specific moves will be made. The conclusions that emerge are these: First, group size and movement are, as one might guess, tied to environmental variation, but the relationship is a surprisingly loose one because of changing individual food preferences and group perceptions. Second, the distinction between the group and the individual evident in broad demographic patterns is reflected on this smaller scale as well. I then note differences in the spatial and temporal organization of subsistence and manufacturing activities. In the third and final part of this chapter, I examine the camp itself from an archaeological point of view. Typological methods for categorizing !Kung campsites are evaluated and consideration is given to the difficulties an archaeologist would face in attempting to reconstruct seasonal round and activity patterning on the basis of well-preserved sites. I focus attention specifically on the causes of sample bias and on the kinds of extreme variability between camps that result from very short-term occupation. The conclusion is that several basic sampling problems have often been overlooked and that in some cases "absolute" typologies, which group sites by supposed activities, may best be replaced by parametric approaches, where units may be ordered on a single scale of complexity. The commonly accepted distinction between "base" and "work" camps is examined to illustrate this point.

THE DOBE GROUP: THEIR TERRITORY AND COMPOSITION AND THE METHOD USED TO STUDY THEM

The group that spends the dry season at Dobe moves within the territory shown in Map 4. This region includes about 320 square km, located mostly to the north and west of Dobe, which provides the only permanent water for

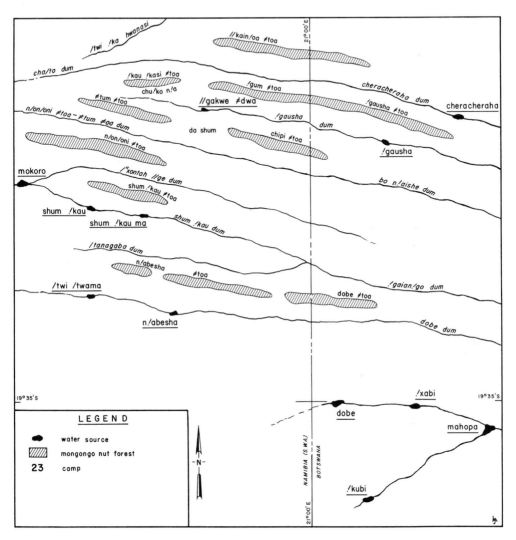

MAP 4. Area utilized by the Dobe group.

the group. Dobe itself lies between an extensive low-lying area of exposed hardpan to the south and the rolling dune and *molapo* system stretching to the north. While the southern area is extensively exploited for several months during the dry season, no camps are established south of Dobe. People primarily rely on the areas to the north and northwest, where

numerous camps are constructed and occupied. This northern area includes
five pans which may hold water for several months during and immediately
after the rains; one additional pan, !gausha, lies just to the east and is used
primarily by !kangwa-based groups. Nine groves of mongongo trees stretching roughly east–west along the dune crests, and the nuts they yield, provide
the dietary mainstay for the Dobe group. In the far northern reach of this
region, stretch a series of *hwanasi,* or salt pans, which attract herds of large
game during the rains.

I include in the Dobe group or band all nuclear families or individuals
who at one time or another traveled with the core sib group, and thus found
their way into the records compiled jointly by DeVore and myself. I have
already shown why it is difficult to equate a "band" with a specific
constellation of individuals over the long run, and would note that similar
considerations apply, with slightly less force, over spans as brief as one
year. A family may construct a hut at Dobe and occupy it for only brief
intervals spending most of its time at other waterholes. Thus, my criteria
for group membership derive largely from pragmatic considerations. Figure
4 details the genealogical relationships of all group members, while Figure 5
contains the same information in slightly amplified form to show which
individuals share a single hut. The vertical lines in Figure 4 indicate how the
nuclear families tended to group themselves at the time of this study and are
based on observed personal interactions rather than any formal set of
genealogical rules. Since the horizontal divisions serve to indicate social,
rather than biological age, sibs may fall in different categories.

/″xashe n!a's[2] group, which has the longest and most consistent ties with
the Dobe area, provides the core to which the other families, with the exception of those in the far right-hand column have attached themselves.
/″xashe n!a's wife, n//au n!a, is considered the *n!ore gau* or "owner" of the
Dobe area, but in fact, it is her three sons—all adults in or near their prime
as hunters who form the nucleus of the Dobe camp. From this point of
view, n≠isa and debe may be seen as half sibs through marriage, while
kã//ka n!a's group as well as dam and his father are in-laws of n!aishe, the
eldest brother. This type of arrangement around the sib group is clearly
described by Lee (1972 b). The families in the far right-hand column play
only a marginal role in the study. They centered on several permanent
waterholes located to the east, and none had a hut at Dobe.

At the outset, I must explain that much of the data on which the following analysis is based were collected almost as an incidental byproduct of my
main study. At the start of my fieldwork I intended to obtain information
on a series of !Kung camps to study intracamp patterning; it was the indi-

---

[2] I employ pseudonyms throughout.

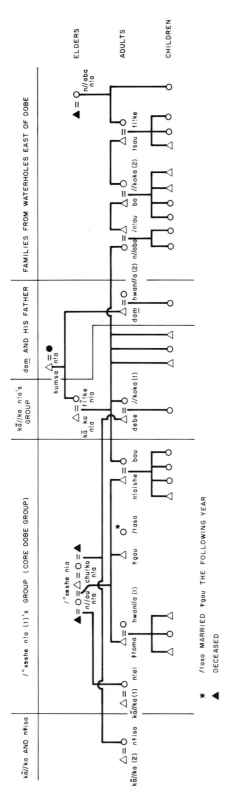

FIGURE 4. Occupants of mapped camps (excluding Camp 8).

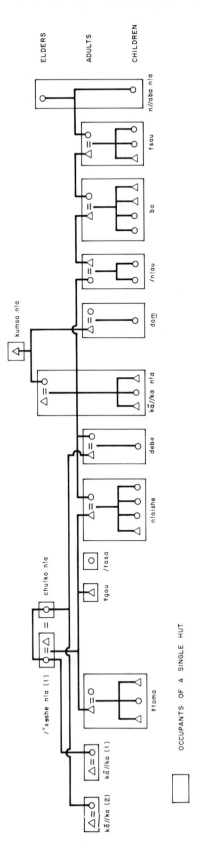

ELDERS

ADULTS

CHILDREN

FIGURE 5. Occupants of mapped camps (excluding Camp 8) grouped by hut residence.

OCCUPANTS OF A SINGLE HUT

vidual sites *per se* which held my attention. At some point in time after their occupation, Irven DeVore and I would sit down with an interpreter and reconstruct the day-by-day activities at a particular site through interviews with several of the people who lived there. This often took place at the very site, so that informants could answer specific questions that might arise as I mapped it and plotted the position of each feature and every scrap of bone. As my own familiarity with the !Kung language increased, I was able to conduct the interviews myself and dispense with the interpreter. As my fieldwork drew to an end, I realized that our data also documented the movements of a hunting and gathering group over the major part of the year and could be used to examine the whole range of subsistence-related questions considered in this chapter. But, for this end, I had stirred the pot more than I might have wished, because the effect of my own actions on group movement can be seen.

What we do have are fairly complete records on the movements of ≠toma and n!aishe, two married members of the Dobe sib group during the periods they camped away from Dobe between January 27 and July 11, 1968. This includes the season of heavy rains, autumn, and the first half of the winter, and thus comprises almost all of the moves made by them during the yearly round. If the start of a yearly cycle is marked by the first rains, it is likely that prior to January 27, 1968, the brothers made no more than one trip of perhaps 8 to 10 days to the north of Dobe. After July 11, 1968 we know that no other extended trips occurred until the next rains, because I was living near their dry season camp. A total of 37 moves were made, and 28 different camps were occupied. This information is summarized in Table 3 and Map 5 and is presented in detail in Appendix B.

I mapped 13 of these 28 camps—all those that contained faunal remains—and identified them consecutively both by sequence in the studied sample and by number in a specific geographical area. The numbering reflects the order in which the camps were mapped, not occupied. Thus "Camp 16, shum !kau 3" refers to the sixteenth camp I studied in detail, and the third of these camps located in the shum !kau *molapo*. I mapped sixteen camps in all. Thirteen were occupied by the brothers between January 27 and July 11, 1968. One, Camp 2, dates to an occupation from the previous year, while another, Camp 1, was inhabited by /n!au and bo and their families during the study period, just before they joined the two brothers at Camp 3. Since Camp 8, the final camp in this series, is located at !gwi dum south of the Aha Hills and was inhabited by an entirely different !Kung group, it is not relevant here. Basic information on this 16-camp series, is summarized in Table 4 and Map 6 (with the exception of Camp 8).

TABLE 3.   Camps Occupied by Dobe Group: January 27, 1968–July 11, 1968

Place	Location of site	Date of occupation	Number of days occupied	Site
1. Dobe	O	?	?	base camp
2. n/on/oni ≠toa	G	Jan. 27	7	*
3. ≠tum ≠toa	G	Feb. 3	8	new site (ns)
4. n/on/oni ≠toa	G	Feb. 12	2	reoccupy 2
5. /tanagaba	M	Feb. 14	2	ns
6. /twi /twama	M	Feb. 16	3	ns
7. n!abesha	M	Feb. 19	2	ns
8. Dobe	O	Feb. 21	17	reoccupy 1
9. n!abesha	M	March 9	5	ns
10. shum !kau	M	March 14	2	ns
11. n/on/oni ≠toa	G	March 16	2	reoccupy 2
12. ≠tum ≠toa	G	March 18	2	reoccupy 3
13. hwanasi	SP	March 20	3	ns
14. chu!ko n!a	O	March 23	2	ns
15. /twi !ka hwanasi	SP	March 25	1	ns
16. /twi !ka hwanasi	SP	March 26	1	ns
17. chu!ko n!a	O	March 27	2	reoccupy 14
18. !gum ≠toa	G	March 29	2	ns
19. Dobe	O	March 31	11	reoccupy 1
20. Dobe ≠toa	G	April 11	1	ns
21. ≠tum ≠toa	G	April 12	3	ns
22. //gakwe ≠dwa	M	April 15	12	ns
23. !gausha ≠toa	G	April 27	1	ns
24. Dobe	O	April 28	26	reoccupy 1
25. n!abesha	M	May 24	5	reoccupy 9
26. shum !kau	M	May 29	1	ns
27. n/on/oni ≠toa	G	May 30	5	ns
28. ≠tum ≠toa	G	June 4	3	ns
29. ≠tum ≠toa	G	June 7	1	ns
30. Dobe ≠toa	G	June 8	1	ns
31. Dobe	O	June 9	14	reoccupy 1
32 North of Dobe	O	June 23	1	ns
33. n!abesha	M	June 24	1	ns
34. shum !kau	M	June 25	6	ns
35. mokoro	M	July 1	2	ns
36. n/on/oni ≠toa	G	July 3	1	ns
37. //gakwe ≠dwa	M	July 4	8	ns
38. Dobe	O	July 11		reoccupy 1

* This camp was built in May 1967.
  G = Site in nut grove
  M = Site in molapo
  SP = Site near salt pans
  O = Other

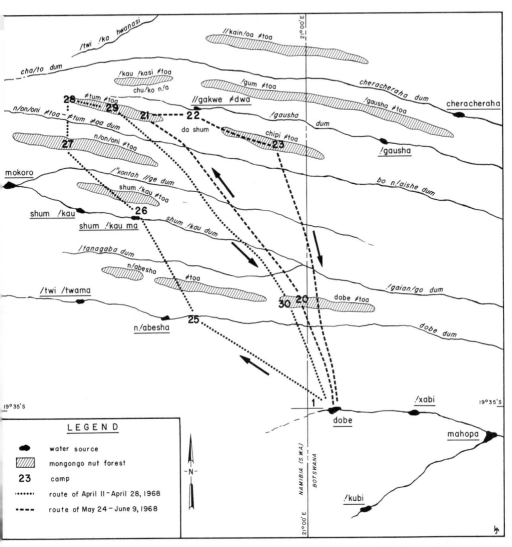

MAP 5. All camps occupied by the Dobe group, January 27–July 11, 1968 (from Yellen 1976:58).

In fairness, I must emphasize three kinds of problems with data quality. The first involves uneven coverage in the day-by-day records, men served as the primary informants and thus hunting activities have been strongly over-emphasized. In practice it is much easier to talk to the men because each day is in some way unique and stands out in the hunter's mind. Asking

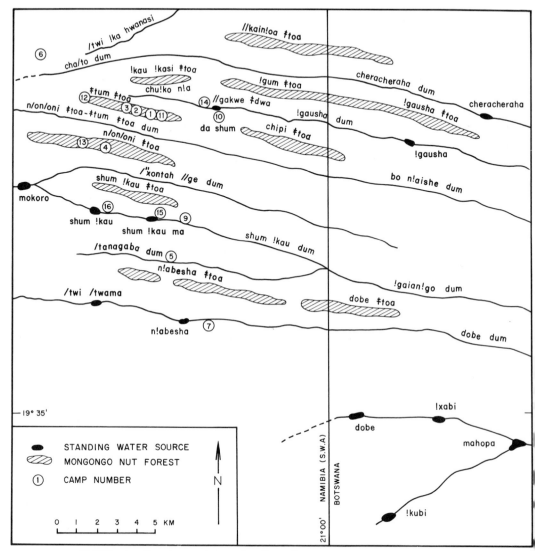

MAP 6.   Location of mapped camps (less Camp 8).

women where they went produces much less detailed and reliable information. Second, the bias caused by the presence of DeVore and myself has been mentioned earlier. At Camp 5, /tanagaba, I met the group, persuaded them to march north and retrace their route, and then drove them back to Dobe. The following two camps (6 and 7 in Table 3) were never, in fact, occupied, but I included them because the group was anxious to return to Dobe and had definitely decided to spend three days at /twi /twama and two days at n!abesha on their way back. At !gum ≠toa, (18 in Table 3) the group walked to the border road between Botswana and Namibia hoping I would meet them and give them a ride back to Dobe, which I did. And finally, at Camp 14, //gakwe ≠dwa 2, one assistant, one colleague, and I were present throughout the occupation and then drove the group back to Dobe at their request.

The third and most serious source of bias results from the presence of Bantu with their crops and their herds at all waterholes in the !kangwa valley except Dobe. During their stays at Dobe, group members could make daily trips to !kabi to visit relatives there and to drink milk. For this reason, no records were kept while group members were at Dobe. Once they moved to the north, however, food and water were obtained only by traditional methods, and in that context Bantu influence was insignificant. Had neither Bantu nor anthropologists been there, I believe that the basic pattern would have been the same but less time would have been spent at the permanent waterhole. I would also assume—and I emphasize this is only an assump-

TABLE 4. Summary of Mapped Camps

Camp designation	Initial date of occupation	Length of occupation
Camp 1, ≠tum ≠toa 1	a. Mid-Jan. 1968	several days
	b. Feb. 12, 1968	5 days
Camp 2, ≠tum ≠toa 2	June 3, 1967	9 days
Camp 3, ≠tum ≠toa 3	a. Feb. 3, 1968	9 days
	b. March 18, 1968	2 days
Camp 4, n/on/oni ≠toa 1	a. May 19, 1967	4 days
	b. May 25, 1967	1 day
	c. Dec. ?, 1967	6 days
	d. Jan. 27, 1968	7 days
	e. Feb. 12, 1968	2 days
Camp 5, /tanagaba	Feb. 14, 1968	2 days
Camp 6, hwanasi	March 20, 1968	3 days
Camp 7, n!abesha	a. March 9, 1968	5 days
	b. May 24, 1968	5 days
Camp 8, !gwi dum	Late March, 1966	ca. 30 days
Camp 9, shum !kau 1	March 14, 1968	2 days
Camp 10, //gakwe ≠dwa 1	April 15, 1968	12 days
Camp 11, ≠tum ≠toa 4	April 12, 1968	3 days
Camp 12, ≠tum ≠toa 5	June 4, 1968	3 days
Camp 13, n/on/oni ≠toa 2	May 30, 1968	5 days
Camp 14, //gakwe ≠dwa 2	July 4, 1968	7 days
Camp 15, shum !kau 2	May 29, 1968	1 day
Camp 16, shum !kau 3	June 25, 1968	6 days

tion—that decisions to move from one rainy season camp to another were affected indirectly at most by events in the !kangwa valley, and in my analysis of such movement, the "Bantu factor" may be ignored.

THE YEARLY CYCLE OF MOVEMENT: GROUP AND ACTIVITY PATTERNS

A camp's size, location, and length of occupation are determined primarily by environmental variables, and, in large part, reflect conscious choices by group members about how food resources in a given area should be utilized. !Kung subsistence strategy is strongly influenced by the desire to keep hunting and gathering trips as short as possible and to minimize the distances traveled each day. Most, if not all, of a nuclear family's personal belongings can be carried by a single adult, and a serviceable hut can be constructed in little more than an hour; these factors facilitate mobility and permit groups to relocate in more desirable areas with a minimum of difficulty. The major constraining factor is water, which for most of the year is available only at Dobe. But during and just after the rainy season, when smaller pans and hollows in trees are full, people move to take advantage of desirable vegetable resources as well as local and short-lived concentrations of larger game. The desire for a varied diet can be met, given the relative abundance at this time of year. Moves are often made to fulfill this demand, and not because food supply in a single area is exhausted.

I would emphasize this subjective use of resources because it implies, over the short run at least, a very loose quantitative fit between population density and carrying capacity. I would identify three factors responsible for this "subjectivity." First, the !Kung knowledge of potential local resources, though extensive, is not complete. The outside researcher cannot determine the degree of local ignorance, since his own is likely to be far greater and much of what he learns must be taught by local informants. But residents of other parts of the country have shown me that the best material for rope making, while available, is not used by the !Kung, and that substances other than the beetle may make more potent poisons. Second, as Lee (1965:100f) points out, the !Kung display marked food preferences which are based on relative abundance, ease of collection and preparation, taste, and supposed nutritional value. Some foods are avidly sought, while others are eaten only in a pinch. And finally, the !Kung themselves desire variety. Food preferences can change from week to week, since people grow tired of eating the same thing. Given the general ease with which food may be gathered, a group is willing to expend additional energy and either move camp, or walk further on a daily collecting trip than nutritional needs alone would dictate.

On a yearly basis the distribution of surface water exerts the primary influence on group movement. The pattern is one of concentration near the Dobe waterhole in relatively large, long-term camps during the dry months of the year, and dispersal in smaller units to nut groves and seasonal waterholes during and after the rains. Over the 26 week study period, I recorded 37 moves from one camp to another. Excluding the large base camp at Dobe, 27 camps were occupied: 11 of them in nut groves, 14 near pans in *molapos,* and 2 in intervening areas; 23 of them were occupied only once, while 3 were reoccupied a single time, and one was reoccupied twice. Excluding Dobe, an average occupation lasted 3.1 days; variance about this mean, however, is extremely high (see Table 5). The largest number of sites were occupied for only one day, but many of these served only as convenient stops to break longer journeys. I would argue that these may better be regarded as way stations than as camps, with the connotations this latter term implies. This also holds true for many of the sites occupied for 2 days.

As Map 7 illustrates, movements out of Dobe during and after the rains are basically cyclical in nature. Typically, a group heads northwards, occupies a series of camps as it goes, and then turns back again. Frequency of return to Dobe and length of time spent there are based largely on social factors: desire to visit other !Kung, pick up or leave behind individuals or families, visit Bantu cattle posts, or check in at the anthropologist's camp. But during their rounds to the north, the length of time spent in an area reflects decisions that relate primarily to subsistence. !Kung prefer to camp

TABLE 5. Length of Occupation at Camps away from Dobe: January 27–
July 11, 1968

Length of occupation (number of days a site is occupied)	Number of sites occupied a stated number of days
1	10
2	9
3	3
4	—
5	3
6	1
7	2
8	—
9	1
10	—
11	—
12	1

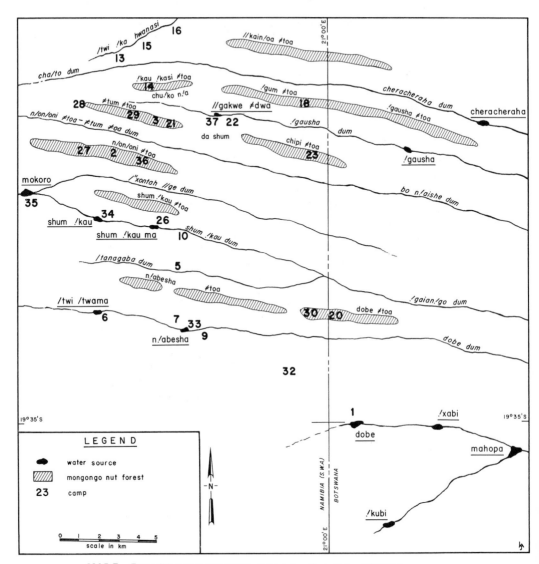

MAP 7. Two rainy-season trips by the Dobe group (from Yellen 1976:59).

in an area where a mix of resources—including water and plant and animal foods—is readily available, and shifts in campsite may reflect changing food preferences, the availability of new vegetable resources, or new knowledge about the location of wide-ranging and constantly moving large game. Thus, a group may spend several days beyond easy walking distance of a nut grove while the hunters scout likely areas for antelope. If none are found, the next stop may be a grove where nuts are plentiful, but the men must go further afield to hunt. If the hunters then see a promising area farther away, or perhaps kill a large buck, the entire group may move toward the kill, camp at the water source nearest to it, and remain there until the meat is finished. Of course in all such moves, water is the major constraining factor.

While the general area to which a move will be made is a matter for careful consideration, there are no hard and fast rules about exactly where the camp will be located. I offer one general observation: A former campsite will not be reoccupied unless the huts are standing in fair repair. The lifespan of a hut is short—often under a year—so generally the reoccupation will occur within several months of the original construction. A family then returns to its own hut. But for two reasons a group usually selects a new site in the same area: Old sites tend to attract fleas, ticks, and other forms of insect life which makes it more pleasant to relocate. Second, if a group returns to an old site in the same season, gathering will be slightly more difficult because the closest and most easily collected resources will be gone. At any rate, I observed no overlapping of new and old but discernible sites. Either a group will reoccupy its old huts or it will start anew somewhere else.

To conclude this discussion on the general seasonal round, I would examine the relationship among three variables: season, the length of time a camp is occupied (for that part of the year when more than one option is available), and number of occupants. Because most 1- and 2-night camps are just way stations and may obscure underlying regularities, I consider only mapped camps occupied by the two brothers between January and July 1968. This gives 13 camps in all, but since 3 of them (Camps 3, 4, and 7) were reoccupied, the total sample equals 16. I define length of occupation as the number of nights spent at a camp during a single stay, and I include both young and adults in determining the number of occupants. Seasonality was converted to a parametric variable by labeling January 27, 1968, as "day 1" and January 28 as "day 2," then numbering consecutively from there. Correlation coefficients between the three variables were then determined by Pierson's r, and the results are presented in Table 6. Since it is possible to predict the direction that the correlation should take, p values are determined on the basis of a single-tailed test.

Statistically, the results are clear-cut. Both the positive correlations—between number of occupants and season and between number of occupants and length of occupation—are strong, while the final r value, between length of occupation and season, strongly suggests no correlation at all. But practically, the results are difficult to understand, since I would have predicted a priori that the three variables would all positively correlate with

TABLE 6.   Correlations: Season, Length of Occupation, and Number of Occupants

	$\bar{x}$	s^2
Season	74.87	2842.65
Length of occupation	4.62	9.05
Number of occupants	16.25	23.53

	Length of occupation	Number of occupants
Season	$r = .05$	$r = .55$
	$p = $ n.s.	$p \le .025$
Length of occupation		$r = .57$
		$p \le .025$

one another. According to this line of reasoning, as "season" increased, the number of temporary water sources would decrease and group options would become limited. Thus, camps at remaining water points would be occupied for longer periods of time and group size would increase. Two of the three predicted correlations are, in fact, observed, but the third—between season and length of occupation—is not. I offer a possible explanation, which is admittedly hypothetical.

I set forth the possible causal relationships in Table 7. Seasonality must be an independent variable, and group size then is dependent on it, increasing as the rainy season gives way to winter. I would suggest that the length of occupation depends on the number of people, and I offer a possible reason for this. The time of year covered by my study is one of relative plenty, and it is possible to assume that obtaining enough to eat was no problem; it is also safe to guess that the variety available in any area was limited. I have argued that people desire variety in their diet and often shift camps to meet this need—and interview data in Appendix B support these assumptions. The deductions I derive from the above facts however are more tenuous in nature. If one assumes that not only overall amount of

TABLE 7.   Causal Relationships: Group Size, Length of Occupation, and Seasonality

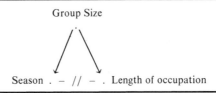

Arrows indicate direction in causal relationships.

food but also variety in any one area remain basically unchanged from January to July, it is reasonable that length of occupation at a specific site is not correlated with season. The one definite seasonal change, however— decreasing availability of water—suggests that group size will increase, since the number of people remains the same and the number of alternate places to camp grows smaller. It only remains to explain the positive correlation between group size and length of occupation, and I offer the following rationale. As the size of a group increases, variety in diet may also become correspondingly greater, and there are two possible reasons for this. First, the larger the group, the greater the number of people who may engage in those hunting and gathering activities that have a relatively low chance of success. For example, given more hunters and more daily hunting parties, the likelihood of supplementing the diet with meat from large animals increases. Other activities with relatively low rates of success, such as honey gathering, may also be pursued. Second, a larger group can obtain a more complete picture of available resources, because small numbers of individuals go out in different directions each day. They are not only gathering food, but they are also collecting incidental information on the location of point resources. The greater the number of such groups, the more extensive is the knowledge of the different resources available likely to be, and thus overall hunting and gathering efficiency will increase. Thus, a large group may mean a greater variety of both meat and plant foods for consumption; as a result, individual groups may be more willing to remain at the same camp for a longer period of time.

Perhaps at this point it is wise to pass from the environmental to the social aspects of settlement pattern. In Chapter 3, I used demographic data to show that individuals and nuclear families are loosely constrained in their movements, and the Dobe group was briefly mentioned. I now return to consider them in greater detail.

In 1964, Lee conducted a census of the Dobe camp (Lee 1965), which was repeated by me in 1968 and 1969. Any !Kung with a hut at the camp was included, whether he was present most of the time or not. Schematic diagrams of the 1968 and 1969 camps are presented in Figures 6 and 7, while in Table 8 Lee's 1964 data are incorporated with my own for 1968 and 1969, to compare camp membership by extended family. As this table indicates, at one time or another, elements of four extended families were represented at Dobe. Three of these (headed by /"xashe n!a, ≠gau n!a, and chu!ko n!a) are linked in the eldest generation by sib ties, while the fourth (headed by kã//ka n!a) is linked by marriage in the next generation to both /"xashe n!a and chu!ko n!a's groups. While two of these families are present in all three years, the overall changes are striking and illustrate in microcosm the kind of individual mobility evident on a wider scale.

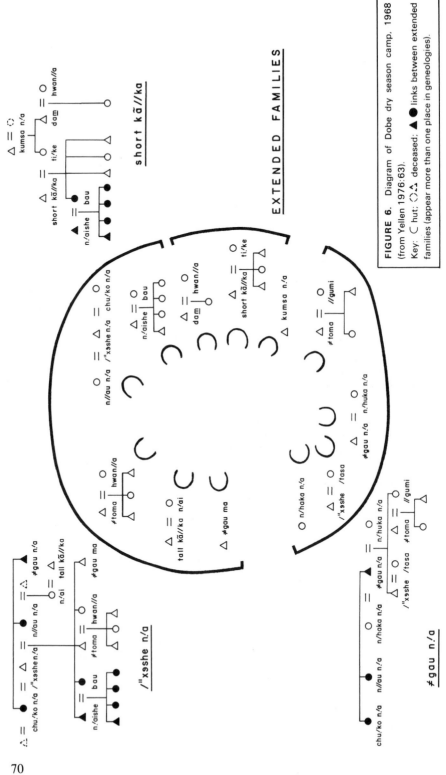

FIGURE 6. Diagram of Dobe dry season camp, 1968 (from Yellen 1976:63).
Key: ⊂ hut; ◐◑ deceased; ▲ ● links between extended families (appear more than one place in geneologies).

70

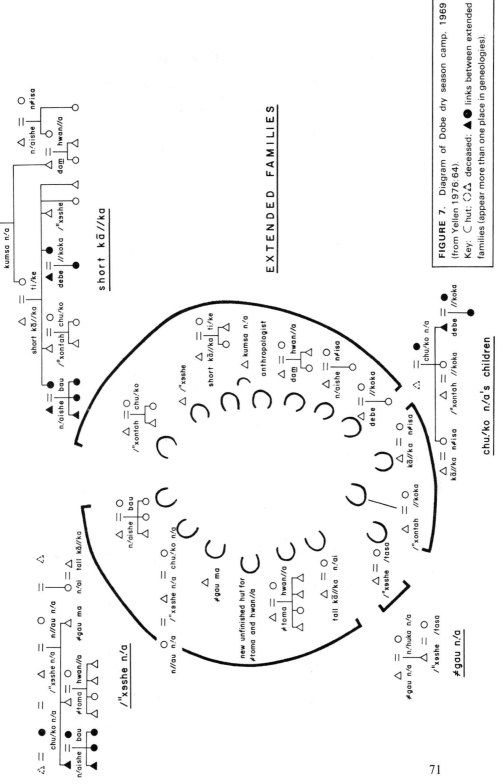

FIGURE 7. Diagram of Dobe dry season camp, 1969 (from Yellen 1976:64). Key: ⊂ hut; ○△ deceased; ▲● links between extended families (appear more than one place in geneologies).

EXTENDED FAMILIES

short kā//ka

/"xₐshe n./a

≠gau n./a

chu./ko n./a's children

TABLE 8. Occupants of Dobe Dry Season Camps: 1964, 1968, 1969, Tabulated by Extended Family

| | Extended families of: | | | | |
	/"xashe n!a	≠gau n!a	kã// a n!a	chu!ko n!a 's children	Total
1964					
adults	12	13	—	—	25 (+11 young)
huts	?	?	—	—	?
1968					
adults	10	7	5	—	22 (+13 young)
huts	5	4	3	—	12
1969					
adults	10	2	10	6	28 (+15 young)
huts	5	1	6	3	15

Of the 13 adults of ≠gau n!a's family present in 1964, only 2 remain in 1969; kã//ka n!a's group are not represented in 1964, but in the 1969 camp they have the greatest number of huts; and chu!ko n!a's 3 married children first appear in 1969. Five adults who have huts in the 1968 camp have none in 1969, and 11 adults present in 1969 are absent in 1968. In all, 33 different individuals live in the 1968 and 1969 Dobe camps, but only 17 of them are present both years. During the overall 6-year period, the core family of /"xashe n!a and his adult sons remains fairly stable, but around it great changes take place. One should note, however, that while the turnover of individuals is significant, the total number of inhabitants changes only slightly from year to year. There are 12 adult males and 13 adult females in 1964; 12 males and 10 females in 1968; and 15 males and 13 females in 1969. This suggests to me that constraints on individual movement are weak, but that overall settlement size is tightly controlled.

Even in one dry-season camp, turnover can be considerable, and very rarely are exactly the same individuals present for more than several days running. People make extended visits as well as very brief visits to other camps, and a hut may stand empty for a month or longer. Likewise, people may maintain a hut at more than one camp. The construction of a hut emphasizes the absolute right of a person to live at a certain place, but it is far from certain he will be there at any given time.

When one examines changes in group composition over my 1968 study sample, this same looseness in group bonds is reflected in a slightly different way. I divided rainy-season movement into "trips," with the Dobe waterhole as the starting and end point for each of them. Five trips in all were made. Table 9 shows group composition by nuclear family for each of them, and, since the two brothers n!aishe and ≠toma (with their wives and children) form, by somewhat arbitrary definition, the basis for my entire study, they are present in all camps. From this point of view, Table 9 only indicates that the brothers do in fact travel together. But note the changes that take place around this core: of the seven other social units represented, none is present on more than three (i.e., 60%) of the trips. Two of them move with the brothers 60% of the time, one shows an association of 40%, and the remaining families travel only once with the brothers. On no two trips is group membership identical, and even when group size on different trips is about the same, composition may vary markedly. Compare the mid-April trip with the late May–early June trip. In each case group size is about the same; but the turnover in group composition by social unit exceeds 50%.

The final question I would examine in this section concerns similarities and differences between camps in regard to specific activities that occurred in each of them. A camp may be defined, if one wishes, as a spatial locus for specific kinds of tasks, and likeness between camps may be based on activity comparisons. One obvious point to examine is the division between activities that take place in the camp itself and those that occur elsewhere. A second, less obvious distinction involves the differences in patterning between subsistence and manufacturing activities, since my own prolonged observation of !Kung indicates this division to be a useful one.

Dealing first with the inside–outside camp dichotomy, one may note that activities taking place away from the campsite are limited almost entirely to hunting, gathering, and collection of the raw materials for manufacturing goods. This latter task is generally incidental to food collecting. Age and sex primarily determine these task-specific groups, although there are a few exceptions: All members of a camp, for example, may collect honey together. The size of such groups largely depends on the task at hand. Thus, men usually hunt alone or with a single partner, but all men in camp may cooperate to follow a wounded animal, help butcher it, and carry the meat back to camp. Women generally set off to gather in a large group and then spread out a bit as they go, maintaining voice contact all the while.

I would categorize the raw materials that are carried back to a camp according to their eventual use either as food (subsistence items) or as the basis for manufactured goods. While the !Kung sun-dry meat from large animals to prevent spoilage, they do not store or hoard food in any regular way, and subsistence needs are met on a more or less day-by-day basis. Since camps are located to minimize hunting and gathering distance and food is not stored, it should surprise no one to find a close relationship

TABLE 9. Participants in Trips from Dobe, 1968

Dates of trip	Families[a]									Number of participants
	n!aishe	≠toma	≠gau	/'xashe n!a	kã//ka (1)	Kã//ka n!a	dam	debe	kã//ka (2)	
January 27–February 20	x	x								4 adults 7 young
March 9–March 30	x	x	x							5 adults 7 young
April 11–April 27	x	x		x		x				12 adults 11 young
May 24–June 8	x	x	x	x	x					10 adults 7 young
June 23–July 10	x	x	x[b]	x	x			x	x	15 adults 8 young

[a] The names refer to heads of nuclear families, with two exceptions: ≠gau is an adult unmarried male and dam is accompanied by his very elderly father.

[b] During this trip, ≠gau was accompanied by his future wife, /tasa.

74

A simple stick is used to carry wildebeest meat from kill site to camp.

between the area in which a camp is situated and the specific kind of subsistence activities carried out there. And these activities are reflected in the debris found within a camp.

This tight correlation may be illustrated by comparing series of camps in three slightly different environmental settings: the open southern *molapos* of n!abesha and /tanagaba, the extensive n/on/oni ≠toa mongongo grove, and the *hwanasi* area in the northern part of the Dobe territory (see Table 10). I include in this sample all camps occupied in the n!abesha, /tanagaba, and *hwanasi* areas during my study but eliminate one camp at n/on/oni ≠ toa, with a 50 man-hr occupation, in order to equalize as closely as possible man-hours of occupation in each of the three areas. The distances between these places are not overly great; only 7 km—less than a 2-hr walk—

separates the *hwanasi* area from n/on/oni ≠ toa; and/tanagaba lies only 3 km further to the south. A !Kung can easily cover this much ground in a day's hunting or gathering trip. A comparison of the southern *molapos* with the nut grove camps shows that while small game was eaten in both areas, few if any mongongo nuts were consumed in the *molapo* camps. In all n/ on/oni ≠toa camps mongongo nuts were the prime source of food. At the *hwanasi* camps, within easy walking distance of the nut groves, no mongongo nuts were eaten, but only there was the flesh of a large antelope consumed.

Manufacturing activities, however, do not conform to this pattern. One can find no neat correlation between the area in which a raw material is collected and the camp in which processing takes place. I would explain this through reference to both the kinds of materials involved and the !Kung way of making things. Without exception, the raw materials—dried animal skins, pieces of bone and ostrich egg shell, sinew and vegetable fiber for twine, wood for spear shafts, bows, mortars and pestles, and the like—are light and even in their unaltered form may be easily transported. Manufactured articles often take a long time to complete; people work sporadically for brief periods and carry the partially finished goods from one camp to another. Also, it strikes me that the spacing of manufacturing activities is irregular and not possible to predict; at some camps occupied by several families for longer than a week, none took place. And the end result is the

TABLE 10.   Game and Major Vegetable Foods from Camps in Three Areas

	n!abesha and /tanagaba (*molapos*)	n/on/oni ≠toa (nut grove)	hwanasi (salt pans)
Number of camps in sample	5	4	4
Number of adult man days spent in area	60	58	25
Game killed and eaten in area	Small game 5 porcupine 7 springhare 1 hornbill	Small game 5 porcupine 9 springhare 1 steinbuck 1 duiker	Small game 1 steenbok
	Large buck none	Large buck none	Large buck 1 gemsbok
Notes on vegetable food	Mongongo nuts eaten at two camps only in limited numbers	Mongongo nuts major vegetable food at both camps	No mongongo nuts eaten

A tanned animal skin serves to carry mongongo nuts.

lack of a relationship between the source of a raw material and the camp or camps at which its transformation takes place. Thus, while one can predict how particular subsistence activities correlate with area, the same does not hold true for manufacturing processes. I would offer only one general rule: The longer a camp is occupied, the greater the probability that any particular activity will occur there.

SOME IMPLICATIONS OF INTERCAMP VARIABILITY

The site, which is the closest archaeological counterpart of the ethnographically observable camp, serves as the basis on which most reconstructions of prehistoric life ways are attempted. For this reason I must consider the camp as a discrete entity (comparable to the archaeological site), rather than as an almost incidental byproduct of different activity systems. Archaeologists, either consciously or otherwise, generally devise an a priori site typology and then classify individual cases accordingly. Such terms as "kill site," "base camp," "temporary collecting station," "summer camp," and so on dot the archaeological literature, and it proves a valuable exercise to examine !Kung campsites from this point of view.

The place to start is outside the camp itself. Both hunting and gathering activities take place away from the living site, and they leave few if any marks on the landscape. An eland, for example, may weigh up to half a ton, but the site of its killing is marked immediately afterward by only a few bones, the horns, the stomach and intestinal contents, and the scattered pieces of charcoal used to cook the liver and other pieces of meat. From an archaeological point of view, it most likely would prove invisible.

Turning next to camps themselves, one may distinguish between the dry-season base camps and their smaller rainy-season counterparts. The dry-season camps are larger, and, because they are occupied for much longer periods of time, the huts are better constructed and more evenly arranged. For the same reason, more debris piles up in them, and the ash of winter fires (fed through the entire night and part of the day) is carted away and dumped behind the huts. People may live in such a camp as long as 6 months, and only if a death occurs there or it becomes extremely rank and bug ridden will it be abandoned for a nearby site, generally less than 100 m away. In contrast, the rainy-season camps are smaller; they have fewer huts and occupants, are more briefly inhabited, and consequently are marked by less debris and fewer if any dumps. After the main rains are over, these more rudimentary huts are placed to incorporate small trees and leafy

A large Dobe dry-season camp.

A small two-hut, rainy-season camp.

Occupants of a small rainy-season camp.

bushes and thus minimize construction. To keep clearing to a minimum, they are placed so as to avoid thick clumps of bushes and take advantage of small open spaces, with the result that huts are more irregularly arranged and their spacing does not necessarily have an even circular pattern.

With one exception, differences between the largest rainy camps (such as Camps 8 and 14) and their dry-season counterparts are of degree rather than of kind. On the basis of size, number of occupants, and overall configuration, they could easily be confused with dry-season sites. The only crucial difference lies in location: Dry season camps are always near permanent water, rainy season ones only rarely so. But from an archaeological perspective, even this criterion may become relative, for reconstruction of past water distribution is by no means an easy task. !gausha and //gakwe ≠dwa, for example, both lie on a feeder tributary to the !kangwa valley. Both pans probably held year-round water sometime in the past, but we have no idea just when this might have been. If a prehistoric site were found near the !gausha pan and one assumed that its inhabitants followed a "!Kung pattern," one still could not be sure whether the site was occupied in the dry season or not.

Because of their basic similarities, rainy- and dry-season camps can be arranged on a single scale ranging from small, short-term camps marked by scant amounts of debris, at one end, to larger counterparts occupied for longer periods and more densely covered with assorted kinds of remains, at the other. It is then possible to speculate on the degree of likelihood that an individual camp will be preserved in such a form to permit discovery by some future archaeologist. Is there some minimum level of archaeological visibility? I suggest that there is, and I think that it is most likely that none but the largest !Kung dry-season camps would be found by the future archaeologist. During the course of my own work, I noted the location of all Late Stone Age surface scatters. Almost certainly a Khoisan people are responsible for them, and geological and faunal evidence indicates that environmental conditions at the time of deposition were as dry as or drier than the present. Using !Kung informants, I surveyed the !kangwa valley and most of the Dobe area and found that all sites were in areas near permanent water—where !Kung construct their dry-season camps today. If one makes the likely assumption—but an assumption nonetheless—that these Late Stone Age peoples utilized the environment in much the same way as their modern counterparts, this implies that none of their smaller, rainy-season sites were discovered by surface survey techniques, that the archaeological visibility of such sites was nil. It is worthwhile to add that trial excavation at the site of modern rainy-season camps near larger seasonal water points did yield a few scattered Late Stone Age lithic remains, but I had to search very hard and know just where to look to find them. This shows that these

Late Stone Age peoples did camp away from permanent water sources. It also implies that, all else being equal, a close correlation exists between site size—including both the extent and the density of debris—and likelihood of archaeological discovery. In part, this conclusion is commonsensical, but, interpreted in light of a modern !Kung settlement pattern, the Late Stone Age data suggest that, as site size decreases, the likelihood of discovery lessens at a remarkably rapid rate; also, that the bias is much higher than I personally would have suspected. And this gives rise to obvious difficulties in reconstructing seasonal movement on the basis of excavated data.

A second problem is also directly related to camp size and length of occupation; it involves lack of activity overlap from site to site and the difficulty this raises in intercamp comparisons. The smaller a camp and the briefer its occupation, the more greatly it will differ from its immediate neighbors in terms of similarity of remains. The divergence will be most marked and most difficult to understand when byproducts of manufacturing activities are compared, while differences in subsistence remains may be explained in light of a more meaningful pattern. Recall the difference in patterning between subsistence and manufacturing activities and then consider the likelihood that any specific activity will take place in a camp on any given day. For some activities, such as drinking water or eating food, the probability is quite high; for others, such as carving a spear shaft, it is extremely low. The relevant variables are how often the activity generally occurs, how many people in the group perform it, and total group size. Next, compare subsistence and manufacturing activities. The former occur daily and take place in all camps. They are closely tied to resources of a particular region, so that variation in subsistence activities between camps reflects differences in local resource utilization. Chance does enter; large antelope are sometimes killed and eaten in the southern *molapos* and nut groves, but the likelihood that such an "untypical activity" will occur on any one day is relatively slight. For manufacturing activities this same kind of pattern does not hold. If one knows, for example, that the Dobe group will camp in a particular place on a certain day, one can reasonably predict what subsistence activities will take place. But the distribution of manufacturing activities in time and space conforms to no such pattern, and even if one knows what took place in one camp it is still very difficult to predict what will transpire in the next one.

Over the course of a year, a certain number of each of these activities will occur. The question is, what is the likelihood that any one of them will be carried out in a specific camp? Four variables must be considered. First, the relationship between an activity and a geographical area; for subsistence activities the tie is a close one, and on the basis of camp location one can hazard a pretty good guess whether or not a specific subsistence activity will occur. For a manufacturing process however, the chance of a correct guess is much lower. Second, one must have some idea how often during the year a specific activity is carried out; generally, the rarer the action the less predictable it becomes, and again this applies with particular force in manufacturing activities. Some subsistence acts, such as honey gathering, although uncommon, are strictly seasonal, and, given this knowledge, the likelihood of occurrence at a specific camp can be predicted. The last two variables, group size and length of occupation, must be considered together. If one assumes that most activities are initiated by a specific individual, and this most often is the case, the greater the number of man-days spent at a camp, the greater the likelihood of any specific activity happening. Again, examine subsistence activities first. The longer a group remains in a nut grove and the more hunters that are available, the greater the likelihood that a larger buck will be killed and consumed at that camp. Thus, a more complete range of the available food resources, including the less common ones, will be represented the longer the site is occupied. And for manufacturing activities not closely tied to geographical area, the likelihood that a specific one will take place is very closely related to the number of man-days of occupation.

What are the archaeological implications of this pattern? At camps occupied for only a brief period of time, the range of subsistence activities represented are likely to be "typical" for a camp located at that specific area during that particular season. Thus, intercamp comparisons are likely to yield valid information about how particular areas are used, and differences from one camp to another are likely to reflect culturally and environmentally significant facts. As the number of man-days increases and more kinds of subsistence activities are represented, the overall picture will be drawn in finer detail but probably not be drastically altered. For manufacturing activities, however, this relationship will not hold. The smaller a camp and the briefer its occupation, the more difficult it will be to predict what, if any, manufacturing activities took place. Comparisons among camps will likely give misleading results. Differences among camps will be both great and culturally meaningless. If a group camps at some place and then departs and the same individuals return for the same length of time a year later, it is quite possible that none of the manufacturing activities carried out the first time will be repeated the second.

The archaeologist, speculating on the basis of a limited number of sites, may find his conclusions going badly astray. It would be possible perhaps to identify "ostrich egg shell bead making sites," "twine making sites," "quiver making sites," and so on. While these identifications would be valid, the natural tendency to leap from there to a site categorization would do little to elucidate cultural patterning. The effect would be to codify what may best be conceived as an almost random process and best be appreciated through rules of probability and chance. And the smaller the camp and the briefer its occupation, the greater the problems of comparison.

A detailed typology of camp types, derived a priori on the basis of activities is unlikely to be suitable in the !Kung situation. One can actually see what kinds of problems arise when such an approach is attempted by applying one specific deductive formulation of this type. And because the model is deductive, meant to be applied as an analytic framework to all hunter and gatherer settlement patterns regardless of their position in time and space, its usefulness may be tested against a controlled single case.

Binford has suggested that two main kinds of hunter and gatherer camps may be postulated. One type, the base camp, is "selected primarily in terms of adequate life-space, protection from the elements, and central location with respect to the distribution of resources. [Maintenance activities] related to the preparation and distribution of subsistence goods already on hand and to the processing of on-hand raw materials in the production of tools" take place primarily at base camps, which are distinguished by the presence of such activities [1966:268]. The second type, the work camp, is characterized primarily by extractive tasks—"e.g., kill sites, collection stations, and quarries for usable flint [1966:268]." Binford goes on to suggest that maintenance and extractive tasks, and thus base and work camps are

> not isomorphic in their distribution, extractive tasks more commonly being performed by work groups and minimal segments of the society at locations determined by the distributions of resources within a territory. Maintenance activities, on the other hand, would tend to occur at locations selected principally in terms of space and shelter requirements of the residence group [1966:291–292].

In one way, Binford's distinction does fit the !Kung because extractive activities are generally undertaken by special work groups in specific locations where, of course, the desired resources are available. But this has nothing to do with camps per se, since these activities take place away from any kind of camp at all. It is possible to distinguish between !Kung dry-season camps occupied for long periods of time and their more temporary wet-season counterparts, and to show for the latter that location influences the subsistence activities that occur, but one cannot fit this division into the base camp–task camp pattern.

Based on the !Kung data, I would suggest the following approach. First, distinguish between activities that occurred within a campsite and those that took place away from it. (The latter would include most of Binford's "extractive activities.") Next, separate the food preparation and manufacturing activities that took place within a camp (both considered maintenance by Binford) and proceed to analyze as to camp variation on this basis. It may be most profitable to think in terms of a single scale of complexity measured by the number and variety of supposed activities that occurred at a site. Compartmentalization into discrete types is popular in archaeology because such typologies are relatively easy to handle. Each case can be fitted into a separate named box and comparisons can then proceed on this basis. The utility of such a technique is obvious, but the validity depends on the distortions that take place as category assignations are made and final conclusions are drawn. I would suggest that, for comparisons of hunter–gatherer activities, the utility is rarely great enough to justify such an approach.

5

INTRACAMP PATTERNING:
AN OVERVIEW

THIS IS THE first of two chapters in which I examine intracamp patterning. Based primarily on field observation, it describes how activities and individuals are arranged within a !Kung camp. The archaeological implications of these observed patterns are considerable, and, on the basis of them, one may seriously doubt the validity of many present-day approaches to the spatial analysis of excavated sites. I start by showing how a !Kung camp is arranged and then examine the nature and spatial ordering of social units within a camp. Within this general framework I then consider the factors that determine where specific kinds of activities will take place. Finally, I critically examine one approach to the spatial analysis of Paleolithic living floors, which archaeologists often tacitly accept. Several conclusions may be drawn: The most parsimonious way to understand the relationship between a specific activity and where it occurs is to distinguish first between areas that belong jointly to everyone in a camp and those that are the property of a single nuclear family. Next, to draw a sharp line between "nuclear family areas" and areas where special tasks take place. The location or locations for any particular kind of activity may then be predicted if such factors as the social context in which it takes place, its messiness, the amount of space it requires, and the time of day are known and considered. I would argue that this rather complex set of interactions precludes the simplistic notion that a straightforward correlation exists

Rainy-season hut in process of construction.

between a specific activity and a unique location. Unfortunately, it is just such an assumption that underlies most of the technically sophisticated interpretations that regularly appear in the archaeological literature.

I have been forced to relegate illustrative and supporting data to the appendixes. This organization may indicate questionable judgment on my part, since it is necessary to flip back and forth between this text and camp plans but because the camp plans themselves and related explanatory data form a cohesive and integrated package, I decided against breaking this mass into small and uneven segments, and I apologize for any difficulties this decision may cause.

!Kung camps are generally circular in shape, and the greater the number of huts a camp contains, the more nearly it conforms to this pattern. Huts are located along the circumference of the circle, with their entrances facing inward toward the center, and vary in type according to the season and the length of time they will be occupied. At the one extreme are rainy-season and Dobe camp structures, which are circular in shape, slightly under 2 m in height and about 2 m in diameter. These domed houses are constructed from branches set around the circumference, bent inward, and tied to form the high point of the roof. This frame is then covered with a thick layer of grass tied loosely in place, with a small area left open for the entrance. At the other extreme, at temporary camps not occupied during the rains, a hut may consist of no more than a few leafy branches stuck into the ground to

"Hut" occupied in short-term camp after the rains.

provide shade. The hut also serves as a place to store belongings, and it demarcates the area belonging to a single family. Very few activities take place inside a hut; only during a rainstorm do people sleep in them at night.

The hearth provides warmth in winter, is used for cooking, and serves as a focus for activities. Located in front of the hut, each is marked by charcoal as well as by a small depression, which results from raking coals, ash, and hot sand during cooking. Other pits or scatters of surface charcoal, which usually lie outside the hut circle, may also be present and these result from special activities. One other characteristic of all camps are scatters of debris generally confined to the area immediately around each hearth. For the most part, this debris consists of vegetable remains (generally nut shells

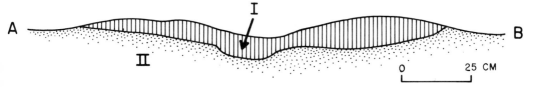

Cross-section of a hearth (Feature F, Camp 1). I: homogeneous mixture of ash, charcoal and sand; II: Light yellow, undisturbed sand.

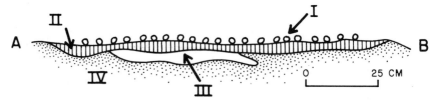

Cross-section of a charcoal scatter (Feature N, Camp 1). I: surface of scatter charcoal; II: Light grey sand with infrequent charcoal inclusions; III: Brown, stained sand with charcoal inclusions; IV: Light yellow, undisturbed sand.

and fruit and melon skins), bone fragments, and the waste products of manufacturing activities. The latter include bits of ostrich egg shell, bone and wood shavings, and fiber used for making string. Two fist-sized (or slightly larger) nut-cracking stones are the only items of value left at a campsite when it is abandoned, they are either used again when the camp is reoccupied, or are carried to the new camp when one is established nearby. Iron knives, axes, and adzes, which form the core of the !Kung tool kit are never left behind, and only once in the course of my work did I discover a lost tool.

Rainy season hut with hearth and associated debris.

The longer a camp is occupied or the more substantial the huts, the greater the likelihood that a circular arrangement will result. In early winter camps, occupied for brief periods after the rains have ceased, natural vegetation is often incorporated into the hut structure and nuclear family activities center on small natural areas of shade. Extensive ground clearance is rare, and camp shape—which tends to follow the distribution of leafy bushes and small trees—may thus be quite irregular. Conversely, in camps occupied by greater numbers of families and for longer periods of time, the ideal circular shape more nearly obtains. One may note that !Kung themselves are aware of this "ideal." They employ a set of six circular discs of dried animal skin to divine the future, basing their prediction on the relative positions of the discs after they have been tossed on the ground. I have observed tosses where five of the discs formed a circle and the sixth lay in the center. This arrangement is described as *chu/to,* or camp. Informants told me that the outer discs represented the huts and associated hearths and the central disc was a fire—perhaps a dance fire—which served as a focal point for the entire camp.

It follows that a !Kung camp may be divided into public and private areas. The public, or communal, part includes both the center of the hut circle as well as the space outside of it. The private, or family areas—in most cases the domain of a single nuclear family or adult—include the hearth, the hut, and the immediately surrounding space. An individual then sees a threefold spatial division: the area belonging to him and his family, the similar places occupied by other families, and the area shared by all camp members.

Huts are generally occupied by nuclear families, with a husband, wife, and immature children sharing a single hut and hearth. Young unmarried adults of the same sex usually live together in a separate hut, while widowers and co-wives have huts of their own. At the 1969 Dobe camp, 12 of 14 huts were occupied by nuclear families, 1 by two young men, and 1 by an elderly widower. Placement of huts around the circle is generally by extended family, with the huts of such a group contiguous to one another; in analyzing the placement of families in larger dry-season camps, the extended family concept proves useful. The 1968 and 1969 Dobe dry-season camps (Figs. 6 and 7) illustrate this point; in both, members of extended families occupy adjacent huts. The location of particular families is also of special interest. The genealogical link between the extended families of /"xashe n!a and kã//ka n!a is provided by the marriage of n!aishe, who is /"xashe n!a's son, to bau, kã//ka n!a's daughter. In both the 1968 and 1969 camps, these two extended families occupy adjacent positions in the hut circle, and in both the hut of n!aishe and bau form the spatial link between the two. Genealogically, this husband and wife may be considered as members of either extended family. The position of debe and //koka in the 1969 hut circle illustrates this same basic point. Through this marriage the link between chu!ko n!a's children and kã//ka n!a's family is established, and, again, the hut of debe and //koka provides the link between these two groups.

Given this division of a camp into a communal and a private area, and the division of the latter among individual nuclear families, I can now show how individual activities are patterned. The easiest way for me to do this is to present first an idealized picture and then consider in turn the factors that distort it.

Just where a specific activity takes place is determined first by whether the entire group or only individual nuclear families are involved. Some activities, such as dancing or the first distribution of meat, are communal and involve either representatives of more than only family or most, if not all, of the camp members. These generally occur in the camp's center and, incidentally, leave few if any material remains. Conversely, individuals sleep and generally eat in nuclear family groups, consequently these activities take place around individual family hearths. It is there that meat is cooked, divided into individual portions, and finally consumed; the resultant bone

A man scrapes dried skin with adze in front of his hut.

Multiple activities take place in the family hearth area.

scatters reflect the last stage of this process. Manufacturing activities are also carried out in this context, and the incidental byproducts of such work are also localized around the individual hearths. Often several men will work together to make and poison arrows, or several women and girls will cooperate to fashion beads from a broken ostrich egg shell; but these joint ventures usually do not take place in distinct and separate areas. They are centered about the hearth of one participant, with the other workers there as friends and visitors.

One consequence of this clustering of activities in individual nuclear areas is the presence of the discrete but very similar clusters of material remains associated with each of them. The site plan of Camp 5 shows this clearly.[1] A hearth, located in front of each hut, is surrounded by such remains as bean pods, bone fragments, and melon skins. In the site plan of the larger and more complex Camp 12, one may observe this same general association of hut, hearth, and the surrounding concentration of debris—byproducts of activities that take place within the context of the nuclear family. Because of this activity clustering, some parts of a camp are essentially empty, and this is evident at larger sites—see site plan of Camp 8—where the center of the hut circle is devoid of remains. In camps with one, two, or three huts,

[1] For site plans and scatter distribution of Camps 1–16, see separate packet accompanying this book.

no center-of-the-circle exists, and the pattern cannot hold. Since few activities, other than sleeping during the day, take place inside the hut itself, these interiors contain little if anything in the way of debris.

Let me now enumerate the factors that blur this simple division of activities between community and family and the related distribution between the camp center and the individual nuclear area. Some activities require a lot of space, and others are so messy that they would disturb the nuclear family area if carried out there. Fresh skins of large buck for example are pegged out horizontally to dry, and this takes up a good deal of room. Such skins attract both vermin and carnivores. Although conceived as a "family" activity, skin drying takes places outside of the hut circle, generally behind the hut of the person who owns the skin. Activities that involve heating in pits are segregated in the same way; ash-filled depressions in which animal heads are roasted for eating, or roots warmed in the process of transforming them into quivers, are also set outside the camp circle. The site plans of Camp 13, where a skin was dried, and Camp 6, where roasting and quiver making took place, illustrate this general point.

Most of the year, the sky is clear and the sun hot. For obvious reason, then, people try to stay in the shade, and this involves moving in accordance with the continually shifting pattern of sun and shadow. The hut itself shades the hearth area for part of the day, but when the sun is in the wrong

Pegging fresh kudu skin to dry in special activity area outside of hut circle.

A man sits inside hut for shade from afternoon sun.

place, people go elsewhere. At times the shift may only be to a different side of the hut, as evidenced in the site plan of Camp 12, where charcoal and nut scatters lie to the east and north of most of the huts. Movement to these areas is in response to a hot, late afternoon summer sun (in the southern hemisphere). But in most camps people move farther at certain times of day, relocating in shady spots close to the camp yet outside the hut circle. For a good example of this, observe the site plan of Camp 2. Thus, the same general areas used for skin drying, head roasting, and so forth are also occupied to take advantage of shade; exact location depends on the distribution of individual trees and shrubs. For this reason the very same kind of activities that take place around the nuclear family hearth are also carried out for much briefer periods of time in these shady spots outside the hut circle.

Children run and play where they please. They not only scatter debris about, but their play areas may lie either within or outside the hut circle; often such spots are marked by discarded debris, such as smoothed sticks, or water root shavings and one may see evidence of such activities in the site plans of Camps 5, 6, and 9. There are also some adults who have their own huts, and usually hearths as well, but are largely dependent on others for food, and they constitute a final disruptive factor. One widower and one

A husband and wife work in a shady area away from the family hearth.

A group of three children playing away from the hearth.

unmarried younger man are represented in the Dobe sample, and in many if the camps I mapped they ate and spent most of their time at the hearths of their closest relatives. Camp 6 provides a perfect example of this. Shelter 2, which was occupied by ≠gau, an unmarried male, has neither hearth nor debris associated with it, since ≠gau spent most of his waking time in camp near the fires of his brothers. In other camps, such as 12, both hut and hearth may be present, but associated debris either scanty or absent.

With all these complicating factors thrown in, it is difficult to predict what will happen in a particular camp; but there are several generalizations I would make. First, a pattern *does* underlie the spatial distribution of specific activities; the location or locations in which an activity takes place are not scattered at random, and the byproducts from many kinds of activities do form clusters that one can distinguish on the ground. On the basis of function and location, I would define four different kinds of activity areas. The first, located in the center of a camp is the *communal activity area* and in not one of my 16 camp samples are remains of communal activities present; it is marked by negative evidence only, and no further consideration is accorded to it. I term the second type the *nuclear activity area;* it includes the hut, the hearth, and associated debris, and it is within it that most family activities take place. Outside the hut circle, one may define two kinds of space: one used for shade, the other for skin pegging and the like. I label both kinds *special activity areas,* to differentiate them from their nuclear area counterparts.

When one sees just where any particular activity may occur, it becomes immediately obvious that in relation to intra-camp patterning a distinction between subsistence and manufacturing activities serves no useful purpose. An individual may cook meat, prepare vegetable foods, make ostrich egg shell beads, poison arrows, or make mortars and pestles within the nuclear activity area—because all involve relatively clean, non–space-consuming processes involving only the nuclear family. Thus the debris from manufacturing activities will lie intermixed with discarded bones, nut shells, and other food remains. And if the !Kung did have stone tools, one might guess that many of these also would be produced, used, and discarded after use in these very same places. Special activity areas that result from movement into the shade are very similar to the nuclear areas; but since less time is spent in them, fewer activities will be represented. The !Kung relegate only a few tasks, such as skin pegging, head roasting, and quiver making unique to areas; in very few instances are individual activities strictly segregated.

Finally, consider a single activity such as cracking nuts. This usually takes place within the nuclear family context, and at camps where nuts are eaten it is almost certain to occur around each hearth. But people also crack nuts in the shady areas outside the hut circle. There is a second

A woman cracks mongongo nuts in front of family hearth.

context, then, for nut cracking, and because of its importance in most camps, it is likely to be represented in all special activity shade areas. Now, consider a less common task such as making ostrich egg shell beads; in many camps it is not performed at all, but assume that one episode of bead making did take place. The tiny shell fragment byproducts may then be located either in any one of the individual nuclear areas or in any one of the special activity shade areas. Because of the relatively greater amount of time people spend around the family hearth, more likely than not the fragments will be found in that context, but one can be no more specific than that.

Against this background, one may evaluate models archaeologists often use to examine activity patterning within an excavated site. What underlies many of them is the a priori assumption that most activities are performed by special-purpose, job-specific groups, and that individual tasks are spatially segregated from one other. This is the underlying belief of Watson, Le Blanc, and Redman when they say

> Various members of a single culture may perform different activities in different parts of the same site at about the same time. The resulting horizontal distribution of cultural debris and features might indicate or delineate butchering, cooking, sleeping and tool-making activity areas [1971:119].

The most misleading aspect of this statement lies not in its overly simplistic nature but its implication that the primary nature of an activity itself rather than its social context uniquely determines the location at which it will be performed.

A direct correlate of this kind of assumption is that objects found in association in an archaeological context are related to a single task or form part of a single tool kit. Longacre and Ayres, for example, in their analysis of an abandoned Apache ramada (campsite) accept this from the outset and note, "The cluster of tools near the ramada presented us with a problem. Because they were found together, we inferred that they were used in a single task, but we were unable to suggest the exact nature of the task [1968:156]." While their assumption proved correct in that instance, it provides a dangerous a priori base from which to proceed. Whallon (1973:266) discusses the widely accepted concept of the "tool kit" as a basis of spatial analysis. At its heart lies the belief that the types of stone tools found in spatial association are likewise associated with a single task. Note, however, that at !Kung campsites stone hammers and anvils used to crack mongongo nuts are regularly found in nuclear areas, which also have relatively high concentrations of bone. But there is no direct relationship between the stones and the faunal remains. Each are physical markers of quite different activities, linked only by the identical social contexts in which they took place. In societies with relatively simple technologies—and this includes most hunters and gatherers—and lack of craft specialization, where an individual produces goods primarily for himself and for his immediate family, I would hypothesize that a large number of activities do occur in the context of the nuclear family. Thus, there is reason to suspect that the !Kung pattern I have observed is not limited to one time, place, or environment.

Let me end on an encouraging note. Activities in a !Kung camp are carried out in "corporate" settings and not in "special purpose groups." And this makes it likely that the archaeologist may move directly from scatters of debris to questions of basic social organization. Paradoxically, the seemingly easier step of reconstructing specific activities based on association of stone tools and other types of remains may prove more difficult and not serve, as many have suspected, as a necessary step or building block for more abstract kinds of speculation.

6

INTRACAMP PATTERNING:
A QUANTITATIVE APPROACH

IN THIS CHAPTER I try to do two things. The first is to use quantitative data to sketch, in finer detail, the pattern I have already outlined, and to show how such social variables as group size, composition, and length of occupation are reflected in the scatter of debris in abandoned campsites. Second, I consider the archaeological implications of these observed ethnographic patterns and suggest ways in which conclusions may be directly useful to the archaeologist. Here the ability to make predictions is of prime importance. In the present context, the bundle of numerical data, statistical analysis, and associated speculation is too tightly interwoven for the data and the archaeological implications to be examined separately, and thus two closely related lines of inquiry are developed side by side. The problems raised by differing perspective affect my analysis in a number of ways which range from the most expedient way to define categories to the much more basic question of just how these may be logically derived. I offer three examples to illustrate this point.

A first and fairly trivial consideration involves the different ways in which units of analysis are defined. The variable to which the size of a camp most closely relates is the total number of inhabitants (counting both adults and young), and the correlation between camp area and group size thus defined is extremely high. In an archaeological context, however, the individual is difficult to discern, and it is very hard to estimate the total number of inhabitants. On the basis of the number of hut rings, cooking fires, or the like, it may be possible, however, to determine archaeologically the number of larger social units represented at a site. So in my analysis I use the concept of "social unit," defined on the basis of hut occupation, even though a slightly better correlation would be obtained on the basis of number of individuals.

A second and more important concern involves the relationship between correlation and causality. In a site where natural features of the landscape impose no constraints on the size or arrangement of a camp, it is obvious that in any correlation between group size and total camp area, the former is the independent variable and the latter the dependent one. Thus, in a regression equation that expresses the relationship between group and site size, area will be the y variable and be placed on the left hand side of the equation. But, for the archaeologist, area or estimated area is the known variable, since it may be estimated by the scatter of debris, while group size is unknown. To change the proper descriptive equation to a predictive one, the dependent variable must be treated as if it were the independent one. In the sections that follow, regressions are often stated in both ways, depending on the immediate question at hand.

A final problem involves the way in which analytic categories are derived. On the descriptive or ethnographic level, when only the !Kung are considered, this question is irrelevant. The concept of a *nuclear area,* for example, is valid because it is based on observation of group members. If one examines a !Kung campsite abandoned perhaps 25 years ago, a practical difficulty may arise in trying to isolate individual nuclear areas, but one need not question the validity of the concept itself. To examine an archaeological site with no direct historical ties to the !Kung however, one must ask whether or not the idea of a nuclear area is even applicable, and it is not possible to assume a priori that such is the case. Of course, observed scatters may be crammed into such a framework, but the validity of such an approach is tenuous at best. Thus the question one must ask is: Is it possible from a specific set of archaeological data to determine whether or not a nuclear area concept is, in fact, appropriate? This involves identifying the basic and unique characteristics of nuclear areas and showing how these may be distinguished from their *special activity area* counterparts. And this most fundamental problem, of deriving a general system from a specific case or, from a more realistic point of view, determining the analytic usefulness of such a specific formulation, is crucial. Thus, for descriptive purposes, the validity of analytic categories established on the basis of observation may be assumed; for archaeological goals, techniques for the empirical derivation of these same units must constantly be sought.

I group variables into two general categories: social and material. Group size, organization, and length of occupation at a particular site fall within the *social* category, while the term *material* refers to actual remains left at a camp after the site is abandoned. At the heart of this analysis lies an attempt to establish the relationship between these two categories of variables: the number of people or social groups involved and the length of occupation, on the one hand, and the observable byproducts of the occupation, on the other.

To establish predictive relationships of this nature can provide a valuable tool in archaeological interpretation, and several prior studies have been directed toward one part of this goal. However, I believe that none of them can be successfully applied to Paleolithic data. The relationship between settlement size and number of occupants, for example, was first examined by Naroll (1962), who noted an allometric relationship between the area of a settlement under covered or roofed-over space and total population. He suggested that "The population of a prehistoric settlement can be very roughly estimated by archaeologists as of the order of one-tenth of the floor area in square meters occupied by its dwellings [1962:588]." Cook and Heizer (1968) repeated Naroll's study on a sample drawn from aboriginal California populations and also found an allometric relationship between total floor space and population. They noted that

> In aboriginal California the floor space per individual house was based upon a minimum average of 6 persons, with 20 square feet available to each. Additional persons involved an increase of 100 square feet each, such that as the mean number of occupants increased, the floor space per person approached a limit of 100 square feet [1968:114f].

Cook and Heizer also concluded that while a direct logarithmic correlation may exist between total settlement size and population within relatively restricted or limited regions, this association tends to disappear with increased sample heterogeneity. The direct applicability of Naroll's or Cook and Heizer's work to the interpretation of Paleolithic sites is slight. The most useful predictive variable, covered floor space, can only rarely be determined in an archaeological context, and in many instances it is not present at all. In terms of !Kung activity patterning, the area inside the hut is rarely used and is generally devoid of debris. Archaeologically, the very presence of !Kung huts, much less their size, would be impossible to discern. Two weakness of a more general nature characterize both these studies. First, control over data is fairly loose; both Naroll and Cook and Heizer rely on extremely varied and disparate sources. Naroll draws his sample on a worldwide basis; Cook and Heizer limit theirs to aboriginal California. But, in both instances, variation within a single society is not considered, and the latter authors postulate the existence of "controlling factors . . . derived from both the physical and the biotic environment, and from the cultural background of the people concerned [1968:115]," which they are not able to identify or isolate. Second, in both studies, only correlations are noted and no attempts are made to suggest underlying mechanisms. Yet, if some basic causal relationship could be found, it would then become easier to attack the larger problem of cross-cultural variation.

While several researchers have examined the relationship between settlement size and population, not one to my knowledge has tackled the problem of predicting length of occupation on the basis of observable remains. Again, obvious value derives from establishing a correlation of this type, but the problem of sorting time-dependent effects from others that may best be explained on the basis of group size is formidable. The total amount of debris at a particular site, for example, may vary directly with both the number of individuals present and the length of occupation.

A brief word about organization is necessary at this point. In the following section I describe the basic data employed in this study, their weaknesses, their value for direct archaeological comparison, their subdivision into analytic units, and the coding scheme employed. Next, nuclear and special activity areas are compared and intragroup variation is then examined for each. Correlations are then sought between larger areas within the camp and the social variables. Several interesting trends are noted and a *ring model* is proposed that permits group size to be predicted on the basis of an *inner ring* length of occupation to be estimated on the basis of an *outer ring*. This order of presentation follows the steps involved in the original research, since I devised a ring model to explain unexpected patterns noted in the earlier phases of the study. Let me admit at the outset that I can *prove* nothing, since the hypotheses generated from this single body of data require independent testing. But the present organization of materials permits one to view this model as a post hoc explanation, capable both of explaining previously observed patterns and of being directly confirmed or rejected, given and independent sample.

UNITS AND MEASURES OF DATA ANALYSIS

The same series of 16 camps previously discussed form the basis for this present study. For 15 of them, the length of occupation and the numbers of adults and young are known, and these camps are used consistently in the analyses that follow. For the remaining site, Camp 8, I do not have these data; consequently I included it in the total sample only when scatters observed on the ground are compared directly to one another without reference to social variables. I visited each of the 16 camps after the occupants had departed, and the interval between abandonment and study varied from several hours to 32 weeks. I would note parenthetically that no obvious relationship exists between the length of time a camp is deserted and the destruction or dispersal of faunal and other remains within it (see Yellen in press a). Future work hopefully, will, document the decomposition of camps over a span of time measured in years rather than months.

I treated each camp as comparable to a living floor uncovered through excavation. For each, a grid system was established, and all features were described and plotted to the nearest centimeter. These plans are presented in Appendix B. In all cases, at least one of the original occupants of the camp was present to answer questions that might arise during mapping. For scatters of very abundant vegetal remains such as mongongo shells, only the areal extent of the scatter was noted. Such scatters were accorded an alphabetical designation, as were such other features as huts, cooking hearths, and thin scatters of charcoal. Other kinds of floral remains—melon skins, for example—were treated as discrete pieces because only a few specimens were represented at any site; accordingly, they were numbered and noted on the camp plan. All other objects, such as nut-cracking stones, broken digging sticks, tin can lids, and ostrich egg shell fragments, were numbered (starting from "l" at each site) and their position recorded. All bone fragments were collected, labeled, and identified according to species, anatomical position, and the way in which each fragment was broken; a highly condensed summary of this information is also present in Appendix B.

One must consider the extent to which the 16-camp series may approximate excavated archaeological sites, since conclusions derived from this sample will hopefully be useful in archaeological interpretation. But the question is impossible to answer. Just as one cannot speak of a "typical" prehistoric hunter–gatherer lifestyle, so does the concept of a "typical" Paleolithic site lack meaning. Geological conditions, soil acidity, the speed with which material remains were originally buried, rodent activity, and similar factors determine in each specific instance the degree of disturbance or preservation of cultural material. Thus, I can only give some relevant particulars for the !Kung series; similarities or important distinctions between this and a potential archaeological counterpart will need to be judged on a case by case basis.

As one might expect, preservation of vegetal remains, especially hard nut shells, bean pods, and melon skins was excellent in all sites; but over the long run most if not all of these remains would disappear. For faunal remains, however, short-term destruction proceeds more rapidly. Although dogs were present only at Camp 14, all sites were picked over by hyenas and jackels in the interval between abandonment and mapping. More serious disturbance of faunal remains, however, resulted from porcupine and ungulate activity because, in the Kalahari, large antelope share the worldwide penchant of the porcupine for eating bone itself. And for this reason very little in the way of faunal material was recovered in some sites. Another relevant class of archaeological data is tools themselves; stone artifacts or byproducts of their manufacture form a major component of material recovered in many Paleolithic sites. The !Kung, however, use iron tools, which they meticulously care for and husband. In the entire 16-camp series I found only one such tool left behind by accident—a knife. No discarded specimens were found. Thus, one major and relatively nondestructable class of data is absent from the studied series. A final consideration involves the fact that only material observable on the surface was plotted. Since the uppermost several centimeters of sand on which these remains lie is soft and dry, fragments of bone and other debris can work downward to the base of this layer. Test excavations indicate that a fair amount of material is buried, smaller objects being the most susceptible to such downward movement.

The coding of *social variables* is a fairly simple and straightforward affair; the original and then reduced data are presented in Appendixes B and C, respectively. For reoccupied camps, the length of occupation was calculated as the sum of the individual occupations, and group size was based on the largest number of people present at any one time. The only exception to this latter rule is Camp 3, where membership changed drastically between the first and second occupations; here, group size was figured as the total number of different individuals present at one time or another. Married persons and sole occupants of huts were counted as *adults,* while all children who shared a hut and hearth with their parents were counted as *young.* I would emphasize that this latter category includes both teenagers and tiny infants. A *social unit* is defined by ownership of a hut and/or hearth and ranges in size from one adult to two adults and four young.

I used two different systems to subdivide space within a camp. The first is based on delineation of a series of progressively smaller units, starting with the entire camp and moving inward until only the scatter within the hut circle is included. Four separate areas, abbreviated "ALS," "LMS," "LNAT," and "LNAS," are defined as follows (Figure 8, a simplified plan of Camp 5, shows what each represents):

ALS (absolute limit of scatter): This line is drawn to include *all* of the camp debris. The outermost remains are marked by dots, which are then connected by the shortest possible lines.

LMS (limit of most scatter): A subjective judgment is involved in determining the LMS, which is meant to include all but those few odd remains and scatters of charcoal that lie clearly outside the camp area. In all cases the materials located between the ALS and LMS constitute less than 5% of the total remains.

LNAT (limit of nuclear area, total): This area includes all huts, their associated hearths, and the debris surrounding the hearth. This corresponds to what I term the hut circle.

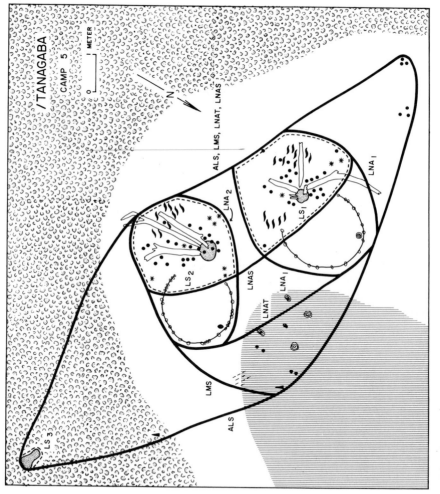

104

FIGURE 8. Division of Camp 5 into units for analysis

LNAS (limit of nuclear area, scatter): Since huts disappear much more quickly than the hearths and other debris associated with them, it is useful to recalculate the LNAT area, removing huts from consideration, and the LNAS is defined on that basis. Since evidence of shelter presence or exact location is rarely preserved in Paleolithic sites, this measure is of potentially greater use to the archaeologist than is LNAT.

The definition of ALS is precise. LMS rests on a slightly subjective base, but experience has shown that students, once shown how LMS is calculated on one or two plans, will show a very high level of agreement when each delimits this same area on the remaining camps in the series. In most instances the boundaries of LNAT and LNAS may likewise be established with little difficulty or disagreement. In the analysis of fully excavated Paleolithic sites, two of these four measures, ALS and LMS, may be determined in a fairly objective manner if excavation is extensive enough. The remaining two may or may not be relevant, and probably only in rare cases is tentative delineation possible.

I based the second system for areal subdivision on the identification of discrete clusters of debris. A hearth with associated bone fragments and nut shells, or a skin preparation area with a grass mat alone or mat and associated pegs illustrate the cluster concept. I ignore the odd bone fragment or melon skin seemingly unassociated with other remains in this clustering process. The extent to which clusters may be defined on an objective basis is crucial from an archaeological viewpoint, and it must be admitted that in this present study no such claim for objectivity can be made. I drew these clusters by eye, with prior knowledge of their social significance. From that point of view they are correct, but they are subjective to the extent that they would not be exactly duplicated by a second researcher. And from an archaeological perspective, herein lies the greatest weakness of this formulation. These clusters of debris are termed *limited scatters* and designated "LS," followed by an identifying number. Huts themselves are ignored in the LS determination. As Appendix C shows, I subdivide limited scatters depending on whether they are associated with nuclear family or special activity areas. The "LS:NA" (*limits of scatter, nuclear area*) are numbered starting with "1"; thus, LS 1 includes the hearth area associated with Hut 1, LS 2 with Hut 2, *etc.* This consecutive numbering is then continued to include the "LS:SA" (*limits of scatter, special activity areas*). Thus, in a site with four huts and associated hearths, LS1–LS4 will designate the limits of scatter of these nuclear areas, while the remaining LS designation will indicate other areas of special activity.

To provide maximum archaeological usefulness, huts themselves are ignored when LS areas are computed; thus, one final measurement includes both the hut and the LS associated with it. A space thus encompassed is termed a *limited nuclear area* and designated "LNA" plus a number. As with LS:NA, the LNA number including Hut 1 on a camp plan is labeled "LNA$_1$," and so on. Thus, at any site, LNA$_1$ will include LS$_1$ or coincide with it if no hut was present.

In summary, space within each camp is subdivided on the basis of two systems. The one may be idealized as a series of concentric rings designated "ALS," "LMS," "LNAT," and "LNAS." The other is based on clusters of debris, excluding huts themselves from consideration; each cluster is termed a limited scatter and is given an LS designation. A second set of nuclear area clusterings, which include the hut itself, are labelled LNA.

For each of the defined areas, two measures—the size and the "richness"—amount and variety of debris—are calculated. (There is only one exception; richness measurements are unnecessary for LNA scatters.) I express size in square meters (m^2), calculated by laying a m^2 grid of the appropriate scale over each area, counting the number of boxes that fell entirely within a delimited space, and then using a similar grid marked in centimeters to determine what portion of each remaining box fell within the circumscribed limit. For each area I also noted the maximum diameter (d), since in an archaeological context it is sometimes easier to determine or estimate this latter measurement. The correlation between diameter and m^2 for each kind of area is extremely high; in all cases a p value of equal to or less than .005 suggests that predictions made on the basis of m^2 could also be formulated by using relevant diameters in their place, although predictive value of this latter measure would probably be lower. Table 11 gives com-

TABLE 11.   Correlation between Diameter and m^2 [a]

		ALS	LMS	LNAT	LNAS	LS:SA	LS:NA	LNA
$\bar{x}$	m^2	198.44	150.04	122.23	116.11	2.91	10.66	13.33
	d [b]	19.56	16.84	14.91	14.64	2.09	4.45	4.90
s^2	m^2	8794.39	6165.41	7229.21	7532.54	15.60	37.19	43.12
	d	21.80	22.22	34.11	32.51	1.93	2.03	1.54
n		15	15	15	15	38	68	68
r^2		.8403	.8935	.9285	.9320	.9151	.8373	.8223
r		.9167	.9453	.9636	.9654	.9566	.9150	.9068
p	$\leq$	.005	.005	.005	.005	.005	.005	.005

[a] m^2 = meters squared.
[b] d = diameter.
ALS: $d = .05\ m^2 + 10.50$
LMS: $d = .06\ m^2 + 8.33$
LNAT: $d = .07\ m^2 + 6.82$
LNAS: $d = .06\ m^2 + 7.28$
LS:SA: $d = .34\ m^2 + 1.11$
LS:NA: $d = .21\ m^2 + 2.17$
LNA: $d = .17\ m^2 + 2.62$

putations of Pearson's r to show this high degree of correlation in all cases. In each camp I made two additional measurements: the distance from hut extrance to hut entrance and from hearth to hearth (see Appendix C).

Thus one series of observations for each defined area involves the measurement of size and distance. A second type of calculation, to estimate "richness," was also made for each area. Observation of spatial patterning of activities suggested to me that very few tasks are segregated on account of the nature of the process itself; skin drying, head roasting, and quiver making are the few exceptions. Most other tasks, however, can occur in more than one spatial context, and the likelihood that a certain activity will occur in a particular spot is directly related to the length of time people spend there. Thus, the longer one area is occupied, the greater the number of activities likely to occur and be repeated there. I guessed that nuclear areas and special activity areas could be distinguished on this basis and sought an index that could quantitatively measure the relative richness of any particular area within a site. I wanted *richness* to be based on two factors: the number of different kinds of remains present and the relative amount of each one. It is essential to note that, from this perspective, the identity of any kind of debris per se is irrelevant. Stated in these terms, the richness of an area can be considered equivalent to the biological concept of "species diversity" for a given geographical region. Buzas, discussing biological use of this concept, states: "Today many researchers consider number of species and species abundance as two aspects of the same thing. When they speak of "species diversity," they refer to both number and abundance of species [n.d.:1]." Applied to campsite analysis, it is possible to equate any particular kind of debris—porcupine bones, grass mats, nut-cracking stones—with an individual species, and the amount of any particular kind of remain is equal to the abundance of that species.

From a number of measurements available, I finally settled on the Shannon–Weiner *information function* (see MacArthur and MacArthur 1961). This function—termed H'—is expressed by the equation:

$$H' = \sum_{i=1}^{s} \frac{n_i}{N} \log\left(\frac{n_i}{N}\right),$$

where

> s is the number of species,
> N is the total number of individuals, and
> n_i is the number of individuals in the ith species.

The H' value is, in effect, a measure of uncertainty. As the number of species increases, and as the distribution of members among species becomes more nearly even, the value of H' increases. The higher the H', the more difficult it becomes to predict the identity of any individual chosen at random from the cluster. The H' value is not the ideal measure for LS richness, since it does not take the absolute amount directly into account, but I considered it adequate because it could be applied to site analysis without assuming that discarded nut shells, ostrich egg shell fragments, and the like act according to the same rules as biological populations; the resultant H' measures seemed reasonable by intuitive assessment. Finally, H' can be easily calculated.

The one problem in applying the H' value to campsite analysis involves the treatment of scatters. Discrete objects such as porcupine bones or nut-cracking stones can be counted; for scatters of such items as charcoal and mongongo nut shells, which do not lend themselves to this treatment, the size of the feature must be considered. To do this I used a scaled grid to measure scatter size to the nearest 10 cm^2. A scatter that covered one meter was given an arbitrary rating of 10. For example, if one LS contained 12 porcupine bone fragments, 4 hornbill bones, 0.72 m^2 of charcoal and 0.58 m^2 of mongongo shell scatter, the total number of species represented is equal to 4, and the number of individuals within each species is 12, 4, 7, and 6, respectively. With this data, H' can then be determined; calculations for each LS are presented in Appendix C. A corrected version of H', termed H' (C), has also been computed, and it alone is used in the analyses that follow. In $H'(C)$, scatters are multiplied by a constant, so that on the average their weight is equal to that of "species" composed of discrete individuals.

Thus, any circumscribed area may be evaluated on the basis of size and richness. In neither of these measures is the actual nature of the "species" or kinds of debris considered; two LS will have the same H' (C) if each has the same number of species and an identical distribution of individuals or areas among species. That one area may contain porcupine bones and mongongo shells while the other has charcoal and ostrich egg shell fragments is irrelevant. A third and final way, then, of describing and comparing individual areas is by type of constituent; data necessary for such an undertaking are presented in Appendix B. I would suggest that either dendritic or two-dimensional cluster analysis can easily be adapted for this end.

ANALYSIS OF LIMITED AREAS OF SCATTER

I define *limited areas of scatter* (LS) as areas of concentrated debris observable on camp plans and delineated by eye. Scatters associated with family hearths and resulting from activities carried out in a nuclear family

TABLE 12. Comparison of LS:NA and
LS:SA on Basis of Richness

	LS:NA	LS:SA
$\bar{x}$	1.31	0.51
s	0.47	0.50
n	74	52

Student's $t = 9.17$.
$p \leq .001$.

context I term *nuclear area scatters* (LS:NA), while all others are classed as *special activity areas* (LS:SA). Within this framework, it is valuable first to compare LS:NA as a group to their LS:SA counterparts and then to examine intragroup variation for each of these categories.

On the basis of either size or richness, the differences between LS:NA and LS:SA are immediately apparent (see Tables 12 and 13 and Figure 9). These results are not surprising. Nuclear areas are markedly richer than special activity areas, as one might predict, since much less time is spent by fewer people in the latter. For similar reasons, it is not surprising to find that nuclear areas are also significantly larger. These results are also gratifying because they support the validity of the original distinction (based on direct observation of !Kung activity patterning), between these two types of area. Fairly good separation between nuclear and special activity areas may be obtained when each is plotted on a graph, with area on one axis and richness on the other (see Figure 9). Note the effect of social unit size; units composed of only a single adult fall within the range of special activity areas.

The most significant questions to ask are these: If one were given all the LS units undifferentiated as to type, would it be possible to divide the total sample into its two constituent parts with any degree of accuracy or even realize its heterogenous nature? I would answer a qualified "yes," since the total sample, when plotted on the basis of H' (C), assumes a bimodel pat-

TABLE 13. Comparison of LS:NA and
LS:SA on Basis of Area

	LS:NA	LS:SA
$\bar{x}$	10.93	2.49
s	6.28	3.49
n	74	52

Student's $t = 8.78$.
$p \leq .001$.

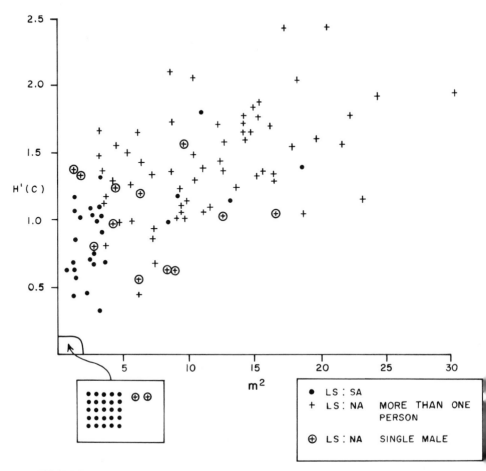

FIGURE 9.   Distribution of LS:NA and LS:SA against area and richness.

tern that reflects the only slightly overlapping distributions of LS:NA and LS:SA. This suggests that the potential applicability of this division may be evaluated in any specific archaeological context. When area, however, is plotted in a similar fashion, no hint of bimodality can be detected (see figures 10 and 11).

Let me shift focus and consider only LS:NA. If Camp 8 (with incomplete data) is excluded, the remaining 15 camps provide a sample of 68 nuclear areas for study. For each, size and richness are known, and one may demonstrate the close correlations between these two dependent measures and the independent variables of social unit size and length of occupation. I must note at the outset that the number of individuals in a nuclear area varies independently from the length of occupation (see Table 14).

Starting with the relationship between length of occupation and area, Table 15 shows that the two variables are closely correlated regardless of the size of the associated social unit. And when the size of the social unit is held constant (see Table 16), this same correlation holds. Thus, ≠toma's family, which includes two adults and three young (2A + 3Y), was present at 14 of the camps in the sample. And when LS:NAs occupied by only ≠toma are considered, the correlation between area and length of occupation is significant. It is extremely interesting to note that of the four social units I analyze in this way, significant correlations obtain only for the two true nuclear families—composed of a husband and wife in the prime of life and their immature offspring. In the corresponding areas, occupied by ≠gau, unmarried adult, and the elderly /"xashe n!a and his equally old

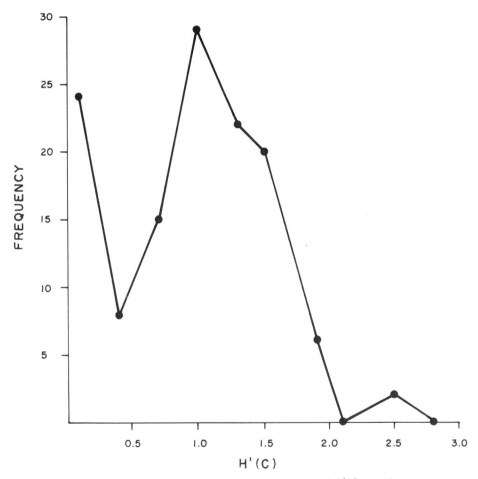

FIGURE 10.   Distribution of LS:NA + LS:SA by richness, plotted at 0.3 H' (C) intervals.

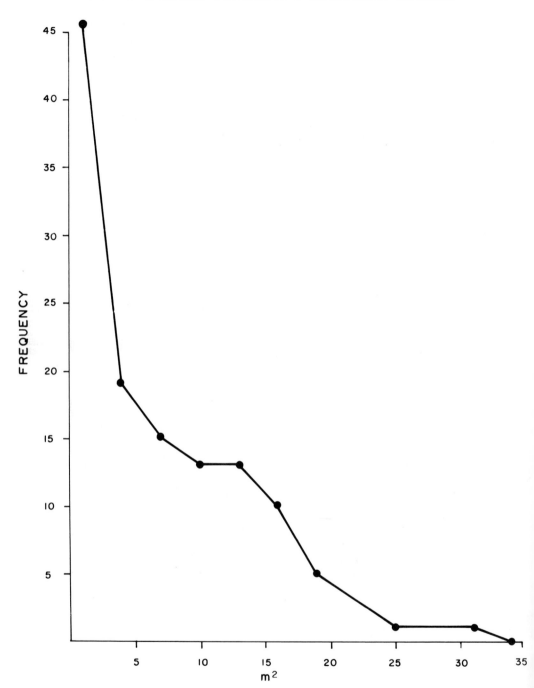

FIGURE 11.   Distribution of LS:NA + LS:SA by area, plotted at 3.0 m₂ intervals.

TABLE 14.   Correlation between Length
of Occupation and Number of Occupants
(Calculated by LS:NA)

$\bar{x}$	days	6.98
	individuals	3.66
s^2	days	23.33
	individuals	3.66
n	68	
r^2	.0001	
r	.0075	(not significant)

wives, no such correlation exists. I would suggest a social explanation: Neither of these groups really comprises an independent social unit; all the individuals involved spend a disproportionately large amount of time at other people's hearths. Again, these conclusions are not particularly surprising, one might guess that the longer an LS:NA was occupied, the more its margins would tend to creep outward. It is slightly unexpected, however, that a significant correlation is noted between area and length of occupation, when social unit size is not controlled.

Just as it is possible to demonstrate a close correlation between the length of time an LS:NA was occupied and its size, so too it is clear that richness as measured by $H'(C)$ is also time dependent (see tables 17 and 18). This relationship holds both when the size of the social unit is ignored and when camp to camp variation is analyzed for individual social units. One would expect this, because the longer a nuclear area is occupied, the more likely it is that a greater variety of activities will occur; also, common tasks will be carried out a greater number of times. Thus, richness would be expected to increase accordingly.

Thus far, in the analysis of LS:NA variation, I have considered only the independent variable of time. A second such variable—size of the social unit—must also be examined. (I have already shown that length of occupa-

TABLE 15.   LS:NA: Correlation between
Area and Length of Occupation

$\bar{x}$		m^2	10.65
		days	6.98
s^2		m^2	37.14
		days	23.33
n		68	
r^2		.1676	
r		.4093	
p	$\leq$	.001	

$m^2 = .52 \text{ (days)} + 7.05$

TABLE 16.   LS:NA: Correlation between Area and Length of Occupation, by Social Unit[a]

		≠toma (2A + 3Y)	n!aishe (2A + 4Y)	≠gau (1A)	/"xashe n!a (3A)
$\bar{x}$	m^2	11.50	12.38	5.70	10.93
	days	6.71	6.71	6.92	5.87
s^2	m^2	16.04	57.64	22.68	41.47
	days	27.76	27.72	30.26	13.84
n		14	14	12	8
r^2		.5151	.3361	.0013	.0272
r		.7177	.5797	.0363	.1650
p	≤	.005	.025	n.s.	n.s.

[a] A = adult
Y = young
≠toma: m^2 = .55 days + 7.83
n!aishe m^2 = .84 days + 6.77

tion and group size, in this context, vary independently of each other.) As one might guess, both the area and the richness of an LS:NA are directly correlated with the number of individuals who occupy it (see tables 19 and 20). The more interesting question to consider is just how these dependent variables are related to group size. Cook and Heizer (1968:114f), although they used data not directly comparable to my own, concluded that addition of individuals—up to a certain point—is reflected in even and equal incremental increases in floor area. Given the LS:NA data, it is possible to determine whether two adults do take up twice as much space as one, and if three adults occupy a 3:2 larger area than do two. The effect of children may also be incorporated into such a study.

To examine this relationship, I grouped social units by size only, and reasonable samples were obtained for the following categories: 1A (one

TABLE 17.   LS:NA: Correlation between Richness and Length of Occupation

x	$H'(C)$	1.32
	days	6.98
s^2	$H'(C)$	0.20
	days	23.33
n		68
r^2		.1433
r		.3785
p	≤	.01

$H'(C)$ = 0.04 (days) + 1.08

TABLE 18.   LS:NA: Correlation between Richness and Length of Occupation, by Social Unit

		≠toma (2A + 3Y)	n!aishe (2A + 4Y)	≠gau (1A)	/"xashe n!a (3A)
$\bar{x}$	$H'(C)$	1.32	1.35	0.8475	1.55
	days	6.71	6.71	6.92	5.87
s^2	$H'(C)$	0.11	0.15	0.26	0.06
	days	27.76	27.76	30.26	13.84
n		14	14	12	8
r^2		.2115	.3895	.3427	.1874
r		.4599	.6241	.5854	.4329
p	≤	.05	.01	.025	n.s.

≠toma $H'(C)$ = 0.03 (days) + 1.13
n!aishe $H'(C)$ = 0.05 (days) + 1.04
≠gau $H'(C)$ = 0.05 (days) + 0.47

adult), 2A, 3A, 2A + 3Y (two adults + three young), and 2A + 4Y. I computed the average areas and richnesses for the LS:NA of each of these units (Table 21). Differences between averages were then evaluated by student's t, and these results are presented in tables 22 and 23.[1] The results are intriguing. Consider area first: Average area increases with the size of the social unit, but the increments are clearly not additive as one would expect in light of the Cook and Heizer model. Also, differences are surprisingly slight, although one adult occupies significantly less space than any larger social unit, the differences in area between any of the larger units are not significant. Two adults do not take up significantly more space than two adults and four young. Thus, one cannot divide an LS:NA by the number of occupants, imagine that each individual then takes up one portion of that space, and establish a simple incremental system.

When richness is examined this same way, the results are surprisingly similar. For adults alone, richness varies directly with social unit size, but children seem to have a surprising negative effect—as their numbers increase, the richness of the LS:NA drops. (Perhaps children spread the debris around.) But student's t again shows that only a social unit of one adult stands out significantly from the crowd.

---

[1] In determining p values in Table 22, it was assumed that area varied directly with number of adults if the number of children were held constant, and that the same applied for children given a constant number of adults. No a priori guess as to the number of children necessary to equal the effect of a single adult could be made. For this reason, p values are determined on the basis of a one-sided test for all comparisons except 3A:2A + 3Y, and 3A:2A + 4Y. In Table a3, p is determined on the basis of a one-sided test for all A:A comparisons, and a two-sided test for all others, since the actions of children are difficult to predict ahead of time.

TABLE 19.   LS:NA: Correlation between Area and Number of Individuals (A + Y)

$\bar{x}$	m^2	10.66
	individuals	3.66
s^2	m^2	37.19
	individuals	3.66
n		68
r^2		.1308
r		.3617
p	$\leq$	.01

$m^2 = 1.15$ individuals $+ 6.43$

An important point emerges: Individuals cannot be treated as discrete additive units, and any archaeological formulation that makes such an assumption is probably doomed to failure. Individuals interact with one another, and one cannot assume that a husband and wife will take up twice as much space as one of them alone. In the United States, a standard single mattress is 38.5 inches wide, while the best-selling double mattress—the queen size—measures only 60 inches from side to side. Additive models take for granted that an individual will act the same way in a variety of social circumstances, but unfortunately this assumption does not always hold. Attempts to assign values to individual units (in this case, single people) through examination of combinations of units have been termed "disaggregation studies" by Rau (personal communication). Tea and rice consumption by different family members (i.e., husband versus wife) in India, and feed requirements for different aged cattle in Brazil, have been analyzed this way, and Rau has noted that all such studies have ended in failure because each assumes that the actions of one group member are not

TABLE 20.   LS:NA: Correlation between Richness and Number of Individuals (A + Y)

$\bar{x}$	$H'(C)$	1.32
	individuals	3.66
s^2	$H'(C)$	0.20
	individuals	3.66
n		68
r^2		.075
r		.2739
p	$\leq$	.05

$m^2 = 0.06$ individuals $+ 1.09$

TABLE 21.   LS:NA: Area and Richness by Size of Social Unit

Size of social unit		m^2	$H'(C)$
	$\bar{x}$	6.12	0.89
1A	s^2	22.84	0.24
	n	14	14
	$\bar{x}$	9.88	1.48
2A	s^2	29.68	0.06
	n	9	9
	$\bar{x}$	10.93	1.55
3A	s^2	41.47	0.06
	n	8	8
	$\bar{x}$	11.61	1.31
2A + 3Y	s^2	15.11	0.10
	n	16	16
	$\bar{x}$	12.78	1 41
2A + rY	s^2	54.57	0.20
	n	16	16

TABLE 22.   LS:NA: Comparison of Area by Student's t, on Basis of Social Unit Composition

	1A	2A	3A	3A + 3Y
2A	$t = 1.73$ $p \leq .05$			
3A	$t = 2.00$ $p \leq .05$	$t = 0.37$ (n.s.)		
2A + 3Y	$t = 3.45$ $p \leq .005$	$t = 0.93$ (n.s.)	$t = 0.33$ (n.s.)	
2A + 4Y	$t = 2.86$ $p \leq .005$	$t = 1.02$ (n.s.)	$t = .60$ (n.s.)	$t = 0.56$ (n.s.)

TABLE 23. LS:NA: Comparison of Richness by Student's *t*, on Basis of Social Unit Composition

	1A	2A	3A	3A + 3Y
2A	$t = 3.33$ $p \leq .005$			
3A	$t = 3.54$ $p \leq .005$	$t = 0.59$ (n.s.)		
2A + 3Y	$t = 2.82$ $p \leq .01$	$t = 1.39$ (n.s.)	$t = 1.88$ (n.s.)	
2A + 4Y	$t = 3.04$ $p \leq .01$	$t = 0.43$ (n.s.)	$t = 0.82$ (n.s.)	$t = 0.73$ (n.s.)

affected by actions of another. A mother will take food from her own plate to feed her child. My own conclusion is that the question "How much space does a person occupy?" is not, at least in this context, a meaningful one.

Thus far, I have compared nuclear and special activity areas to each other examining variation within nuclear areas alone. To round out the picture, I afford special activity areas (LS:SA) similar consideration. Table 24 provides a breakdown of special activity areas by camp and type, with Camp 8 excluded. The 11 kinds of LS:SA areas represented may be divided into two categories. *Shade areas* result from a shift of general activity from the hearth area to a more shady spot during certain times of the day. The same general range of activities that take place near the hearth also take place in the shade areas. The second category of LS:SA consists of those *unique* kinds of *activities,* such as skin drying, which are spatially segregated for other reasons. Of a total of 39 LS:SAs in my sample, 21 are classed as shade areas and for these alone is statistical analysis possible.

Table 25 ranks the different kinds of LS:SA by frequency. The 15 camps were occupied for a total of 103 days. Since three skin preparation areas for example are represented, they occur with a frequency of 1 every 34.3 days. Viewed from a slightly different perspective, on any particular day, the odds that skin preparation will take place are about 1 to 34. I believe that all such unique activities are best viewed this way—as infrequent events, with a likelihood of occurrence directly related to length of occupation.

An examination of the shade areas yields a clear-cut and unexpected pattern. At the start of my analysis I believed that each social unit had its own

TABLE 24.   Tabulation of LS:SAs by Camp and Type of Activity

Camp	\ LS:SA by type of activity 1	2	3	4	5	6	7	8	9	10	n
1	5										5
2	3		2								5
3		1									1
4	6	1									7
5				1							1
6	1		1	1	1						4
7										2	2
9							1				1
10	3							1			4
11		1									1
12											0
13	1		1								2
14	2			1					1		4
15						2					2
16											0
Total:	21	3	4	3	1	2	1	1	1	2	39

Type of activity:
- 1—shade
- 2—skin preparation
- 3—skin pegging
- 4—quiver making
- 5—head roasting
- 6—skin roasting
- 7—play area
- 8—meat drying
- 9—guest sleeping
- 10—?

TABLE 25.   Frequency of LS:SAs, Grouped by Type of Activity

LS:SA by type of activity	Frequency $\dfrac{103 \text{ days}}{\text{number of LS:SAs}}$
Shade	4.9
Skin pegging	25.7
Skin preparation	34.3
Quiver making	34.3
Skin roasting	51.5
Purpose unknown	51.5
Play area	103
Meat drying	103
Guest sleeping place	103
Heat roasting	103

TABLE 26. Correlation between Number of LS:SAs (Shade Only) and Number of Social Units

$\bar{x}$	LS:SAs (shade only)	1.40
	social units	4.10
s^2	LS:SAs (shade only)	3.97
	social units	4.41
n	15	
r^2	.0042	
r	.0649	
p	n.s.	

shade area or areas. But Table 26 dispelled this view, since there is no significant correlation between the two. The number of shade areas is, however, closely related to length of occupation (see Table 27). The only reasonable explanation I can find is that individuals, regardless of family affiliation, sit together in shady areas and that after a certain number of days the group moves from one spot to another, as the first becomes littered with debris. Nuclear areas cannot be moved in a similar way, because each is placed in regard to its immediate neighbors and to shift one would affect all the rest. But for these shade areas—which can be located anywhere shade exists outside the hut circle—similar problems do not arise. Given this hypothesis, one would expect to find no significant correlation between the length of time a camp was occupied and either the richness or size of any shade area located within it, and, as tables 28 and 29 show, testing confirms these predictions.

Finally, when all LS:SA are considered as a single sample, it is not surprising to observe that the total number of LS:SAs are closely related not to the number of social units present but to the length of time a camp was occupied. Tables 30 and 31 document this fact. Later in this chapter I consider the important archaeological implications which such a pattern may have.

TABLE 27. Correlation between Number of LS:SAs (Shade Only) and Length of Occupation

$\bar{x}$	LS:SAs (shade only)	1.40
	days	6.87
s^2	LS:SAs (shade only)	3.97
	days	26.12
n	15	
r^2	.5505	
r	.7419	
p	$\leq$ .005	

LS:SAs (shade only) = 0.29 days − 0.59

TABLE 28.   LS:SA (Shade Only):
Correlation between Length of
Occupation and Richness

$\bar{x}$	days	11.90
	$H'(C)$	0.79
s^2	days	31.79
	$H'(C)$	0.24
n	21	
r^2	.0337	
r	.1835	
p	(n.s.)	

TABLE 29.   LS:SA (Shade Only):
Correlation between Length of
Occupation and Area

$\bar{x}$	days	11.90
	m^2	3.82
s^2	days	31.79
	m^2	23.50
n	21	
r^2	.0776	
r	.2785	
p	(n.s.)	

TABLE 30.   Correlation between
Number of LS:SAs (Total) and Length of
Occupation

$\bar{x}$	days	6.87
	LS:SAs (total)	2.60
s^2	days	26.12
	LS:SAs (total)	4.40
n	15	
r^2	.4456	
r	.6676	
p	$\leq$ .005	

LS:SAs (total) = 0.274 days + 0.7187

**TABLE 31.   Correlation between
Number of LS:SAs (Total) and Number of
Social Units**

$\bar{x}$	social units	4.10
	LS:SAs (total)	2.60
s^2	social units	4.41
	LS:SAs (total)	4.40
n	15	
r^2	.0009	
r	.0292	
p	(n.s.)	

ANALYSIS OF ALS, LMS, LNAT, AND LNAS

Think of the areas designated "ALS," "LMS," "LNAT," and "LNAS" as four circles set one inside the other. Not surprisingly, the size of each is closely correlated with that of the other three, and, if the area of one is known, it is possible to estimate the others (see Table 32). At the start of the analysis my guess was that the size and richness of each of these areas would be correlated positively with both the length of time a particular site was occupied and the number of inhabitants present. I then computed a number of coefficients of correlation and corresponding simple lineal regression equations to see if such relationships did, in fact, exist.[2] For each area, size and richness were tested against length of occupation, and the size of the group, which I computed in four different ways: First, all occupants were counted; next, adults only were considered; then young only; and, finally, the correlations were repeated on the basis of the number of social units (see tables 33 and 34). A similar analysis of richness gave no significant results, and one may only note that H' (C) is, in a general way, positively correlated with length of occupation for each of the different areas, but in no case is r significant. No correlation exists between H' (C) and group size.

Examination of the coefficients in Table 33 reveals an intriguing pattern which reaches well beyond the expected result that area and group size are positively correlated. While the highest correlations are obtained when

---

[2] It is clear in retrospect that simple linear regressions are not adequate, since the possibility must be considered that some relationships between variables are exponential in nature. Since most of the camps in the sample are relatively small, the predictive value of lineal regressions is probably about the same as their exponential counterparts, but if larger, dry-season camps are to be considered, the possibility of serious bias arises.

group size is calculated on the basis of total number of individuals, it is satisfying from an archaeological point of view to observe that the correlation with the number of social units is almost as strong. But it is the overall pattern of these correlations that merits consideration because, regardless of the group measure employed, as "area" decreases, the correlation becomes stronger. For example, using "all occupants" as a measure, as one moves from ALS to the smaller LMS, the value increases from .7050 to .8092; the value for LNAT, which lies wholly within LMS is higher still, and the highest value, .9048 is obtained for LNAS. Much to my surprise, I discovered that when length of occupation and area are analyzed in the same way, exactly the reverse holds true. As Table 33 shows, while both ALS and LMS are significantly time dependent, the former is more so, the size of LNAT and LNAS are not greatly affected by this variable. A little further on I offer a likely explanation for these facts. It should be noted at this point, however, that, in this sample, length of occupation and group size are not positively correlated with each other ($r = .0972$, p = n.s.), and in the relationship between area and time, group size is irrelevant. Partial correlations (see Table 35) bear this out. When group size is controlled and thus effectively removed from the picture, the correlation between area and length of occupation actually increases.

While the reasons may be unclear, these correlations do exist, and both length of occupation and group size can be predicted once the area of scat-

TABLE 32.   Correlation among, and Relative Areas of, ALS, LMS, LNAT, and LNAS

	ALS	LMS	LNAT
LMS	$r = .9360$ $p \leq .0005$		
LNAT	$r = .8016$ $p \leq .0005$	$r = .9303$ $p \leq .0005$	
LNAS	$r = .7996$ $p \leq .0005$	$r = .9360$ $p \leq .0005$	$r = .9960$ $p \leq .0005$

LMS/ALS = .7560; LNAT/LMS = .8147; LNAT/ALS = .6160; LNAS/LMS = .7739; LNAS/ALS = .5851; LNAS/LNAT = .9499

TABLE 33.   Correlation between Area and Social Variables for ALS, LMS, LNAT, and LNAS

		ALS	LMS	LNAT	LNAS
All occupants	$r =$	.7050	.8092	.8986	.9048
	$p \leq$	.005	.0005	.0005	.0005
Adults only	$r =$	.6110	.7264	.7919	.8164
	$p \leq$	.01	.005	.0005	.0005
Young only	$r =$	.6096	.6511	.7500	.7205
	$p \leq$	.01	.005	.005	.005
Social units	$r =$	.6634	.7674	.8112	.8362
	$p \leq$	.005	.0005	.0005	.0005
Length of occupation	$r =$	.6373	.4581	.2425	.2212
	$p \leq$	.01	.05	(n.s.)	(n.s.)

ALS: $m^2 = 13.4$ occupants $- 25.30$
$\quad\quad m^2 = 32.4$ social units $- 49.04$
$\quad\quad m^2 = 11.7$ days $+ 117.85$

LMS: $m^2 = 12.87$ occupants $- 64.42$
$\quad\quad m^2 = 31.39$ social units $- 5.66$
$\quad\quad m^2 = 7.04$ days $- 101.71$

LNAT: $m^2 = 15.47$ occupants $- 135.66$
$\quad\quad m^2 = 35.93$ social units $- 43.03$

LNAS: $m^2 = 15.9$ occupants $- 148.96$
$\quad\quad m^2 = 37.8$ social units $- 57.77$

TABLE 34.   Mean and Variance for Social Variables and Area of ALS, LMS, LNAT, and LNAS

	$\bar{x}$	s^2	n
All occupants	16.67	24.38	15
Adults only	8.73	13.64	15
Young only	7.93	4.07	15
Social units	4.60	3.68	15
Length of occupation	6.87	26.12	15
ALS: m^2	198.44	8794.39	15
LMS: m^2	150.04	6165.35	15
LNAT: m^2	122.23	7229.22	15
LNAS: m^2	116.11	7532.54	15

TABLE 35. Partial Correlation between Area and Social Variables for ALS, LMS, LNAT, and LNAS

		ALS	LMS	LNAT	LNAS
All occupants	$r =$	.8385	.8644	.9062	.9101
(time held constant)	$p\leq$	.0005	.0005	.0005	.0005
Length of occupation	$r =$	.8059	.6488	.3554	.3145
(occupants held constant)	$p\leq$	.0005	.01	(n.s.)	(n.s.)

ter is known. Thus, in many archaeological contexts, area can be accurately assessed, and both ALS and LMS determined. I offer the most useful predictive equations, calculated with group size and length of occupation as the dependent variables:

$$
\begin{aligned}
\text{ALS: occupants} &= .04\ m^2 + 9.28 \\
\text{social units} &= .01\ m^2 + 1.90 \\
\text{length of occupation} &= .03\ m^2 - .02
\end{aligned}
$$

$$
\begin{aligned}
\text{LMS: occupants} &= .05\ m^2 + 9.03 \\
\text{social units} &= .02\ m^2 + 1.78 \\
\text{length of occupation} &= .03\ m^2 + 2.39
\end{aligned}
$$

THE RING MODEL

To make sense of the data presented thus far, imagine that a camp is subdivided into two concentric areas or *rings* (see Figure 12). The inner ring coincides with the LNAT or hut circle itself. The outer ring includes the area between ALS and LNAT and thus consists of the total area outside of the hut circle. While the area of the inner ring provides a measure of group size, the area of the outer ring primarily reflects the length of time a camp is occupied. The number of special activity areas it contains determines the outer ring area, and this number, as I have shown, is time dependent only. Thus, in one part of a !Kung camp, area is dependent on group size; in another portion, time is the determining factor, and one may conclude that these two independent variables may each be determined on the basis of observed remains.

Several of the trends observed in the previous section serve to buttress my contention. For example, as one moves from ALS to LNAS, it is reasonable that the correlation between area and group size increase because each successive area measurement more nearly corresponds with with inner ring.

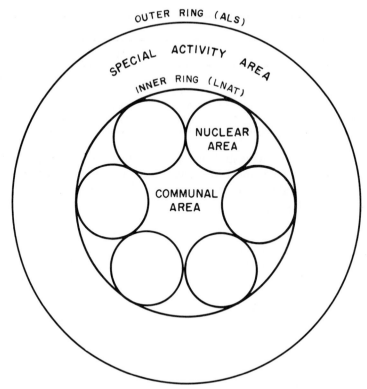

FIGURE 12.   Inner and outer rings in a !Kung camp.

Extraneous, nongroup-related areas are successively removed, thus decreasing statistical noise. Conversely, one would expect that the ALS, then LMS areas would provide the best and next best correlations with the length of occupation, since only these include the time-dependent outer ring; and this is in fact the case. Partial correlations also support my interpretation. Within the inner ring, the correlation between group size and area changes very little when time is controlled, and this indicates that time has little effect on inner ring dimensions. But when ALS and LMS are treated the same way, correlations are higher when time is controlled, indicating that, in this larger area, time acts as a factor working to obscure the group size–area relationship. Now consider the partial correlations in which group size rather than time is controlled. Outer ring size is, of course, influenced by the inner ring which it surrounds. When group size—in effect, the inner ring area—is held constant, the correlation between ALS and LMS (both indirect measures of outer ring size), on the one hand, and time, on the other, increase significantly. Unfortunately, I must emphasize that none of this constitutes "proof." As I "played" with these data, trying the different kinds of correlations that I present here, a "picture" gradually emerged, and the ordering of material in this chapter reflects this process. Yet I find the results intuitively satisfying and note that, with additional data, they could easily be verified or refuted.

The Inner Ring

I would offer a model to explain the relationship between group size and inner ring area, using the number of social units, rather than total number of individuals, as the measure of group size. To review briefly, in Chapter 5 I argued that the area of any social unit is marked by a hut and, almost always, a hearth. Since most social units consist of a single nuclear family, I termed this area of hut, hearth, and surrounding debris a "nuclear family area." Each such area is the private domain of a single social unit (although this does not preclude extensive visiting), and usually the units are placed in a circular arrangement with the hut entrances facing inward.

Although the size of a nuclear area does vary somewhat with the size of the social unit, let me assume that this area is constant and circular in shape. Since nuclear areas are arranged to form a circle, one may devise a simple model for camp growth. In smaller camps, occupied for short periods of time, however, I have shown that this ideal is rarely obtained, and for this reason the model must remain hypothetical at best. Conceive of nuclear areas as beads, tightly strung on a necklace. As a new bead is added, the circumference and diameter of the necklace will increase, the empty space in the center will grow proportionately larger, and the total circular configuration will be maintained. Thus the inner rings of camps with four, five, and six social units would follow the pattern set out in Figure 13, and in each case the size of the individual nuclear area would remain unchanged. The circle that encompasses all of the nuclear areas of a camp coincides with the LNAT, or Inner ring.

Each of the nuclear area circles in Figure 13 includes not only the hut, hearth and surrounding debris, but a certain amount of buffer space between social units. These spatial relationships are decided upon when a camp is first established, and, barring some late and unexpected arrival who may squeeze his hut between two others, these relationships hold throughout the entire occupation. Wiessner (1974) uses my data to demonstrate this fact convincingly.

Note that the area in the center of the inner ring expands as the hut circle grows larger and that it is just "empty space." Geometry dictates the presence of this area when social units are placed in a circular arrangement,

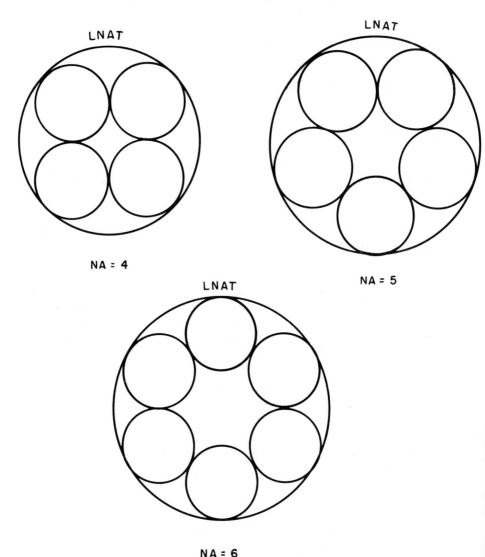

FIGURE 13.   Inner rings of camps with four, five, and six nuclear areas.

and the !Kung use this space for communal ends. Although, the area actually utilized by each individual or each social unit remains constant as the number of nuclear areas increases, dividing the total area within the hut circle by the number of individuals or social units yields the result that area per unit or per person grows larger as group size increases. The implications of such an observation can easily be misleading. Similarly, I would note that if individuals or social units share and live or sleep within a single roofed structure, and if the living areas are arranged along the walls of the structure, then the same general principle will apply within the structure. Hut size and number of individuals or social units will stand in an allometric relationship with each other. Cook and Heizer (1968:144f) point out that floor space per individual within a house increases with the number of occupants, and this may well be explained by the mechanism suggested above. It is also possible that the allometric relationship between total covered floor space per village and population noted both by Naroll (1962) and by Cook and Heizer (1968) may result from the same cause.

The Outer Ring

I have shown that inner ring area correlates closely with group size and that the size of the outer ring is time dependent. This latter relationship may be directly demonstrated, since total outer ring area may be measured by subtracting the LNAT area from the similar ALS measurement. In the same way, the area ALS minus LMS can also be determined. For each of these spaces, I calculate the correlations with group size and length of occupation and present the results in tables 36 and 37. Clearly, the outer ring size closely reflects length of occupation and is not dependent on group size.

In a true archaeological situation, or even in an old abandoned !Kung site where all evidence of huts had disappeared, it would be hard to draw a dividing line between the inner and outer rings. But one could determine the limits of the ALS and the LMS by fairly objective means. Luckily, the correlation between ALS − LMS and length of occupation is nearly identical

TABLE 36.   Correlation between Length of Occupation and Two Outer Ring Measures

		ALS–LMS	ALS–LNAT
$\bar{x}$	m^2	48.41	76.12
	days	6.87	6.87
s^2	m^2	1175.69	3240.61
	days	26.12	26.12
n		15	15
r^2		.4799	.4717
r		.6928	.6868
p	≤	.005	.005

ALS–LMS: area = 4.65 days + 16.50
ALS–LNAT: area = 7.65 days + 23.68

TABLE 37.   Correlation between Group Size and Two Outer Ring Measures

		ALS–LMS	ALS–LNAT
$\bar{x}$	m^2	48.41	76.21
	individuals	16.67	16.67
s^2	m^2	1175.69	3240.61
	individuals	24.38	24.38
n		15	15
r^2		.0065	.0315
r		.0830	.1175
p		(n.s.)	(n.s.)

to that obtained using ALS – LNAT, or the entire outer ring; thus, for practical reasons it may be substituted for its larger counterpart. A partial correlation between this outer portion of the outer ring and length of occupation (with group size held constant) gives an r of .6903, and a $p \leq .005$. And since this value is nearly identical to the simple correlation for the same two varibles, it can again be seen that group size has no effect on the area of this outer ring.

If the relationship between ALS – LMS and length of occupation is calculated in archaeologically useful form, with time as the dependent variable,

$$\text{Number of days} = 0.1 \text{ area} + 1.87$$

On this basis, one can enter an abandoned !Kung camp, take a few measurements, and estimate the length of occupation.

Archaeological Implications

To what extent, one may ask, is the ring model useful to the archaeologist. Clearly it will not apply where natural constraints—the limit of a rock overhang or conformation of a beach ridge—restrict either the borders of the shape of a settlement. Second, such an approach may be used only when all or almost all of a site is excavated and its boundaries determined since it is just those remains near the outer margins that reflect the length of the occupation. And, finally, I would guess that, once a site surpasses a certain size, the ring model will no longer hold, because as the size of the inner ring increases, the empty central space also grows proportionately larger, and when the number of social units becomes too large, another form of arrangement will be employed.

Given those excavated sites that do meet these criteria, a basic question still remains. With only a seemingly meaningless scatter of stone tools and faunal remains, when is it useful to think in terms of "rings." I would suggest several guidelines. First, I would see if fairly distinct clusters of debris are present or if all material is randomly distributed across the site. If such clusters are definable, I would measure the size and richness of each and then determine similarities between clusters on the basis of specific kinds of remains. If activities were patterned along the !Kung model—even though the activities themselves were quite different—one might predict the kind of cluster arrangement that would result. The larger, richer clusters would lie nearer the center of the site and would share basically the same components. Outlying clusters would likely be smaller and less rich. Some of these latter would contain the same kinds of remains as the central clusters, while others might be quite distinct. The more nearly the patterning of debris conformed to this ideal, the greater the likelihood that a ring analysis would produce meaningful results.

What I have tried to do is provide a concrete approach to the analysis of living floors. With the ring model, an archaeologist may start by asking a series of very specific questions of his data to see if they conform to a particular pattern. If they do, then interesting and anthrpologically valuable questions can be answered. There is a certain sense and reasonableness about the way the !Kung arrange themselves and their activities on the ground. The circle permits maximum face to face interaction, and such a pattern has been observed over and over again in the ethnographic present. It would be most surprising if the ring was not represented in the archaeological record.

One must realize, however, that my formulation will often provide only a starting point, and a very real danger arises if one tries to force all archaeological scatters into a framework of this kind. I must frankly admit that, in the event that data do not fit into this mold, I am uncertain just what the next step should be, but I can envision some very interesting questions that might arise. The ring model, for example, is partially based on the fact that a group subdivides itself into conceptually identical units. For the !Kung and all the other hunter–gatherer societies with which I am familiar, these subunits coincide with the nuclear family. Perhaps the archaeologist can try to establish, at least roughly, that point in time when the nuclear family first appeared and attempt to trace social evolution by analyzing large numbers of sites, which may be vastly separated in time and space, with just this kind of question in mind.

7

A FEW CONCLUSIONS

I HAVE TRIED to examine the relationship between ethnographic data and archaeological assumptions, methods, and goals, and have relied heavily on !Kung material for examples. More specifically, I have offered several general models and provided what I hope are techniques that may prove useful to others. In this concluding chapter, the main points in this book are summarized and evaluated in light of my stated goals. In Chapter 1 I argued that the archaeologist could use ethnographic data in four separate ways, which could be conveniently summarized under the head *general model, buckshot, spoiler,* and *laboratory* approaches. And these provide a useful framework for a final summation.

In an ethnographic situation where the "causes" (answers) are known from the start, one can look at the "effects"—in this instance observable remains—and see what techniques offer the best route from the one to the other. And since the answer or cause is known beforehand, it is the methods of analysis and associated assumptions that can in fact be examined. In each of the four interpretive chapters, which span the range from broad-scale demographic organization to intracamp patterning, this *laboratory* approach has been employed.

This is most obvious in Chapter 6, where a priori knowledge permitted me to devise and evaluate a number of techniques for estimating group size and length of occupation from debris. It is these techniques themselves that are of concern. Considering the patterning of activities within a single camp—the subject of Chapter 5—it was again possible to start with a controlled situation; given such knowledge at the outset, one may look at a !Kung site through an archaeologist's eyes, see what interpretive assumptions he is likely to make, and then evaluate them against the previously determined pattern. In Chapter 4 I treated a series of camps, to isolate the factors responsible for variation between camps; and in Chapter 3 I played the same game on an even larger board and used known, long-term, broad-range !Kung movements to evaluate often-made analytic assumptions and suggest alternative approaches.

Unfortunately, it is easier to direct ethnographic data to negative rather than positive ends—to assume the role of *spoiler*. One cannot legitimately make absolute generalizations on the basis of a single society, but it is valid to evaluate statements, models, and assumptions of a generally deductive nature meant to encompass all hunting and gathering societies in this way. Such balloons may be punctured by a single pin, and they must then be recast, qualified or discarded. Here, even limited ethnographic data can serve an extremely valuable, though negative, function, and a regrettably large part of my work has been directed toward this end.

These negative conclusions are summarized as follows. First, because the archaeologist has only a loose control over time, it is best not to use the individual as an analytic unit. For the !Kung, the group or band is a long-lived, archaeologically relevant phenomenon, but individuals and nuclear families move with relative ease from band to band and region to region. Thus, any model that a priori ties people closely to places must be viewed with extreme caution. One cannot deny that valued items—obsidian, pottery, iron knives, and the like—may cover great distances through trade, but I believe that formulations that posit exchange of information, women, or material goods for the primary purpose of maintaining relations between neighboring groups or bands are chancy at best. Of necessity they rest on the assumption that most people stay put, and the !Kung data reveal that the seemingly constant and random movement of individuals and families in themselves can provide the necessary social lubricant. I elaborated this argument in Chapter 3.

Second, the !Kung data graphically illustrate the danger of oversimplified camp typologies. Binford (1966), for example, has suggested a distinction between base camps that are occupied for longer periods of time and collection or extraction stations. This distinction is not applicable to !Kung sites, and sampling problems make any inter-camp comparisons formidable. In Chapter 4 I also argued that any reconstruction of a seasonal round on the basis of excavated sites alone is extremely hazardous because differing archaeological visibility among sites can create a strong and systematic bias. This is not a heartening conclusion.

Third, I have suggested that it is unfounded to assume that activities are spatially segregated or arranged by type within a single camp. Most tasks may be carried out in more than one place and in more than one social context; and, conversely, in any single area, one can find the remains of many activities all jumbled together. Unfortunately, many archaeological analyses are based on just such an erroneous assumption, and their resulting conclusions must be called into question. A corollary of this simple area–activity assumption is that associated remains are functionally related, and Whallon (1973) indicates that this single idea underlies all present-day spatial analyses. !Kung data makes this a priori model untenable.

Finally, in Chapter 6 I showed that individuals cannot be treated as simple aggregations. Two people do not take up twice as much space as one, and it is meaningless to divide total site area into number of square meters per person. While area and group size are positively correlated, the ratio is not one to one, and because of this fact estimates of group size cannot be made by dividing total area by the area required by the hypothetical "ideal" individual.

Let me turn from negative to positive uses of ethnographic data. The role of specific, unprovable analogy was examined in Chapter 1. While such a hit-or-miss approach is scientifically inconclusive, specific ethnographic analogy is hard to avoid and may play a useful, if only suggestive, role. I termed this the *buckshot approach* and provided several pellets of potential value. For example, !Kung campsites are generally circular; nuclear families have areas that include a hut and an associated hearth generally viewed as "private property." Hut entrances face inwards and most family activities take place around the hearth. The center of the hut circle, as well as the area behind the huts, is viewed as communal space, and the latter is used both for shade during certain times of the day, and for messy, space-consuming activities such as pit roasting and skin drying. Because of this, a camp may be described in terms of nuclear and special activity areas, and specific activities may be localized in terms of this bipartite division. I discussed this in detail in chapters 5 and 6.

Quantitative analysis indicates that the size of the hut circle, or inner ring, is closely and directly related to group size, while the outer ring, which encompasses special activity areas, reflects length of occupation. On this basis, I offered predictive equations for group size and length of occupation and put them in an archaeologically useful form. This constitutes an original piece of research and is perhaps the single most important contribution of this book. The major portion of Chapter 6 deals with this analysis.

The final use to which ethnographic data may be put involves the construction of general models. I offered an example of this in Chapter 3, where the dichotomy between the group and the individual was examined. I suggested that a band–territory model may serve as a useful construct for examining some kinds of relationships between man and environment, but that such bands are relatively open, or "anucleate," and individuals and families can move with ease from one to the next. Such open social patterning, I believe, probably characterizes most Paleolithic groups. I also delineated general factors, which may be applicable in understanding differences between archaeological sites. I suggested that subsistence and maintenance activities should be considered separately, since the former, by their very nature, must occur daily, while the latter may exhibit a less even chronological distribution.

Any site may be conceived of as a spatial locus containing a sample of the society's total repertoire of activities. As a general rule, the longer a site is occupied and the larger the number of inhabitants, the greater and more varied will be the activities that occur there. This raises severe statistical problems in making comparisons among small sites and among very small and very large sites. For subsistence-related activities, these difficulties are far less serious than for those that involve manufacturing. Given the limited number of sites with which archaeologists generally have to work, large intersite differences may signify less than one might suppose. When sites are compared on the basis of their contents, I suggest a single scale, ranging from simple to complex, may prove more useful than a typological approach that posits, a priori, discrete and, often, named categories.

Although unique activities are rarely relegated to mutually exclusive areas within a camp and most may occur in more than one place, I have demonstrated that underlying social rules are clearly reflected in the spatial patterning of activities. Because of this, it is possible that the seemingly "abstract" aspects of social organization may be more easily reconstructed from camp debris than such supposedly more simple aspects as delineating the nature and range of activities that took place. To analyze the observed scatter of remains within a camp, I have suggested that the first step should involve identification of debris clusters. The contents themselves are irrelevant in this initial stage. When such clusters have been isolated, they may then be described in terms of area, richness, and the kinds of remains they contain. With these three variables, comparisons may be made and culturally meaningful patterns sought.

In the final analysis, how can one evaluate the web of observation, criticism, and hypothesis that forms the intellectual core of this work? I am painfully aware of a number of specific weaknesses and areas that require additional work. The general models, for example, are too fuzzy to be of specific use. Empirical clustering techniques should have been developed and evaluated in detail; but they were not. And spatial analysis stopped short of cluster comparison based on individual kinds of remains. The essential observable characteristics of !Kung spatial arrangement within a camp have not been stated in such a form that the question may be asked: Can the distribution of remains at any archaeological site be shown to fit a nuclear area–special activity area model? I can only offer the apology that future work will proceed along these lines. Further fieldwork must expand the sample to include larger dry-season camps and must consider in detail differential scattering and burial of various kinds of remains. Finally, the value of cross-cultural information on this level of specificity is also evident. Unfortunately, little exists, and, again, directions for future fieldwork are suggested.

But, if I have done no more than indicate some of the unsuspected limitations and problems that confront the archaeologist, noted a few fruitful lines for further investigation, and offered several techniques and approaches that will further these ends, then I believe this contribution to be a useful one.

APPENDIX A

DESCRIPTIVE SUMMARY OF FAUNAL, FLORAL, AND OTHER REMAINS[1]

FAUNA

In the campsite series, 14 species of mammals, reptiles, and birds are represented (see Table 38, Appendix B). These include 10 species of mammal, and 2 each of reptile and bird. With the exception of the few fragments of giraffe bone, used for making arrow linkshafts, and several kudu bones of unknown origin, remains of the other 12 species are the incidental, discarded byproducts of butchering and food consumption. For descriptions of the individual animals and the techniques for hunting, butchering, sharing, and cooking them, see Lee (1965), Yellen (1972b, in press a) and Yellen and Lee (1976).

FLORA

Descriptions of the kinds of plants the !Kung utilize for food are included in Lee (1965), Yellen (1972a), and Yellen and Lee (1976). Remains of eight species are represented in the campsite series and, of these, the seven used for food are discussed here. Wild sisal is discussed under "twine" in the next section. While these seven, especially the mongongo nut, represent the overwhelming majority of the plant food eaten, a number of species known to have been consumed at these sites have left no visible remains.

[1] The data in Appendix A are keyed to the site plans contained in the packet.

137

BAOBAB (*Adansonia digitata*)

The baobab fruit ripens and falls to the ground in early winter. The elongated, roughly elliptical pod averages about 30 cm in length, and its white, dryish meat is surrounded by a thick, woody casing. The pods may be carried whole into a camp and cracked by striking with a stick or against a rock. The resulting pod fragments are large and are discarded after the meat is eaten.

MONGONGO (MANGETTI) NUT (*Ricinodendron rautanenii*)

Mongongo trees grow only on dune crests, and the nut they bear provides the single most important item in the Dobe group's diet. The nuts, which fall after the end of the rainy season but before the start of winter, approximate a small walnut in size. The nut itself may survive on the ground for an entire year and still be edible, but the fruit surrounding it gradually dries, leaving a leathery skin that finally falls away. When nuts are fresh, they are either roasted briefly in coals, and then the fruit is eaten, or they are boiled with water to form a fruit soup. In either case the nuts are later eaten. Later in the year, when only the outer skin remains, it is removed by brief roasting. The nuts are then cracked using a hammer and anvil; the shells are left where they fall, and the nut meat is eaten.

SOUR PLUM (*Ximenia caffra*)

The sour plum ripens during the rains and is approximately 4.0 cm in diameter. Since its numbers are not great, it is most often eaten where found and is only infrequently carried back to a camp. The skin, said to be poisonous, is removed with the teeth and discarded. The meat and the large, soft nut are eaten together.

MONKEY ORANGE (*Vangueria spp*)

The monkey orange approximates a large apple in size and includes more than one species of fruit, produced by the parent trees at irregular intervals. During some years few if any trees bear. !Kung often pick the fruit before it is completely ripe and store it in camp until the extremely thick, woody skin turns an iridescent turquoise color. The shell is then cracked with a stick, the sweet and sticky meat removed, and the durable shell fragments discarded. Often when a campsite is abandoned, unripened collected fruit is not carried away.

SPINY MELON (*Citrullus naudinianus*)

This small melon with a leathery, spiny outer covering, although extremely abundant during the rainy season, is of minor dietary importance. It is most often cut in half with a knife and the tart flesh is eaten directly from the skin together with the seeds. The skin is then discarded.

Tsin Bean (*Bauhinia esculenta*)

While relatively rare in the Dobe area, the tsin bean, which approximates a fauva bean in size, provides a staple winter food in other !Kung areas. The beans grow on a low shrub and are contained two beans to a pod. The entire pod is usually collected and carried back to camp where it is split and the beans removed. An opaque covering surrounds each bean and this is also discarded. The beans are then roasted directly in the coals and eaten.

Water Root (*Fockea monroi*)

This large tuber contains a pulpy interior high in water content even when no other source of water is available. Children like to collect water roots and fashion toys from them, since the meat is easy to carve with a knife yet strong enough to retain its shape for a considerable period. All water roots in the mapped camp series were gathered by children for this purpose.

OTHER MATERIAL REMAINS FOUND IN ABANDONED CAMPSITES

Adzes

The small !Kung adze is used both to chop wood and to scrape skins. The iron blades are obtained through trade, while the wooden handles are carved by the !Kung themselves. The valuable blades are carefully saved and treated, but the handles, which often split, are discarded, and these may sometimes be recovered at abandoned campsites.

Arrows

Arrows are composed of three main segments: the shaft, made from a segment of thick, straight grass stalk; a head and foreshaft, which is now fashioned from a single piece of iron wire; and a bone or wood linkshaft, which is set between the foreshaft and the shaft itself. This permits the shaft to fall away upon impact and makes it difficult for an animal to remove the foreshaft by rubbing it against trees or the ground. Shaft segments are sometimes found at abandoned campsites and most often represent "rejects" that were collected and carried back to camp but on closer examination noted to be faulty in one way or another. Also recoverable at campsites are small pieces of bone, most often giraffe, intended for linkshafts, that have been discarded for the same reason, and bone shavings that are the byproduct of trimming and shaping bone fragments into linkshafts. Iron wire is difficult for the !Kung to obtain, and none was recovered on abondoned sites.

Carrying Nets

Twine carrying nets, up to 1.5 m in length, are constructed by the !Kung and can be used to transport almost anything that is nonliquid. When small objects such as mongongo nuts are carried, the net is lined with a thick layer of grass to prevent them from slipping out, and these grass mats, which are discarded when the net is emptied, are sometimes observed at abandoned sites. The piles of grass are similar to those on which small animals are usually skinned and butchered.

Containers

Most familes in the Dobe group have an iron three-legged cooking pot obtained through trade either with Bantu or with anthropologists, and these have replaced the traditional clay pots made by Bantu. Iron pots are extremely rugged and of course are not thrown away. However, they are sometimes stored at an abandoned camp if the owners expect to return to the area in the near future. Metal cans are replacing the ostrich egg shell as a water container, but shells are still widely used. On breaking, the fragments may either be saved for making beads or discarded. Broken shell fragments are sometimes found in abandoned camps. Bark trays, although rarely used if metal cans are available, are sometimes cut and used to carry honey. The trays are nothing more than a section of roughly trimmed, undecorated bark, and they are discarded after use.

Digging Sticks

Digging sticks are fashioned from straight, slender branches 1.0–1.5 m in length. The sticks are smoothed, and one end is shaped to form a flattened point. Through use, the point is worn away, and continual resharpening reduces the length of the stick. When finally discarded, it is often left at the camp where last used.

Fire-Making Materials

Matches, flint and steel, and fire sticks are all employed by the Dobe group. Pads of fine grass stems, used to catch the spark when the flint and steel technique is employed, are sometimes found in abandoned camps.

Fire Paddles

Implements used to stir and remove vegetable foods from the coals where they are cooked vary from simple sticks of convenient length to small paddles flattened at one end and pointed at the other. These may be made relatively quickly and easily and are often discarded when a camp is abandoned.

KNIVES

Metal knife blades, like adze blades, are obtained from outside sources, and the !Kung carve their own handles and sheaths for them. The pointed blades of which both edges are sharpened, average about 15 cm in length and are never knowingly abandoned. The wooden handles and sheaths, which are carved in a Bantu fashion, are discarded when broken. Often they crack while being made, and both used and unused broken pieces are regularly found on abandoned campsites.

MONGONGO NUT CRACKING STONES

Most mongongo nut cracking stones consist of slabs and rounded fragments of hardpan (calcrete), which is abundant around the Dobe waterhole and the areas to the south. These vary from fist-sized chunks to flat slabs up to 50 cm in length. While, in a few instances, some pieces may definitely be called hammers and others anvils, most in the intermediate size range may be used for either purpose and classification depends on context. When two are found together, the larger is the anvil. In use, the larger piece is placed on the ground with the flattest surface facing upward, and the nut is held on top of it. A second rock then serves as hammer. Some anvils which have had extensive use show signs of dimpling. Anvils often serve as a base on which ostrich egg shell fragments are placed for drilling and fashioning into beads; rarely, they are used for pounding other materials as well. There is no exposed rock in the immediate environs of the mapped camps, and all the cracking stones used at them were carried from the Dobe area (with the exception of Camp 8) at some uncertain time in the past. When a camp is abandoned, the stones are left there, and when another camp is established in the same general area, individuals return to the old site and carry the stones to the new one. Thus a number of old camps have only one or two stones or none at all.

MORTARS AND PESTLES

Wooden mortars, which obtain a maximum size of about 30 cm in length, and pestles, which the !Kung carve from the same wood, are used for pounding a number of vegetable foods. Mortars crack during manufacture and also from extensive use. When badly broken, the mortar is discarded, and fragments are sometimes found on abandoned sites.

OSTRICH EGG SHELL BEADS

Making beads from ostrich egg shell involves a number of steps. The shell from a broken ostrich egg is first further subdivided into a number of small fragments. Each piece is then roughly rounded by striking along its edges with a stone or some other hard object; a hole is then drilled in the center using a sharpened bit of wire set in the end of a wooden shaft. The roughly rounded beads are then strung tightly together; the resultant string is held against the thigh and rubbed lengthwise with a smooth piece of hardpan. This serves to round and smooth the beads. At any stage of this process, a blank may be lost in the sand, break, or be discarded because of faulty workmanship. Thus, beads in various stages of manufacture are found on abandoned sites.

PIPES

Smoking pipes are made from bone or wood or from cartridge casings. Wooden pipes, which may be either straight wooden tubes or carved in imitation of Western pipes, often break and are discarded. Bone pipes consist of a section of hollow long bone, often goat, which has a plug of grass stuffed into one end to keep the tobacco from the smoker's lips. The outside of the pipe may be decorated with incisions. When pipes crack, they are discarded, and these may be found on abandoned sites.

QUIVERS

The !Kung select a section of straight, thick root from one species of tree, remove the pith, leaving the bark intact, and cover one end to form a quiver. A cap is then placed in the other end. To remove the pith, they build a small fire and, after it has burned out, bury the root segment in the hot ash and sand. The bark expands more rapidly than the pith, permitting removal of the latter. In the process however, the bark itself often splits badly and is discarded. Quivers are made in camp, and whole roots, split bark, and discarded pith are sometimes found in this context.

SPRINGHARE HOOKS

Springhare are long-legged, hare-sized animals which spend their days in long, narrow, curving burrows. To hunt them, the !Kung use a metal hook set at the end of a pole which may be 4 m in length. A duiker horn, tied backward against the pole may also serve as hook. The poles themselves are formed of four or five lengths of thin, straight, supple branches tied end to end and tightly bound with gum and sinew. Poles are light but awkward to carry; they are often left for a time at a camp and retrieved at a later date. Sections of pole may be discarded in the process of manufacture and be left at a camp when it is abandoned.

TOY CARS

Children in the Dobe group enjoy carving small toy cars from water root, placing them at the end of long sticks, and pushing them around a campsite, to the accompaniment of appropriate noises. Byproducts of these activities—water root shavings carved car wheels and bodies, and pushing sticks—are found at a number of abandoned sites.

TWINE

The short, thick, fibrous leaves from a small plant that resembles sisal are used to make twine. The outer covering is stripped from the leaves, using the pointed end of a digging stock. Next the inner fibers are separated in a similar way and then spun against the thigh to give a two-ply twine which may vary in thickness. Discarded outer fibers, and a certain amount of inner fiber as well, mark areas within a camp where twine making has taken place.

FEATURES

ASH AND CHARCOAL PILE

In contrast to scatters, discussed later in this section, piles of ash and charcoal are most frequently found in camps occupied during the winter months. At these times, fires are kept burning throughout the night and individuals sleep around them for warmth. Residue rapidly builds up in the hearths, and it is regularly removed and dumped outside of the camp circle to form small, usually isolated, piles.

HEARTH

Hearths (see figure on p. 87) occur in all camps, no matter how short-lived, and provide the focus for the majority of activities that take place there. Each nuclear family group has one hearth, and only on very rare occasions does a hut not have a hearth associated with it. Hearths, marked by a varying depth of ash, sand, and charcoal, grow naturally through use, and their edges are usually clearly defined. The conformation may differ according to the uses to which the hearth was put and may, in cross-section appear raised, depressed, or raised at the "rim" with a relative depression in the center. Edible roots, nuts, and other foods in the coals involve moving and, often, scooping the hearth contents, and this accounts for observed depressions. The hearth is not only a source of warmth in the winter, of light at night, and of energy for cooking; it serves also as a focus for the nuclear family. The general concentration of nut shell, bones, and other remains around it indicates the numerous activities that occur in its immediate environs. Usually people sleep near the hearth.

HUT

Hut forms vary according to the season in which the hut is constructed and the length of time it is expected to be occupied. During the rainy season, huts tend to be substantial and well thatched, as are huts near permanent waterholes, which are occupied for several consecutive months. Conversely, nonrainy-season, temporary huts tend to be of much more flimsy construction and at times may be considered "symbolic" at best. Generally, each nuclear family builds a hut, as do unmarried adults, widows, and widowers, the structures providing not only some protection from the rain but also very welcome shade during the heat of the day, as well as a private place for storing belongings. Rainy-season huts are circular, with a domed roof, and measure up to 2 m in diameter as well as in height. A hut can be constructed in several hours by a husband and wife. A series of branches are placed vertically in the ground, leaving an open space for the entrance; the tops are then bent inward and tied at the center to form the roof. Thin branches are tied in strips to form two or three horizontal bands around the outside, and armfuls of grass are heaped over the frame to provide a rough thatch, which usually is not tied down. The ground inside the hut is carefully cleared and assumes a slight concave shape; a pile of carefully selected soft grass may be placed on the floor to provide a somewhat softer sleeping place. Dry-season, temporary huts are less substantial, and may be placed so as to incorporate living vegetation as "walls." They often lack roofs, sometimes form only a half circle, and usually are not thatched. Their major functions are to demarcate a private family area and provide shade. Very few activities take place inside the hut itself. Children sometimes construct small play huts.

MERRY-GO-ROUND

At only one of the mapped camps was such a structure built. A small tree was cut, leaving a stump approximately 1 m high, and the top of the stump was then carved to a gently rounded point. A hole was cut part way through a sturdy, slightly longer branch at its midpoint. When the hole in the branch was placed over the pointed end of the stump, a crude but workable two-man merry-go-round resulted.

ROASTING PIT

Small pits, dug outside the camp circle, are used to roast the heads of large animals. A fire is constructed in the pit, the entire head is then added and the coals are heaped to cover all parts of it. After the cooked head is removed, the site is marked by a pronounced depression and associated ash and charcoal.

SCATTER OF CHARCOAL

Thin surface scatters of charcoal (see figure on p. 88) occur on most sites and are easily distinguished from hearths. Often they are associated with other remains, such as similar scatters of mongongo nut shells, and they mark special activity areas. Almost without exception they are situated in places that are in the shade when the hearth area is not so protected—individuals move into these areas for limited periods. The small fires which these charcoal scatters mark are not used enough to develop the characteristics of a hearth but usually char the outer covering of mongongo nuts.

SCATTER OF MONGONGO NUT SHELLS (OR OTHER VEGETABLE REMAINS)

These surface scatters mark places at which mongongo nuts or other vegetable foods are processed and eaten. Most often they are associated with the hearth, where such activities usually occur; but during those times of the day when the hearth is not shaded, activities will be moved to areas protected from the sun, and the resulting, generally dispersed, debris will often be associated with the scatters of charcoal discussed in the preceding paragraph.

SCATTER OF WILD SISAL FIBERS

See "twine" on page 143.

SKIN PREPARATION AREA

The primary treatment of fresh animal skins occurs outside the camp circle, and the area may be marked by scattered hair, grass or brush mats, and short, pointed sticks. The skin from large- and smaller-sized antelopes is dried and later cured to make carrying bags or clothing. The drying process always takes place slightly outside the camp circle, since it takes up a good deal of space, is messy, and is likely to attract both bugs and carnivores. The skin is usually placed on a layer of thin grass matting (hair side down), tightly stretched in all directions, and pegged to the ground with a number of short, pointed sticks. The hair often falls out naturally as the skin dries, and along with the grass mat and pointed sticks, provides the sole evidence as to where this activity occurred.

SUNSHADE

Small, flimsy, and quickly made shelters are sometimes constructed near a nut to provide additional protection from the sun at times when the hearth area is not otherwise shaded. Most often, sunshades consist solely of several leafy branches stuck vertically into the ground to give a slightly curved shape. Rarely, thatch is loosely piled against the outer wall.

APPENDIX B

UNGROUPED DATA FROM SIXTEEN !KUNG CAMPS[1]

TABLE B-1.   Key to Faunal Identification

		Species
Aw:	Aardwolf	*Proteles cristatus*
Dk:	Duiker	*Sylvicapra grimmia*
Gb:	Gemsbok	*Oryx gazella*
Gf:	Crowned guinea fowl	*Numida meleagris*
Gi:	Giraffe	*Giraffa camelopardalis*
Ha:	Scrub hare	*Lepus saxatilis*
Hb:	Yellow-billed hornbill	*Lophoceros flavirostris*
Ku:	Kudu	*Tragelaphus strepsiceros*
Li:	Lizard	Species unidentified
Pc:	Porcupine	*Hystrix africaeaustralis*
Sp:	Springhare	*Pedetes capensis*
St:	Steenbok	*Raphicerus campestris*
To:	Leopard Tortoise	*Geochelone sp.*
Uf:	Unidentified (always fragmentary)	
Wh:	Warthog	*Phacochoerus aethiopicus*

Anatomical part
Ca: Cannon bone
Cl: Clavicle
Cp: Carapace
Cr: Cranium

[1] The data in Appendix B are keyed to the site plans contained in the packet.

146

Table B-1 Continued

F: Femur
Fi: Fibula
H: Humerus
Ho: Horn
Hp: Hoof or paw
M: Mandible
O: Bones from extremity (other than cannon bones)
P: Pelvis
Ra: Radius
Ri: Rib
Sc: Scapula
St: Sternum
Te: Tooth
Ti: Tibia
Uf: Unidentified fragment
Ul: Ulna
V: Vertebra

State
C: Complete
Fr: Fragmentary

CAMP 1 ≠TUM ≠TOA 1
(Mapped February 16, 18, and 19, 1968)

Summary

Occupations

1. Several days only (mid-January 1968) by tsau and family; n//aba n!a and young daughter (3 adults, 4 children).
2. 5 days (February 12–16, 1968) by /n!au, bo, and families (4 adults, 6 children).

Water

Water plentiful and locally available in hollows in trunks and root systems of mongongo trees.

Vegetable foods

The main vegetable food is the mongongo nut, which is present in the immediate area. They had fallen the previous June and remained preserved on the ground since that time.

Animal foods

First Occupation
Porcupine. Adult, killed by tsau, date uncertain.
Porcupine. Adult, killed by tsau, date uncertain.

Second Occupation
Springhare. Adult female, killed by bo, Feb. 13.
Springhare. Adult female, killed by /n!au, Feb. 13.

Springhare. Adult female, killed by bo, Feb. 15.

Springhare. Adult male, killed by /n!au, Feb. 15.

Porcupine. Immature, killed by bo, Feb. 15.

Porcupine. Adult, killed by bo, Feb. 15 (not consumed at site).

Steenbok. Adult male. Recovered almost complete from fresh wild dog kill. The viscera, and meat around genitals and upper thighs missing.

Tortoise. Carried whole to site and eaten by children, date uncertain.

Notes on Occupation

OCCUPATION 1

Camp 1 was originally occupied by tsau and family, including his mo-in-law, and si-in-law, because tsau had agreed to meet bo, /n!au, and families in the ≠tum ≠toa grove at about this time, and the families wished to travel together. They wait there for several days with no sign of bo and /n!au and then leave. During their brief stay tsau kills two porcupines.

OCCUPATION 2

/n!au, bo, and their families move from Camp 3, where they had been camping with ≠toma and n!aishe, to Camp 2, which is less than 2 km distant. They find it abandoned, move into tsau and n//aba n!a's huts, and remain 5 days in all. On the last day they come to the DeVore–Yellen campsite, which is about 1 km distant, and that afternoon return to Dobe with them. Their day-by-day activities, briefly recorded, are as follows:

FEBRUARY 12

Both families move from Camp 3 to Camp 1. They spend the remainder of the day gathering mongongo nuts. Neither of the men hunt.

FEBRUARY 13

Both of the men go to hwanasi. Each kills a springhare with a springhare hook. The springhares are carried whole back to camp.

FEBRUARY 14

Both men remain in camp and kill nothing.

FEBRUARY 15

While hunting, bo kills two porcupines and a female springhare and /n!au kills a male springhare. They also see an adult steenbok which is being chased by four wild dogs. The men follow and arrive in time to chase the wild dogs from the fresh kill and retrieve most of the steenbok carcass. They carry the remains back to camp with them.

FEBRUARY 16

Everyone comes to the DeVore–Yellen camp nearby and spends the morning there. In the afternoon, the group returns to Camp 1 and are interviewed. One porcupine is cooked and shared with all present. In the late afternoon, DeVore–Yellen start the 8 km walk to their truck and /n!au, bo, and families decide to accompany them for the free ride back to Dobe. At this time the second porcupine, skinned but uncooked, appears and is taken along. Since the two families plan to return, some belongings, including cooking pots and springhare hooks, are left behind, placed in the crotch of a tall tree.

On February 18 when Yellen returns to continue mapping, Bushmen point out hyena tracks, which indicate that the camp has been carefully picked over for edible remains.

Notes on Site Plan

FLORAL REMAINS

Spiny melon:	skins only
Monkey orange:	both shell fragments and complete unripe fruit
Sour plum:	both skins and nuts
Mongongo nut:	cracked shells only

FAUNAL REMAINS

	Species	Anatomical part	State
1.	Sp	Cr	Fr
2.	Sp	M	C
3.	Pc	V	C
4.	Pc	O	C
5.	Sp	Ri	C
6.	Sp	Ti	Fr
7.	Sp	Cr	Fr
8.	Sp	Cr	Fr

Species		Anatomical part	State
10.	Sp	V&P	Fr
11.	Sp	Ti	Fr
12.	Sp	Ti	Fr
13.	Sp	Ti	Fr
14.	Gf	F	Fr
16.	Pc	Ri	Fr
17.	Pc	Ul	Fr
18.	Sp	F	Fr
19.	Sp	O	Fr
20.	Sp	Uf	Fr
21.	Sp	Uf	Fr
23.	Gi	Ri	Fr
24.	Gi	Ri	Fr
25.	Gi	Ri	Fr
26.	Gi	Ri	Fr
27.	Gi	Ri	Fr
28.	Gi	Ri	Fr
29.	Gi	Ri	Fr
30.	Gi	Ri	Fr
31.	Gi	Ri	Fr
33.	Sp	P	Fr
36.	Uf	Uf	Fr
37.	Pc	Ul	Fr
38.	Pc	V	C
39.	Ku	F	Fr
40.	Sp	Cr	Fr
41.	Sp	Sc	Fr
49.	Sp	F	Fr
50.	Sp	Fi	Fr
51.	Sp	F	Fr
52.	Sp	F	Fr
53.	Dk	F	Fr
54.	Sp	Sc	C
55.	Pc	H	Fr
56.	Pc	Ti	C
57.	Sp	P	Fr
58.	Pk	V	C
59.	Sp	P	Fr
60.	Pc	V	C
61.	Pk	V	C
62.	Dk	Sc	C
63.	St	V	C
64.	Sp	Cr	Fr
65.	Pc	Cr	Fr
66.	St	Ul	Fr
67.	Sp	Ra	C
69.	Pk	V	C
70.	Pc	H	Fr
71.	Uf	Uf	Fr

Species	Anatomical part	State
72. Sp	T	Fr
73. Sp	T	Fr
74. Pc	Ri	Fr
75. Pc	Ri	Fr
76. Pc	Sc	Fr
77. Pc	H	Fr
78. Pc	Ri	Fr
79. Pc	M	Fr
80. Pc	Cr	Fr
81. Sp	Cr	Fr
82. Pc	V	C
83. Pc	O	C
84. Pc	Cr	Fr
85. Pc	M	Fr
86. Pc	Cr	Fr
87. Sp	F	Fr
88. Sp	Ri	C
89. Pc	Sc	Fr
90. Sp	M	Fr
91. Sp	Ri	Fr
92. Pc	Sc	Fr
93. Sp	Ri	Fr
94. Pc	Cr	Fr
95. Sp	Ri	Fr
96. Sp	M	Fr
97. Sp	F	Fr
98. Sp	F	Fr
99. Pc	Ul	Fr
100. Sp	F	Fr
101. Sp	V	C
102. Sp	V&P	V:C, P:Fr
103. Pc	M	Fr
104. Sp	Fi	Fr
105. Pc	Ri	Fr
106. Pc	M	Fr
107. St	F	Fr
108. Pc	Ri	Fr
109. Pc	Ri	Fr
110. St	F	Fr
111. Pc	St	Fr
112. Dk	St	Fr
114. Pc	Ri	Fr
115. Pc	Ri	Fr
116. Pc	Ri	Fr
117. Pc	Ri	Fr
118. Pc	Ri	Fr
119. Pc	Ri	Fr
120. Pc	V	C
121. Pc	O	C

Species		Anatomical part	State
122.	St	F	Fr
123.	Sp	F	Fr
124.	Pc	Cr	Fr
125.	St	V	C
133.	Pc	O	C
134.	Sp	Cr & V	Fr
136.	Pc	Sc	Fr
137.	Dk	V	C
138.	Dk	Ri	Fr
139.	To	Cp	Fr
140.	Pc	Sc	Fr
141.	St	M	Fr
142.	St	M	Fr
143.	St	M	Fr
144.	Sp	Sc	C
145.	Sp	F	Fr
146.	Sp	P	Fr
147.	St	Cr	Fr
148.	Dk	Cr	Fr
150.	To	Cp	Fr
151.	To	Cp	Fr
169.	Pc	M	Fr
170.	Pc	M	Fr
171.	Pc	Te	C
172.	Sp	Cr	Fr
173.	Sp	Cr	Fr
174.	Pc	Cr	Fr
175.	Sp	Sc	C
176.	Pc	Cr	Fr
177.	St	Sc	Fr
178.	St	Sc	Fr
179.	Dk	H	Fr
180.	Sp	Cr	Fr
181.	Pc	H	Fr
182.	St	Ri	Fr
183.	Pc	Ul	C
184.	Pc	Ri	Fr
185.	St	Ri	Fr
186.	Sp	V	C
187.	Pc	Sc	Fr
188.	St	Ri	Fr
189.	Pc	Ri	Fr
190.	Dk	Ri	Fr
191.	Dk	Ri	Fr
192.	Dk	Ri	Fr
193.	St	Cr	Fr
194.	St	Ri	Fr
195.	St	Ri	Fr

Species	Anatomical part	State
196. Dk	Ri	Fr
199. Pc	Quill	Fr
200. Pc	Quill	C
202. To	Cp	C
204. St	Ca	Fr
205. St	Ca	Fr
206. St	F	Fr
208. St	F	Fr
209. Sp	M	C
215. St	F	Fr
216. Pc	Ri	Fr
217. Pc	Ul	Fr
218. Pc	Ul	Fr
219. Pc	Sc	Fr
220. Pc	H	Fr

OTHER REMAINS

Hardpan hammers and anvils for cracking mongongo nuts (15 total).
42.   10 roughly shaped, unfinished ostrich egg shell beads.
43.   49 broken ostrich egg shell fragments.
68.   Fire paddle.
127. Mortar.
128. Fire paddle.
129. Broken, charred pestle fragment.
131. 35 ostrich egg shell fragments.
132. 12 roughly shaped, unfinished ostrich egg shell beads.
152. Digging stick.
154. Digging stick.
155. Digging stick.
156. Fire paddle.
157. Pestle.
167. Tin can.
168. Tin can.
203. 33 ostrich egg shell fragments.
214. Springhare hook attached to pole, with hook end in small tree.
222. Short piece of string.
223. Piece of punk to catch spark from flint and steel.
224. Wooden knife handle.

Since the families plan to return to this camp, other goods are left cached in the thatch of the huts or in nearby trees. They are not noted in the plot and include: 2 pestles, 1 springhare hook, 1 iron bucket, 2 iron pots, 1 knife sheath, a piece of twine, 2 digging sticks, and a dried gemsbok hide.

FEATURES

A.	Thin surface scatter of charcoal, not associated with any hearth.
B.	Scatter of duiker hair. This is residue of drying a duiker skin. The skin was brought from another camp.
C.	Scatter of sour plum skins.
D.	Scatter of sour plum nuts.
F.	Fireplace associated with Hut 1. Its limits are clearly defined by a shallow basin.
G.	Area around hearth. It is slightly raised near the hearth and contains large lumps of charcoal, unroasted mongongo shells, and bone.
I.	Area around fire J. Marked by turned sand and charcoal.
J.	Hearth associated with Hut 2. It has scattered charcoal in the depression.
K–M.	Scatter of charcoal and unburned mongongo shells.
N.	Small scatter of surface charcoal only.
O, P, Q.	Scatters of surface charcoal.
R.	Small scatter of surface charcoal only.
S.	Stack of unburned mongongo shells.
T.	Very thin, diffuse scatter of charcoal.
U.	Scatter of unburned mongongo shells.

Hut 1.   Bo's hut. It is a substantial, rainy-season hut.
Hut 2.   /n!au's hut. Similar to Hut 1.

CAMP 2 ≠TUM ≠TOA 2 (Mapped February 20, 1968)

Summary

Occupation	9 days (June 3–11, 1967) by ≠toma, n!aishe, and families (4 adults, 7 children).
Water	Water present in mongongo trees only.
Vegetable foods	Mongongo nuts are freshly fallen and plentiful; several baobab fruits, a winter, food are present. Honey also eaten.
Animal foods	Gemsbok. Adult male, killed by ≠toma, June 3. Steenbok. Adult, killed by n!aishe, June 3.

Notes on Occupation

Camp 2 is typical of an early winter camp. Water is a major limiting factor, since most of the pans are dry and the mongongo trees, which provide the only source, have little water left. ≠toma, n!aishe, and their families move to ≠tum ≠toa from n/on/oni ≠toa to the south and bring a small amount of dried gemsbok meat with them. The mongongo nuts have just fallen in the ≠tum ≠toa grove and are very abundant: plentiful in the immediate environs of Camp 2. This period also coincides with the brief honey season, and since the two men are lucky enough to kill a large antelope early in their stay, they shift the focus of their attention to honey gathering. This is the last time the group camps in ≠tum ≠toa until the next rainy season. Their day-by-day activities are summarized below:

JUNE 3

In the morning the entire group arrives from n/on/on ≠toa, bringing a small amount of gemsbok meat with them. The two men then leave their families and go north to hunt. On the way, n!aishe shoots an adult steenbok and it dies instantly. In mid-afternoon ≠toma wounds an adult male gemsbok and both men return to camp, carrying the steenbok with them. They arrive about sunset, butcher the steenbok and eat it that night.

JUNE 4

Both men leave camp early in the morning to follow the wounded gemsbok. They chase and tire it, killing it with spears near hwanasi about noon. They skin and butcher it, roasting the liver, some ribs, and the metacarpals, and eat all of these at the kill site. They carry the meat from the four quarters, the heart, lungs, metatarsals, chest, ribs, and backbone to camp that day and leave the remainder in a tree. They also stretch the steenbok skin at the edge of camp to dry.

JUNE 5

The two men again return to the kill site, hunting along the way, and carry the remainder of the meat, except for the skin, back to camp. At the kill site, the head is roasted, and the meat is cut from it.

JUNE 6

N!aishe goes northwest to a forested area, searching for honey, but gets none. ≠toma remains in camp with the children, who are ill.

JUNE 7

The entire group goes after honey, cutting open a first tree to find nothing. In a second tree, which ≠toma sees, they do find honey.

JUNE 8

≠toma and his wife return to the gemsbok kill site to recover the skin, which had been roasted in the fire and placed in a tree. (The skin is later cut into strips and eaten). N!aishe and his family remain in camp.

JUNE 9

N!aishe goes southwest looking for honey. He is successful and brings some back to camp. ≠toma hunts north to //gakwe≠dwa, a pan. He sees nothing.

JUNE 10

Both men go to north to the forest of chu!ko n!a, looking for honey. They find bees in a mongongo tree but don't have time to chop it open; they return to camp.

JUNE 11

Both men hunt southwest to Tsauzedi but get nothing. The women go to chu!ko n!a to chop open the tree their husbands saw the previous day. They find no honey inside.

JUNE 12

The group moves south to n/on/oni ≠toa, a stop on the way back to Dobe. They carry the remaining gemsbok meat with them.

Notes on Site

Floral Remains

Baobab fruit: shell fragments only
Mongongo nut: cracked shells only

Faunal Remains

Species	Anatomical part	State
1. Gb	Ri	Fr
2. Gb	Ri	Fr
3. Gb	Ri	Fr
4. St	Sc	Fr
5. Gb	V	Fr

Species	Anatomical part	State
6. Gb	H	Fr
7. St	Ul	Fr
8. Gb	Ri	Fr
9. Gb	F	Fr
10. Gb	Ti	Fr
11. Gb	V	Fr
12. Gb	Ti	Fr
13. Gb	F	Fr
14. Gb	F	Fr
15. Gb	F	Fr
16. Gb	Ri	Fr
17. Gb	Ti	Fr
18. Gb	Ti	Fr
19. Gb	Ti	Fr
20. Gb	V	Fr
22. Gb	F	Fr
23. Gb	Ti	Fr
25. St	M	Fr
26. Gb	Ri	Fr
27. Gb	F	Fr
28. Gb	F	Fr
29. Gb	V	Fr
30. Gb	F	Fr
31. Gb	V	Fr
32. Gb	V	Fr
33. Gb	V	Fr
34. Gb	H	Fr
35. Gb	F	Fr
36. Gb	V	Fr
37. Gb	V	Fr
38. Gb	Ti	Fr
39. Gb	Ri	Fr
40. St	Ca	Fr
41. Gb	Ri	Fr
42. Gb	V	Fr
43. Gb	Ri	Fr
44. Gb	Ri	Fr
45. Gb	Ri	Fr
46. Gb	F	Fr
47. Gb	Ti	Fr
48. Gb	F	Fr
49. Gb	F	Fr
50. Gb	F	Fr
51. Gb	Ti	Fr
52. Gb	Ri	Fr
53. St	Ca	Fr
54. Gb	F	Fr
55. Gb	V	Fr

Species	Anatomical part	State
56. Gb	V	Fr
57. Gb	V	Fr
59. Gb	V	Fr
60. Gb	Ri	Fr
61. Gb	F	Fr
62. Gb	Ri	Fr
63. Gb	Ri	Fr
64. Gb	V	Fr
65. Gb	Ri	Fr
66. Gb	V	Fr
67. Gb	V	Fr
68. Gb	F	Fr

OTHER REMAINS

58.   Bark tray used for carrying honey. Measures 70 × 20 cm.

FEATURES

A.   Stalks of grass, about two good handfuls, to form a bundle about 1 m long. This is discarded, having been used to line a carrying net.

B.   Scattered charred logs and charcoal. Not compact like a cooking fire. (This was a cooking fire the contents of which had become scattered over the preceding 9 months.)

C.   Pile of 40 sticks, thin, pointed at one end, and about 13 cm long. These were made on the spot, used for pegging the steenbok skin to dry, and then discarded.

D.   Scatter of 22 pieces of cracked baobab shells.

E.   Scatter of cracked mongongo shells.

F.   Small fire marked by scatter of charcoal. It is flat, with no rise or depression.

G.   Baobab shells.

H.   Scatter of charcoal. Same as Feature B.

I.   Very thin scatter of mongongo shells.

J.   3 fragments of baobab shell.

L.   Scatter of charcoal. Same as Feature F.

M.   Scatter of cracked mongongo shells.

Hut 1.   N!aishe's hut. This is a dry-season hut. It has neither roof nor thatching and consists of branches, about 2 m in length set into the ground vertically in a semicircle. It also incorporates living bushes. Some leaves and grass matting are placed on the floor. There is no roof; the hut provides shelter from neither wind nor rain.

Hut 2.   ≠toma's hut. This is similar to Hut 1.

CAMP 3 ≠TUM ≠TOA 3 (Occupation 1 Mapped February 21, 1968; Occupation 2 Mapped April 5, 1968)

Summary

Occupations
1. 9 days (February 3–11, 1968) by ≠toma, n!aishe, and families. During last 2 days of occupation /n!au, bo, and families join group (8 adults, 13 children).
2. 2 days (March 18, 19, 1968) by ≠toma, n!aishe, and families, and ≠gau (5 adults, 7 children).

Water
During both occupations water is locally available and plentiful in the roots and hollows of mongongo trees.

Vegetable foods
During both occupations mongongos are scarce, since the new crop has not yet fallen. Mongongo nuts supplemented by tsin beans, roots, and other, less important plants.

Animal foods
First Occupation
Duiker. Adult female, killed by n!aishe Feb. 4.
Duiker. Killed by ≠toma Feb. 4.
Steenbok. Immature. Killed by ≠toma, Feb. 6.
Springhare. Killed by n!aishe, Feb. 8, and given to /n!au as a gift. (Not consumed in camp).
Porcupine. Immature. Killed by ≠toma, Feb. 8.
Porcupine. Immature. Killed by ≠toma, Feb. 10.
Porcupine. Killed by bo and /n!au, Feb. 11.
1 tortoise and 1 hornbill are also eaten during the first occupation of Camp 3, dates uncertain.

Second Occupation
Porcupine. Adult female. Killed by n!aishe, March 18.

Notes of Occupation

OCCUPATION 1

The first occupation of Camp 3 occurs during the height of the rains. Thus water is plentiful, but mongongo nuts are scarce, since the new crop has not yet fallen. In fact the group is forced to gather nuts from n/on/oni ≠toa, the nut grove immediately to the south. ≠toma and n!aishe move to Camp 3 from Camp 4 to the south, and then return to Camp 4 on their way back to Dobe. Although nuts are scarce in the ≠tum ≠toa grove, hwanasi, a game rich area to the north is within a day's hunting range, and the group moves to ≠tum ≠toa to exploit this latter resource. Thus they must choose between alternative food gathering strategies. At this time /n!au and bo were camping with their families at //gakwe ≠dwa, a pan several miles north of ≠tum ≠toa, and see the tracks of n!aishe and ≠toma on February 8. On February 9 the wives visit Camp 3, and the following day the entire group moves to Camp 3 and builds two huts. (Bau, n!aishe's wife, and n//aba, /n!au's wife, are sisters, but they rarely travel together.) On February 12, when n!aishe and ≠toma move south, bo and /n!au move eastward to Camp 1. Day-by-day activities are as follows:

FEBRUARY 3

N!aishe, ≠toma, and families move to Camp 3 from Camp 4 to be closer to the good hunting grounds at hwanasi. ≠toma and his son go hunting north to cha/to but see nothing. N!aishe and son hunt separately and see the tracks of two duikers, a mother and young, about a mile from camp. They see the young duiker run away, and n!aishe assumes that the mother is nearby. He goes to where the young one was standing and imitates its sound. When the mother appears and starts toward him n!aishe shoots an arrow at her and misses. A second arrow, however, wounds her. After following her for a short distance, n!aishe and son return to camp. The men then help their wives build two huts by cutting poles and grass.

FEBRUARY 4

≠toma and his son return to cha/to and shoot a young duiker there, killing it quickly. It is brought back to camp whole. N!aishe and his son return to follow the duiker wounded the previous day, and, after shooting at it once and missing it, they track it to a tree and find it unable to rise. They kill it with a stick, skin it and crack the cannon bones at the kill site, eating the marrow in them. The rest of the animal is carried back to camp. Both families share the two duikers, and the meat lasts for 2 days.

FEBRUARY 5

≠toma goes to !kau !kasi, a mongongo grove, and sets a snare for a duiker he knows to be in that area. He hunts in the region until noon and then checks the snare. He has caught nothing and returns to camp. N!aishe goes out in morning and sets a snare for the young of the duiker he killed the day before. He returns to camp and in the late afternoon he checks the snare, finding that the duiker had been caught but had had the strength to break the springpole on the trap. On the way out, n!aishe sees a young steenbok but does not get a shot at it.

FEBRUARY 6

N!aishe and ≠toma go out after the steenbok n!aishe had seen the previous day. They track it, and after missing with a first arrow both men wound the steenbok, then chase and kill it with a stick. They carry it back to camp whole and share it among everyone but the two wives, who do not eat steenbok.

FEBRUARY 7

N!aishe and ≠toma hunt north to hwanasi. They see nothing but bring back the horn of a gemsbok they had killed in 1964, to make small bows and arrows from it. These they hope to sell to the anthropologists.

FEBRUARY 8

Both men go with their sons in the direction of the steenbok kill. ≠toma kills a young porcupine and n!aishe a springhare. /n!au and bo's wives visit that day and N!aishe gives the springhare to them as a gift.

FEBRUARY 9

≠toma hunts, killing nothing while n!aishe and his wife go to n/on/oni ≠toa to gather mongongo nuts. They return in midafternoon to find that /n!au, bo, and families have already arrived. The newcomers build two huts in the camp.

FEBRUARY 10

≠toma takes his and n!aishe's son hunting and they kill a young porcupine. The animal is skinned at the kill site and carried back to Camp 3 where it is shared with the newcomers. In the afternoon, n!aishe and family go with /n!au and family to n/on/oni ≠toa to gather nuts.

FEBRUARY 11

≠toma, bo, /n!au, and families go to n/on/oni ≠toa to gather nuts. Along the way, the men kill a porcupine, which is later eaten completely in camp. N!aishe takes his and ≠toma's eldest son hunting. They kill nothing.

FEBRUARY 12

N!aishe, ≠toma, and families move south to n/on/oni ≠toa, Camp 4, while bo, /n!au, and families move east to Camp 1.

OCCUPATION 2

The second, briefer occupation of Camp 3 also takes place during the rains. Again, the mongongo nuts have not yet fallen and the men move to ≠tum ≠toa from n/on/oni ≠toa in the south in order to hunt at hwanasi. This time, however, they wound a gemsbok at hwanasi and the entire group moves north to Camp 6 in order to be near the kill.

When they returned to Camp 3, ≠toma and n!aishe moved into their old huts and built their new fires on top of the old ashes. A new hut, however, was built for ≠gau, and for this both poles and thatch were taken from bo and /n!au's abandoned huts. The two days of the second occupation were spent as follows:

MARCH 18

The three brothers and families move from n/on/oni =toa to reoccupy Camp 3. After arrival, n!aishe and his son hunt in one area of cha/to and kill an adult female porcupine. The other two brothers hunt in another part of the same area and kill nothing.

MARCH 19

All of the men go to hunt in hwanasi. ≠toma and ≠gau hunt together, and ≠toma wounds a young male gemsbok with an arrow. N!aishe, who is hunting alone, wounds two gemsbok but in neither does he place an arrow in a good position. ≠toma also shoots at another gemsbok but misses it. The men return to camp about 4:00 in the afternoon.

MARCH 20

The group moves to hwanasi to be closer to where an eventual kill will be made.

Notes on Site Plan

When Camp 3 was restudied after its second occupation, the new additions were added to the original map. Hut 5 was built during the second occupation, and at that time Huts 3 and 4, which had been abandoned, provided the necessary building materials. Since n!aishe and ≠toma moved back into their old huts and built their new fires on top of the old ones, no additional features, other than Hut 5 were added.

FLORAL REMAINS

Spiny melon:	skin fragments only
Monkey orange:	complete but unripe when camp abandoned
Water root:	complete—probably for carving a toy
Tsin bean:	seed pods only
Mongongo nut:	cracked shells only

FAUNAL REMAINS

Species	Anatomical part	State
	First Occupation	
1. Dk	V	C
2. Dk	Cr	Fr
3. Dk	Cr	Fr
4. To	Cp	Fr
10. Pc	Sc	Fr
11. Pc	P	Fr
12. St	Cr	Fr
13. Hb	Ul	C
14. Pc	Ul	Fr
15. St	Fe	Fr
16. Dk	V	C
17. Uf	Uf	Fr
20. Dk	O	Fr
21. Dk	Ul	Fr
22. Pc	Cr	Fr
23. Pc	Cr	Fr
24. Dk	M	Fr
25. Dk	M	Fr
26. Pc	Cr	Fr
27. Pc	M	C
40. Dk	H	Fr
41. Dk	V	Fr
42. Dk	O	C
43. Dk	Fe	Fr
44. Dk	V	C
45. St	O	C
46. Dk	O	Fr
47. Pc	Cr	Fr
48. Pc	V	C
49. Pc	Ri	Fr
50. Dk	O	Fr
51. Pc	Ri	Fr
52. St	Cr	Fr
53. Dk	O	Fr
54. Dk	O	Fr
55. Dk	Uf	Fr
56. Dk	Ri	Fr
57. Pc	Ri	Fr
58. Dk	P	Fr
59. St	Fe	Fr
60. Dk	O	C
61. Dk	Ri	Fr
62. Pc	Fe	Fr
63. Dk	Ma	Fr

Species	Anatomical part	State
64. Dk	H	Fr
65. Dk	Fi	Fr
66. Dk	Cr	Fr
67. Pc	Cr	Fr
68. Gb	Ho	Fr
69. Dk	Cr	Fr
73. Pc	Sc	C
74. Pc	Sc	Fr
83. Dk	Cr	Fr
97. Pc	P	Fr
98. Dk	P	Fr
99. Pc	Ma	Fr
100. Pc	V	C
101. Pc	Ma	Fr
102. Dk	V	C
103. Pc	P	Fr
104. Pc	Ul	Fr
105. Pc	Sc	Fr
106. Pc	V	C
107. Pc	Fe	Fr
108. Pc	Fe	Fr
109. Pc	P	Fr
110. Pc	Ra & Ul	Fr
111. Pc	Ri	Fr
112. Pc	Sc	Fr
113. Pc	Fe	Fr
114. Pc	Ul	Fr
115. Pc	Ri	Fr
116. Pc	Ri	Fr
117. Pc	Ri	Fr
118. Dk	Ri	Fr
119. Pc	Ri	Fr
120. Pc	Ri	Fr
121. Dk	Ri	Fr
122. Pc	Fe	Fr
123. Pc	P	Fr
124. Pc	Ri	Fr
125. Pc	Ri	Fr
126. Pc	Sc	Fr
127. Dk	V	C
128. Pc	Cr	Fr
129. Dk	Ri	Fr
130. Pc	Cr	Fr
131. Pc	Cr	Fr
132. Pc	Cr	Fr
133. Dk	Ti	Fr
134. Pc	Fi	Fr
135. Dk	Cr	Fr

Species		*Anatomical part*	*State*
136.	Dk	V	Fr
137.	Pc	H	Fr
138.	Dk	V	C
139.	Dk	V	C

Second Occupation

143.	Pc	H	Fr
144.	Pc	Ul	Fr
145.	Pc	H	Fr
146.	Pc	Cr	Fr
147.	Pc	Sc	C
148.	Pc	Ri	Fr
149.	Pc	H	Fr
150.	Pc	P	Fr
151.	Pc	Fe	Fr
152.	Pc	Ri	Fr
153.	Pc	V	C
154.	Dk	V	Fr
155.	Pc	V	Fr
156.	Pc	Ri	Fr
157.	Pc	Ri	Fr
158.	Pc	Ri	Fr
159.	Pc	Ri	Fr
160.	Pc	Ri	Fr
161.	Pc	Ri	Fr
162.	Pc	Ri	Fr
163.	Dk	P	Fr
164.	Pc	Ri	Fr
165.	Pc	Ri	Fr
166.	Pc	Ri	Fr
167.	Pc	Ri	Fr
168.	Dk	P	Fr
169.	Dk	Ma	Fr
170.	Pc	Ri	Fr
171.	Hb	Fe	C
172.	Pc	H	Fr
173.	Pc	Cr	Fr
174.	Dk	Cr	Fr
175.	Pc	Fe	Fr
176.	Pc	Ul	C
177.	Pc	Ti	C
178.	Dk	V	C
179.	Pc	Cr	Fr
180.	St	Cr	Fr
181.	Pc	Hp	Fr
182.	Pc	Cr	Fr
183.	Dk	Fe	Fr
184.	Pc	Ma	Fr

	Species	Anatomical part	State
185.	Pc	Ma	Fr
186.	To	Cp	Fr
187.	Dk	Cr	Fr
188.	Pc	Ri	Fr
189.	Dk	P	Fr
190.	Pc	P	Fr
191.	To	Cp	Fr
192.	Pc	Ri	Fr
193.	To	P	Fr
194.	Pc	Ri	Fr
195.	Pc	Ri	Fr

OTHER REMAINS

Mongongo nut cracking stones (15 total: 13 of hardpan, 2 of flint).
28. A stick about 1 m long. One end is beveled and charred, the other has a small fork. It was used for turning meat cooked directly in the fire.
76. Small pile of ostrich egg shell fragments.
78. A fire paddle, about 1.5 m in length.
141. A broken ostrich egg shell.

FEATURES

A.   Thin scatter of charcoal.
B.   Scatter of duiker or steenbok hair.
C, D, E.   Scatters of cracked mongongo shells.
F.   Scatter of duiker or steenbok hair.
H.   Fire associated with Hut 1. It is slightly depressed in the center and raised around the outside. The surface is a scatter of ash, charcoal, and a few cracked mongongo shells.
I.   Fireplace associated with Huts 2 and 5. It is slightly depressed in the center.
J.   Mounds of ash and charcoal associated with Feature I.
K, L.   Scatters of cracked mongongo shells.
M.   Fireplace associated with Hut 4. Marked by a shallow depression.
N.   Scatter of sand mixed with ash and charcoal.
O.   Scatter of cracked mongongo shells. Some charcoal present.
P.   Scatter of cracked split tsin bean pods.
S.   Fireplace associated with Hut 3. Marked by charcoal and a slight depression.
T.   A slightly raised area of sand mixed with ash and mongongo shells.
U, V.   Scatters of mongongo shells mixed with charcoal.

Hut 1.   N!aishe's hut. A well-constructed rainy-season hut with large entrance. It is made of branches stuck in the ground and bent inward to form a domed roof. Thatch is piled heavily on the outside but not fastened. The hut has a floor of several logs laid parallel, with fine grass piled on top of them.

Hut 2.   ≠toma's hut. Similar to Hut 1 in size and form but no branches under the grass flooring.

Hut 3.   /n!au's hut. Same as Hut 2 but not as well constructed.

Hut 4.   Bo's hut. Built in same way as Hut 3.

Hut 5.   ≠gau's hut. Built from materials taken from Huts 3 and 4. Similar to Huts 1 and 2, but not as large or as well constructed.

CAMP 4 N/ON/ONI ≠TOA 1
(Mapped February 22, 1968)

Summary

Occupations

1. 4 days (May 19–22, 1967) by n!aishe, ≠toma, and families (4 adults, 6 children).
2. 1 day (May 25, 1967) by same group as Occupation 1.
3. 6 days (December 1967) /''xashe n!a and one wife; n!aishe, ≠toma, and families, and ≠gau (7 adults, 7 children).
4. 7 days (January 27–February 2, 1968) by n!aishe, ≠toma, and families (4 adults, 7 children).
5. 2 days (February 12, 13, 1968) by same group as Occupation 4 (4 adults, 7 children).

Water

During all five occupations, water comes solely from the roots and hollows of mongongo trees. During the first two occupations, in May, water is scarce; but the last three occupations occur during the rainy season, and this resource is then abundant.

Vegetable foods

During the first two occupations, the mongongo nuts, which are just falling, are plentiful. In the last three occupations, these nuts are still available but much scarcer than before. Nuts are the main vegetable food during all occupations, although supplemented by honey (Occupation 3) and other minor plants.

Animal foods

First Occupation

No meat eaten.

Second Occupation

Group carries gemsbok meat with them but kill nothing while at Camp 4.

Third Occupation

Springhare. Killed by ≠gau, Day 1.
Springhare. Killed by /''xashe n!a, Day 3.
Springhare. Killed by n!aishe, Day 5.
Red-crested korhaan. Killed by ≠toma, Day 5.

Fourth Occupation

Springhare. Killed by ≠toma en route to camp, Jan. 27.
Springhare. Killed by ≠toma, Jan. 28.
Steenbok. Immature. Killed by ≠toma, Jan. 28.
Springhare. Adult female, killed by n!aishe's eldest son,
    Jan. 29.
Porcupine. Adult female, killed by ≠toma, Jan. 29.
Springhare. Adult female, killed by n!aishe, Jan. 31.
Springhare. Young male, killed by n!aishe, Jan. 31.
Springhare. Pregnant female, killed by n!aishe, Jan. 31.
Duiker. Immature, killed by n!aishe, Jan. 31.
Porcupine. Adult, killed by ≠toma, Jan. 31.
Springhare. Immature, killed by ≠gau, Jan. 31.

Fifth Occupation

Springhare. Killed by ≠toma, Feb. 13.
Springhare. Killed by ≠toma, Feb. 13.

Notes on Occupation

OCCUPATION 1

The data on this occupation are incomplete. The two brothers with their families arrive at Camp 4 from Dobe and build two huts. Although water is scarce, the mongongo nuts have just fallen and are plentiful. Although the men hunt, they kill nothing and eat no meat at this camp. On May 22, however, ≠toma hunts in hwanasi and wounds an adult female gemsbok. The following day both families move north to be closer to the expected kill.

OCCUPATION 2

The camp is occupied for one night only, as a way station by the two families, who are returning to Dobe. After their departure from Camp 4 on May 22, the group had gone north, recovered the dead gemsbok, and cut the meat into biltong. They then started back to Dobe in stages, spending one night at Camp 4 along the way. They carry strips of the dried gemsbok meat, but no bones, with them.

OCCUPATION 3

Early during the 1967 rains in December, a number of Dobe people move to n/on/oni ≠toa to eat mongongo nuts, which have survived on the ground, and to hunt. They reoccupy Camp 4. The original party includes /"xashe n!a and one of his wives, ≠toma and family, and ≠gau. /"xashe n!a and wife move into their son n!aishe's old hut, while ≠toma occupies his old one. ≠gau's mother builds a new hut for him. On the fourth day of occupation, n!aishe and family arrive and build a new hut for themselves. The day-by-day activities are as follows:

DAY 1

All inhabitants but n!aishe and family arrive from Dobe. The men go out to hunt separately, and ≠gau kills a springhare.

DAY 2

≠toma, his son, and ≠gau hunt north to hwanasi. They see a porcupine but are unable to dig it out of its hole. /"xashe n!a hunts alone and gets nothing.

DAY 3

≠toma and ≠gau hunt west to Mokoro. On the way back through /tanagaba they see an antbear but fail to kill it. /"xashe n!a goes to a camp in ≠tum ≠toa to see his son n!aishe, who is camping with kã//ka n!a, and tells him to come and join his brothers at Camp 4. Christmas is fast approaching, and /"xashe n!a wants the group to return to Dobe in time for it. (The anthropologists kill a cow and have a Christmas feast for the Bushmen.) /"xashe n!a kills a springhare that day.

DAY 4

N!aishe and family arrive and build a new hut. ≠toma and ≠gau go out to chop honey from a tree that ≠gau had seen, but they find the tree empty. None of the men kill anything.

DAY 5

≠toma, his eldest son, and ≠gau to to /tanagaba to set a snare for a duiker they had previously seen. On the way they also set a snare over the nest of a red-crested korhaan. They do not get the duiker, but on the way back to camp check the bird snare and find that they have trapped the bird. N!aishe, accompanied by his son, goes to shum !kau and kills a springhare. /"xashe n!a hunts but gets nothing.

DAY 6

≠toma returns to /tanagaba to reset snare for duiker but gets nothing. He also sees a bee tree, which he chops open; he finds a honey comb but no honey. ≠gau goes to !kau !kasi to dig for arrow poison. On the way, he seens another beehive and on his return to camp gets ≠toma to go with him and help open it. The two men do so and find rich honey. N!aishe and his father hunt but get nothing.

DAY 7

The entire group returns to Dobe because they do not want to miss the Christmas celebration.

OCCUPATION 4

As during the previous trip, water is plentiful in n/on/oni ≠toa, and mongongo nuts from the previous year can still be found. ≠toma leaves Dobe on January 27 with his family and goes straight to Camp 4 where he reoccupies his old hut. His brother n!aishe decides to remain at Dobe because his wife is safeguarding some of her father's belongings and does not wish to leave them until her father returns. The following day she reconsiders and leaves the goods with her uncle. Then n!aishe and family join ≠toma at Camp 4 and reoccupy their old hut. The group remains for 7 days in all, but large game hunting has been disappointing so they decide to move north to ≠tum ≠toa because from there they can hunt at hwanasi. They move to Camp 3 for its first occupation. On their later return to Dobe, they move back to Camp 4 again for the final time. Day by day activities for Camp 4 are described below:

JANUARY 27

≠toma and family leave Dobe because "there is no food there." They go straight to n/on/oni ≠toa, and ≠toma kills a springhare en route.

JANUARY 28

≠toma and son hunt to the west in the early morning and kill a springhare and a young steenbok. They return to camp before noon, and a bit later n!aishe and his family arrive. The men spend the remainder of the day in camp.

JANUARY 29

Both men hunt separately, each taking his eldest son with him. N!aishe's son kills an adult female springhare, while ≠toma and son kill an adult female porcupine.

JANUARY 30

The two men hunt west to Mokoro but get nothing.

JANUARY 31

Neither man hunts because they still have meat from the previous day's kills. They go out to gather nuts with the women, and the group finishes the meat from the previous day.

FEBRUARY 1

The men do not hunt and eat much meat from the previous day's kills. They go out and gather nuts with the women.

FEBRUARY 2

Both men hunt to /twi /twama. They see gemsbok tracks and follow until it starts to rain hard. They return to camp.

FEBRUARY 3

The group moves north to Camp 3 at ≠tum ≠toa.

OCCUPATION 5

After the group leaves Camp 3, they return to Camp 4 for two days. This is the first step on the return trip to Dobe. They left Camp 3 because there were no mongongo nuts remaining in the ≠tum ≠toa grove, while there were still some in n/on/oni ≠toa. After two days at Camp 4, the group moves south to Camp 5 at /tanagaba as the next step on their homeward journey. Their activities during this final occupation of Camp 4 are described below:

FEBRUARY 12

The group returns from Camp 3. In the afternoon ≠toma hunts and kills a springhare. N!aishe sees another and tries to hook it from its hole but is unsuccessful.

FEBRUARY 13

N!aishe hunts alone and kills two springhare. ≠toma also hunts; he sees a steenbok, but the animal runs before he can shoot it.

FEBRUARY 14

The group moves from Camp 4 to Camp 5 in the /tanagaba *molapo*.

Notes on Site Plan

FLORAL REMAINS

Sour plum:	skins only
Mongongo nut:	cracked shells only
Monkey orange:	shell fragments only
Spiny melon:	skins only
Water root:	shavings and one complete root—for making children's toys

FAUNAL REMAINS

	Species	Anatomical part	State
4.	Sp	P	Fr
6.	St	Ti	Fr
7.	Sp	V	C
8.	Dk	P	Fr
9.	Pc	V	C
10.	Pc	Ri	Fr
11.	Dk	Fe	Fr
12.	Sp	P	Fr
13.	Dk	V	C
14.	Pc	V	C
15.	To	Cp	Fr
16.	Ha	Sc	C
17.	Pc	U	C
18.	Pc	V	C
19.	Pc	V	C
20.	Pc	U	C
21.	Pc	V	C
27.	Pc	Fi	C
43.	Sp	Ma	Fr
44.	Dk	Cr	Fr
45.	Dk	Cr	Fr
46.	Sp	Fe	Fr
47.	Ha	V	C
48.	Uf	Uf	Fr
49.	Uf	Uf	Fr
50.	Pc	Cr	Fr
51.	Pc	Ri	Fr
52.	Sp	Fe	Fr

Species	Anatomical part	State
53. St	Uf	Fr
54. Sp	Ri	Fr
55. Sp	P	Fr
56. St	Uf	C
57. To	Cp	Fr
58. Pc	V	C
59. Sp	P	Fr
60. St	Fe	Fr
61. Pc	Fe	Fr
62. Sp	Cr	Fr
63. Sp	Fe	Fr
64. Pc	Ri	Fr
65. Sp	Ti	Fr
66. Gf	Sc	C
67. Sp	Cr	Fr
68. Sp	P	Fr
69. Pc	U	C
70. Sp	P	Fr
71. Sp	V	C
72. Pc	Ti	Fr
73. Sp	V	C
74. Pc	V	C
75. St	V	C
76. Sp	Cr	Fr
77. Dk	Cr	Fr
78. Pc	Ti	Fr
79. Sp	Cr	Fr
80. Sp	V	Fr
81. Pc	Fe	Fr
82. Sp	P	Fr
83. St	V	Fr
84. Pc	V	C
85. To	H	C
86. Sp	Cr	Fr
87. Pc	Fe	Fr
88. St	V	C
89. Pc	M	Fr
90. Pc	P	Fr
91. Li	V	C
92. Sp	Cr	Fr
93. Dk	Ti	Fr
94. Sp	V	Fr
95. Dk	Ul	Fr
96. Sp	M	Fr
97. Sp	Cr	Fr
98. Ha	M	Fr
99. Pc	Ri	Fr
100. Li	V	C

Species	Anatomical part	State
101. Pc	Fe	Fr
102. Sp	O	C
103. Pc	Ri	Fr
104. Pc	Sc	Fr
105. Pc	Fe	Fr
106. Dk	Ti	Fr
107. Sp	Cr	Fr
108. Sp	Sc	C
109. St	Fe	Fr
110. Sp	M	Fr
111. Dk	M	Fr
112. Dk	Fe	Fr
113. Pc	Sc	Fr
114. Sp	Cr	Fr
115. Sp	V	C
116. Sp	Cr	Fr
117. Sp	Cr	Fr
118. Sp	Cr	Fr
119. Sp	Cr	Fr
120. Pc	Ti	Fr
121. Sp	P	Fr
122. St	P	Fr
126. Gf	Fe	C
127. Sp	Cr	Fr
128. Sp	V	C
129. To	Cp	Fr
130. Pc	Fe	Fr
131. Dk	V	C
132. Sp	Fe	Fr
133. Sp	V	C
134. Sp	V	C
135. Pc	Cr	Fr
136. Pc	M	Fr
137. Pc	M	Fr
138. Sp	Cr	Fr
139. Pc	V	C
140. Pc	Sc	C
141. Dk	Ti	Fr
142. Sp	Cr	Fr
143. Dk	P	Fr
144. Sp	Cr	Fr
145. Dk	Sc	C
146. Pc	Ri	Fr
147. Sp	Fe	Fr
148. Pc	Ri	Fr
149. Dk	Fe	Fr
150. Ha	Sc	C
151. Sp	Ti	Fr

Species	Anatomical part	State
152. Sp	Ti	Fr
153. Dk	Cr	Fr
154. Sp	O	C
155. Pc	P	Fr
156. Pc	Fe	Fr
157. Pc	P	Fr
158. Sp	O	C
159. Pc	Fe	Fr
160. Pc	P	Fr
161. Pc	Ri	Fr
162. Pc	Ti	Fr
163. Pc	V	Fr
164. Pc	V	Fr
165. Pc	Ti	Fr
166. Sp	Ti	Fr
167. St	V	Fr
168. Sp	P	Fr
169. Sp	Ti	Fr
170. Sp	Sc	C
171. Pc	Ri	Fr
172. Pc	V	C
173. St	M	Fr
174. Pc	V	C
175. St	Ul	Fr
176. Pc	Ri	Fr
177. Pc	Ri	Fr
178. Pc	Ri	Fr
179. Pc	Ri	Fr
180. Pc	Ri	Fr
181. Pc	V	C
182. Pc	V	C
184. Pc	P	Fr
185. Gf	St	Fr
186. Sp	V	C
187. To	H	C
188. St	V	C
189. Sp	V	C
190. Sp	M	Fr
191. St	V	C
193. Ha	M	Fr
194. Sp	Cr	Fr
195. Sp	V	Fr
196. Sp	V	C
197. Sp	Ra	C
198. Sp	P	Fr
199. Sp	Ti	Fr
200. Sp	V	C
201. Sp	Sc	Fr

Species	Anatomical part	State
202. St	P	Fr
203. Sp	Cr	Fr
204. Sp	Fe	Fr
205. Dk	Fe	Fr
206. Sp	Cr	Fr
207. Sp	Ri	Fr
208. Pc	H	C
209. Pc	Fe	Fr
210. Pc	Cr	Fr
211. Sp	Sc	Fr
212. Sp	Cr	Fr
213. Pc	V	C
214. Dk	V	C
215. Sp	Cl	C
216. Sp	V	C
217. Sp	V	C
218. Sp	V	C
219. Pc	Cr	Fr
220. Pc	Sc	C
221. Sp	P	Fr
222. Sp	Cr	Fr
223. Sp	V	C
224. Pc	Fe	Fr
225. St	Fe	Fr
226. Sp	Sc	Fr
227. Pc	Cr	Fr
228. Pc	Cr	Fr
229. Pc	Cr	Fr
230. Pc	M	Fr
231. Pc	M	Fr
233. Sp	Sc	C
234.[a] Sp	M	Fr
235.[a] Sp	Ul	C
236.[a] Sp	Ra	C
237.[a] Pc	Ri	Fr
238.[a] Sp	Cr	Fr

[a] Located in children's play area about 20 m from camp. Not included in plot.

OTHER REMAINS

Hardpan mongongo nut cracking stones (11 total).
1. Discarded wooden mortar.
2. Discarded wooden pestle.
22. Fire paddle.
23. Child's toy car carved from sticks and water root.
30–33. Wheels for toy car. Carved from water root.

192. Stick with wheel set on one end. This is the steering wheel (of water root) for the toy car.
232. Car wheel of water root.

FEATURES

E.   Scatter of cracked mongongo shells and charcoal.
F.   Scatter of cracked mongongo shells.
G.   Scatter of cracked mongongo shells and charcoal.
H.   Scatter of cracked mongongo shells and charcoal. More dispersed and older than Features F and G because shells more weathered.
I.   Water root shavings. Byproduct of making toy car.
J, K.   Scatters of cracked mongongo shells.
L.   Scatter of water root shavings.
M.   Fireplace. Marked by slight depression and raised area around it.
N.   Fireplace. Has same contour as Feature M.
O.   Slightly raised area of ash, charcoal, and cracked mongongo shells. The charcoal is concentrated nearer Features M and N and gradually grades out from there. The reverse is true for the nut shells.
P, Q.   Scatters of cracked mongongo shells and charcoal.
R, S.   Scatters of water root shavings.
T.   Level area discolored by ash and a thin scatter of charcoal.
U.   Scatter of cracked mongongo shells.
V.   Scatter of water root shavings.
W, X.   Scatters of cracked mongongo shells.
Y.   Matting of grass, about 1 m long; two good handfuls. For lining a carrying net.
Z.   Scatter of duiker hair from scraping a skin.
A′.   Scatter of water root shavings.
B′, C′.   Scatters of old charcoal and cracked mongongo shells.
D′–H′.   Scatters of cracked mongongo shells.
I′.   Very thin scatter of cracked mongongo shells.
J′.   Scatter of water root shavings.
K′.   Scatter of sour plum skins.
L′.   Pile of branches on which springhare was placed for skinning and butchering.
Hut 1.   Originally built by n!aishe and later occupied by /″xashe n!a and one wife. It is a large, well-thatched rainy-season hut.
Hut 2.   ≠gau's hut. Same basic plan as Hut 1 but smaller and not as well constructed.
Hut 3.   ≠toma's hut. Same as Hut 1 in size and design.
Hut 4.   Second hut built by n!aishe. Same in size and design as Hut 1.

CAMP 5 /TANAGABA (Mapped February 23, 1968)

Summary

Occupation 2 days (February 14, 15, 1968) by ≠toma, n!aishe, and families (4 adults, 7 children).

Water This is a time of heavy rains, and water is plentiful in a nearby small pan.

Vegetable foods Mostly root foods supplemented by tsin beans and other minor foods.

Animal foods Hornbill. Caught in tree and eaten, Feb. 14.
Springhare. Adult male, killed by ≠toma, Feb. 15.
Springhare. Adult female, killed by n!aishe, Feb. 15.
Springhare. Adult female, killed by n!aishe, Feb. 15.
Springhare. Adult male, killed by n!aishe Feb. 15.

Notes on Occupation

The /tanagaba camp is a very temporary one, an unexpected stopover camp on the way from n/on/oni ≠toa in the north to Dobe. The group left Camp 4 and on the journey southward passed through the /tanagaba *molapo*, where they saw a number of fresh game tracks. Usually this *molapo* is dry, and no member of the group had ever camped there before, but exceptionally heavy rains have filled a small pan to overflowing. Thus the two families decide to break their journey and stay in that area for several days. Their trip is interrupted by DeVore and Yellen, who were camping at ≠tum ≠toa and persuaded them to return north. If uninterrupted, the group would perhaps have spent another day at /tanagaba before moving on toward Dobe. Their day-by-day activities are described below:

FEBRUARY 14

The group passes through /tanagaba on their way from n/on/oni ≠toa toward Dobe. They see a temporary pool of water and many fresh game tracks, and they decide to camp. Rain starts to fall, and the men, instead of hunting, help the women build two huts. Later in the afternoon they go out and gather roots and berries within a mile or so of camp. They catch one hornbill in a tree.

FEBRUARY 15

Both men hunt separately with their springhare hooks. ≠toma kills one springhare and gathers roots. N!aishe kills three springhare while the women gather roots. In the eary afternoon DeVore and Yellen arrive and talk to the two women. Shortly after DeVore and Yellen depart, the two men return.

In the morning, the two men go to ≠tum ≠toa and talk to the anthropologists. They return to /tanagaba and move both their families back to ≠tum ≠toa later in the day.

Notes on Site Plan

At the time Camp 5 was mapped, the entire area was criss-crossed by hyena tracks and hyena dung was found in one of the fireplaces.

FLORAL REMAINS

Spiny melon:	skin fragments only
Monkey orange:	complete fruit, unripe
Water root:	complete—for carving toys
Tsin beans:	seed pods only
Other root foods:	(unidentified)

FAUNAL REMAINS

Species	Anatomical part	State
1. Sp	P & V	Fr
2. Sp	M	Fr
3. Sp	M	Fr
4. Sp	Cr	Fr
5. Sp	Cr	Fr
10. Sp	P	Fr
11. Sp	P	Fr
12. Sp	Sc	C
13. Sp	Cr	Fr
14. Sp	Cr	Fr
15. Sp	M	Fr
16. Sp	Cr	Fr
17. Sp	Fe	Fr
18. Sp	Sc	Fr
19. Sp	Cr	Fr
20. Sp	P	Fr
21. Sp	O	C
22. Sp	Hp	Fr
23. Sp	Ri	Fr
24. Sp	P	Fr
25. Sp	Fe	Fr
26. Sp	H	C

	Species	Anatomical part	State
27.	Sp	Ra	C
28.	Sp	Ul	C
29.	Sp	Ri	Fr
30.	Sp	Ri	Fr
31.	Sp	Ri	Fr
32.	Sp	Sc	Fr
33.	Hb	Uf	Fr
34.	Hb	Uf	Fr
35.	Sp	P	Fr
36.	Sp	P	Fr
37.	Sp	Sc	Fr
38.	Sp	M	C
39.	Sp	Cr	Fr
40.	Sp	Cr	Fr
41.	Sp	Cr	Fr
42.	Sp	Sc	C
43.	Sp	Fe & Ti	Fr
44.	Sp	Fe	Fr
45.	Sp	O	Fr
46.	Sp	O	Fr
47.	Sp	O	Fr
48.	Sp	O	Fr
49.	Sp	O	Fr
50.	Sp	O	Fr
51.	Sp	O	Fr
62.	Sp	P	Fr
63.	Sp	Ri	Fr
64.	Sp	O	Fr
65.	Sp	O	Fr
66.	Sp	O	Fr
67.	Sp	O	Fr
68.	Sp	Fe	Fr
69.	Sp	P	Fr
70.	Sp	H	C
71.	Sp	Ra	C
72.	Sp	Ul	C

OTHER REMAINS

6. Small disc carved from water root. Made by children and probably intended to become the wheel of a toy car.

FEATURES

A. Scatter of water root shavings. The result of children's play.
B. Small scatter of charcoal in a slight depression. This fire was used to heat the root from which quivers are made.

E, F. Fireplaces associated with Huts 1 and 2. Both marked by pronounced depressions with ridges around them. In both hearths, the scatter of charcoal is limited almost completely to the hearths themselves.

G–I. Scatters of burned tsin bean pods.

Hut 1. N!aishe's hut. A large, domed, well-thatched rainy-season hut. Has some grass matting on the floor.

Hut 2. ≠toma's hut. Similar in size and design to Hut 1.

CAMP 6 HWANASI (Mapped April 4, 1968)

Summary

Occupation	3 days (March 20–22, 1968) by n!aishe, ≠toma, and families, and ≠gau (5 adults, 7 children).
Water	Water is plentiful at a small seasonal pan which is located about 0.5 km from the camp.
Vegetable foods	Mainly different species of roots, which are very plentiful in this area. Also some tsin beans.
Animal foods	Gemsbok. Young male, killed by ≠toma, March 20. Steenbok. Young female, killed by ≠toma, March 21.

Notes on Occupation

Camp 6 was occupied for two reasons. First, water was locally available and this is rarely the case. Second, the group expected that a gemsbok would be killed nearby. During the second occupation of Camp 3 in ≠tum ≠toa, three gemsbok were wounded at hwanasi on March 19. The following day the group moved camp to that area, to be close to the expected kill. Had no water been present there the meat would have been carried back to Camp 3. Although the area of hwanasi is rich in game, it lacks mongongo nuts and, usually, water as well, and only rarely do people camp there for any length of time. When a second gemsbok is wounded several days later and it moves south, the group abandons Camp 6 and goes to chu!ko n!a, which also lies in that direction. The day-by-day activities at Camp 6 are given below:

MARCH 20

Early in the morning the group leave ≠tum ≠toa for hwanasi. They agree ahead of time where they will camp and then n!aishe and his son set off alone to hunt. They get nothing and reach Camp 6 late in the day. The rest of the group goes directly to hwanasi and set up camp about 0.5 km from the pan. Then everyone sets out after the gemsbok. After they see that it has gone a long way, however, the women and children, except for ≠toma's eldest son return to camp, while the men continue. They find the half-grown male dead at chu!ko n!a and proceed to skin and butcher it. At the kill site they eat the liver and some ribs and also crack one tibia and all four cannon bones for marrow. The rest of the animal, except for one horn, part of the backbone, and the already cracked bones are carried back to camp.

MARCH 21

≠toma hunts alone and kills an immature steenbok. ≠gau and n!aishe hunt together and get nothing.

MARCH 22

≠toma hunts alone and shoots an adult gemsbok. The animal is well hit and ≠toma follows it far enough to see that it is heading south. N!aishe and ≠gau hunt to the north and ≠gau shoots a young kudu. They see that the poison is working well because the kudu keeps lying down. All the men return to camp and agree to concentrate their attention on the gemsbok, both because it is the larger animal, and because it is heading south in the direction the group wishes to go.

MARCH 23

The group abandons Camp 6 and moves south to chu!ko n!a.

Notes on Site Plan

FLORAL REMAINS

Water root: complete—for carving child's toy
Tsin bean: seed pods only

FAUNAL REMAINS

	Species	Anatomical part	State
1.	St	Fe	Fr
2.	Gb	Fe	Fr
3.	Gb	V	Fr
4.	Gb	Hp	Fr
5.	Gb	Hp	C
6.	Gb	Ri	Fr
7.	St	V	C
8.	St	O	Fr

Species	Anatomical part	State
9. St	O	Fr
10. St	O	Fr
11. St	O	Fr
12. Gb	Fe	Fr
13. St	O	Fr
14. Gb	Cr	Fr
15. St	O	Fr
16. St	O	Fr
17. St	Ul	Fr
18. St	Fe	Fr
19. Gb	Ri	Fr
20. St	Ri	Fr
21. Gb	Ri	Fr
22. St	Ri	Fr
23. Gb	H	Fr
24. St	Ri	Fr
25. St	Ti	Fr
26. St	Fe	Fr
27. St	Fe	Fr
28. St	Sc	Fr
29. St	Cr	Fr
30. St	Cr	Fr
31. St	Ri	Fr
32. St	Cr	Fr
33. St	Fe	Fr
34. Gb	Hp	Fr
35. Gb	Fe	Fr
36. Gb	Fe	Fr
37. St	Fe	Fr
38. Gb	Fe	Fr
39. Gb	Cr	Fr
40. Gb	Cr	Fr
41. Gb	M	Fr
42. Gb	Cr	Fr
43. Gb	V	Fr
44. Gb	Ra	Fr
45. Gb	H	Fr
46. Gb	Cr	Fr
47. Gb	Cr	Fr
48. Gb	Cr	Fr
49. Gb	Ra	Fr
50. Gb	Cr	Fr
51. St	Ul & Ra	Ul:C, Ra:Fr
52. Gb	H	Fr
53. Gb	V	Fr
54. Gb	Fe	Fr
55. Gb	Fe	Fr
56. Gb	Uf	Fr

Species	Anatomical part	State
57. Gb	Ri	Fr
58. Gb	Ri	Fr
59. Gb	V	Fr
60. Gb	Ri	Fr
61. St	Ri	Fr
62. Gb	Cr	Fr
63. Gb	V	Fr
64. St	Ul	Fr
65. Gb	Cr	Fr
66. Gb	V	Fr
67. Gb	Fe	Fr
68. Gb	V	Fr
69. St	H	Fr
70. Gb	Ra & Ul	Fr
73. Gb	Sc	Fr
74. Gb	Cr	Fr
75. Gb	Fe	Fr
76. Gb	H	Fr
77. Gb	V	Fr
78. Gb	Fe	Fr
79. Gb	H	Fr
80. St	Ri	Fr

OTHER REMAINS

Hardpan mongongo nut cracking stone (1 total).

FEATURES:

A. Small hearth with no rise or depression. The charcoal is burned to a fine ash. This is true of the charcoal in all hearths and is because of the kind of wood used, say the !Kung.

B. Thin scatter of tsin bean pods.

C. Remains of small fire, surface level, mostly ash.

D. Scatter of grass with 51 twigs associated, all about 0.3 m long. Some are stuck vertically into the ground but most are lying flat. The gemsbok skin was pegged out here.

H, I. Hearths marked by an irregular ash surface which is level with the surrounding ground. Contain very little charcoal.

J. A cut tree limb, about 1.3 m long with a hole in the middle. The hole goes only half way through the limb.

K. A small tree stump about 1 m high. The top is rounded. The hole in limb J fits into this top and together these form a two man merry-go-round.

L.   A small pit marked by 0.5 m depression and associated ash. The gemsbok
       head was roasted in it.

Hut 1.   ≠toma's hut. It is domed and thatched but fairly crude.
Hut 2.   ≠gau's hut. Similar to Hut 1 but smaller and more open.
Hut 3.   N!aishe's hut. Similar in size and design to Hut 1.

CAMP 7 N!ABESHA (Occupation 1 Mapped April 28, 1968; Occupation 2 Mapped June 30, 1968)

Summary

Occupations	1. 5 days (March 9–13, 1968) by n!aishe, ≠toma, and families, and ≠gau (5 adults, 7 children).
	2. 5 days (May 24–28, 1968) by n!aishe, ≠toma, kã//ka (1), and families; /"xashe n!a and his two wives, and ≠gau (10 adults, 7 children).

Water   During both occupations water is available in the n!abesha
                 pan which is located less than 0.5 km away. During the
                 first occupation it is abundant; in the second the pan is
                 rapidly drying.

Vegetable foods Mongongo nuts provide the main vegetable food during the
                 second occupation. In March the new crop had not yet
                 fallen and nuts in the nearby n!abesha grove are scarce;
                 thus other plant foods, especially roots are more
                 important. During the second occupation the new nuts are
                 on the ground and thus very plentiful.

Animal foods   *First Occupation*

                 Springhare. Adult male, killed by ≠toma, March 9.
                 Springhare. Immature female, killed by ≠toma, March 9.
                 Springhare. Immature female, killed by n!aishe, March 11.
                 Porcupine.)
                 Porcupine.} All killed by ≠toma and ≠gau
                 Porcupine.) in a single burrow, March 11.
                 Porcupine. Adult female, killed by n!aishe and ≠toma,
                      March 12.

                 Second Occupation

                 Porcupine. Killed by ≠toma, May 25.
                 Warthog. Recovered from a leopard kill by ≠toma and
                      ≠gau, May 27. One hind quarter has been eaten
                      by the leopard. The rest is carried back to camp.

Notes on Occupation

OCCUPATION 1:

N!abesha is within easy walking distance of Dobe, and the group moves from Dobe directly to Camp 7 on their way to the nut groves and hunting grounds to the north. They camp in the n!abesha *molapo* close to both a nut grove and a small pan that contains water. They remain long enough to scout the surrounding region for large game and move on when they see that none is present, since this, they state is an important objective of the trip. Thus, from Camp 7 they move north toward hwanasi, with the next brief stopover at Camp 9. At Camp 7, roots and other minor foods provide a major contribution to the diet. The day-by-day activity record is presented below:

MARCH 9

The group goes directly from Dobe to n!abesha, killing nothing en route. After establishing camp, ≠toma and his eldest son hunt and kill two springhare. N!aishe and ≠gau also hunt with their springhare poles but kill nothing.

MARCH 10

≠toma and his eldest son hunt in one direction, while the other two men hunt in another. They see no fresh tracks and kill nothing.

MARCH 11

N!aishe and son go in one direction and kill a springhare. ≠toma, his son and ≠gau make up another party and kill three porcupines which are in a single burrow. ≠gau crawls down the burrow to block off the passage, and then the other men dig down from above and kill the animals.

MARCH 12

≠toma and n!aishe hunt together and kill one porcupine. ≠gau goes out alone and gets nothing.

MARCH 13

≠toma and n!aishe hunt together and ≠gau hunts alone. No one sees anything. On that morning all the meat from the previous kills is finished, and the group decides to move north.

OCCUPATION 2

This visit to n!abesha is planned with the realization that the rains are over, that the pans and water sources in the mongongo trees are rapidly drying up, and that now is the last time that certain areas will be available for exploitation other than on a very brief basis. The group walks directly from Dobe to n!abesha and plans to eat the newly fallen mongongo nuts from n!abesha ≠toa before the nearby pan dries up completely. Eventually the group decides to leave Camp 7 because the hunting is bad, and as they often do, move north toward the areas with more large game. They go first to shum !kau dum and establish Camp 15 there. Day-by-day records of the Camp 7 occupation are as follows:

MAY 24

≠toma leaves Dobe with his family and goes directly to his own hut at n!abesha. On the walk he sees gemsbok tracks but does not follow them.

MAY 25

≠toma and his eldest son hunt and see a porcupine in the open, close to camp. ≠toma spears it and brings it back to camp, hanging it in a tree. He then sets out again with his son, heading north, and he hunts the area between n!abesha and shum !kau dum. He sees giraffe, gemsbok, kudu, and lion tracks but does not follow them because he fears lions. All of the tracks are going north. On the way back to camp he gathers mongongo nuts which he eats that night. During the day, the rest of the party arrives from Dobe. N!aishe and ≠gau reoccupy their old huts while kã//ka (1) and /''xashe n!a build new ones.

MAY 26

The boys stay in camp and the women gather mongongo nuts. N!aishe and kã// ka go west, hunting to /twi /twama, while ≠toma and ≠gau hunt together in that same general direction. Near /twi /twama, n!aishe sees a gemsbok, which he stalks, but the animal runs away. ≠toma and ≠gau turn north toward shum !kau dum, where ≠toma had gone the day before. They see lion tracks and the place where the lion had chased an antbear into a hole. They also try to stalk some warthogs but the animals smell them and run away. /''xashe n!a goes out alone to shum !kau dum to dig for roots. He sees no game.

MAY 27

Several days earlier, one of the anthropologists had driven an empty 44-gallon gasoline drum to a point 9 km from the n!abesha pan. The group planned to roll the drum to the pan, fill it with water, and leave it there to be drunk when the pan was dry. ≠toma and ≠gau go to drum, roll it over half the way to the n!abesha pan and leave it when the strike a very sandy patch of ground. On the way back to camp they see the remains of a warthog which had been recently killed by a leopard. They eat the hind quarter and carry the rest back to camp. N!aishe, his son, and kã//ka (1) hunt to the west but see neither game nor fresh tracks. That day they drink no water, getting moisture only from melons. /''xashe n!a and ≠toma's eldest son remain in camp. The women gather sha, a root, and mongongo nuts.

MAY 28

All the men except /''xashe n!a go to the drum, roll it to the pan and fill it. / ''xashe n!a hunts and sees nothing. The boys remain in camp and the women collect sha roots, mongongo nuts, and melons. Because the hunting is bad, the group decides to move north the following day.

Notes on Site Plan

I first mapped this camp in April 1968, after the first occupation. In late June I mapped it again, after the reoccupation, and made the new additions to the original map. During the second occupation additional huts were built by /''xashe n!a and kã//ka (1), who had not been present the first time. The remainder of the group moved back into their old huts and used their original hearths as well.

FLORAL REMAINS

Mongongo nut:	whole nuts and cracked shells
Wild sisal:	fibers from the outer covering—discarded in the twine-making process

FAUNAL REMAINS

	Species	Anatomical part	State
		First Occupation	
1.	Pc	Cr	Fr
2.	Pc	P	Fr
3.	Pc	Cr	Fr
4.	Sp	Sc	Fr
5.	Sp	Fe	Fr
6.	Pc	Ri	Fr
7.	Uf	Uf	Fr
8.	Pc	V	Fr

Species	Anatomical part	State
9. Sp	Hp	Fr
10. Sp	Cr	Fr
11. Sp	Cr	Fr
12. Sp	Hp	Fr
13. Sp	Cr	Fr
14. Sp	Hp	Fr
15. Pc	V	Fr
16. Pc	P	Fr
17. Uf	Uf	Fr
18. Uf	Uf	Fr
19. Pc	Hp	Fr
20. Uf	Uf	Fr
21. Pc	Ri	Fr
22. Pc	Ri	Fr
23. Sp	Hp	Fr
24. Uf	Uf	Fr
25. Pc	Sc	C
26. Pc	H	Fr
27. Pc	Cr	Fr
28. Pc	O	C
29. Pc	O	C
30. Pc	Cr	Fr
31. Sp	Ti	Fr
32. Sp	V	Fr
33. Sp	O	Fr
34. Pc	Ri	Fr
35. Pc	P	Fr
36. Sp	P	Fr
37. Pc	Fe	Fr
38. Pc	V	C
39. Sp	V	C
40. Pc	V	C
41. Pc	Cr	Fr
42. Pc	V	Fr
43. Pc	V	Fr
44. Sp	Fi	Fr
45. Pc	Ri	Fr
46. Pc	Ti	Fr
47. Pc	Cr	Fr
48. Uf	Uf	Fr
49. Sp	Sc	Fr
50. Sp	Ri	Fr
51. Sp	Ri	Fr
52. Sp	Sc	Fr
53. Pc	O	Fr
54. Pc	H	Fr
55. Sp	V	Fr
56. Sp	Ul	Fr

Species		Anatomical part	State
57.	Pc	Cr	Fr
58.	Pc	V	Fr
59.	Sp	Ri	Fr
60.	Pc	Ri	Fr
61.	Sp	Ri	Fr
62.	Pc	Ri	Fr
63.	Sp	Ri	Fr
64.	Pc	H	Fr
65.	Sp	Sc	Fr
66.	Pc	Cr	Fr
67.	Sp	O	Fr
68.	Uf	UF	Fr
69.	Sp	O	Fr
70.	Pc	Ri	Fr
71.	Pc	V	Fr
72.	Pc	Sc	Fr
73.	Pc	V	Fr
74.	Sp	Fe	Fr
75.	Sp	Ri	Fr
76.	Pc	H	Fr
77.	Sp	Sc	Fr
78.	Sp	Cr	Fr
79.	Pc	P	Fr
81.	Uf	Uf	Fr
82.	Sp	Ri	Fr
83.	Uf	Uf	Uf
84.	Uf	Uf	Uf
85.	Uf	Uf	Uf
86.	Sp	Cr	Fr
87.	Pc	V	C
88.	Sp	P	Fr
89.	Pc	V	Fr
90.	Sp	V	Fr
91.	Pc	V	C
92.	Sp	Fe	Fr
93.	Pc	Fe	Fr
94.	Pc	M	Fr
95.	Pc	Ri	Fr
96.	Pc	Ul	Fr
97.	Sp	H	Fr
98.	Pc	Cr	Fr
99.	Pc	Ri	Fr
100.	Sp	Fe	Fr
101.	Sp	Cr	Fr
102.	Sp	P	Fr
103.	Pc	Ri	Fr
104.	Sp	Fi	Fr
105.	Pc	Ri	Fr
			Fr
			Fr
			Fr

Species	Anatomical part	State
106. Pc	Cr	Fr
107. Pc	Ri	Fr
108. Pc	V	C
109. Pc	Cr	Fr
110. Pc	V	Fr
111. Pc	H	Fr
112. Pc	Fi	Fr
113. Sp	Ti	Fr
114. Pc	H	Fr
115. Pc	Cr	Fr
116. Pc	V	Fr
117. Pc	Ri	Fr
118. Pc	Ra	Fr
119. Pc	Cr	Fr
120. Pc	V	Fr
121. Pc	P	Fr
122. Pc	V	C
123. Pc	Ri	Fr
124. Pc	Ri	Fr
125. Pc	Sc	C
126. Pc	V	C
127. Pc	V	C
128. Pc	Sc	C
129. Pc	Ri	Fr
130. Pc	Ri	Fr
131. Pc	Ri	Fr
132. Pc	Ri	Fr
133. Pc	H	Fr
134. Pc	Cr	Fr
135. Pc	V	C
136. Pc	Ul	C
137. Pc	V	C
138. Sp	M	Fr
139. Pc	Ri	Fr
140. Pc	Ra	C
141. Pc	Ri	Fr
142. Sp	M	Fr
143. Pc	Ri	Fr
144. Pc	V	Fr
145. Pc	Cr	Fr
146. Pc	Te	C
147. Pc	Ti	Fr
148. Pc	V	C
149. Pc	Ul	Fr
150. Pc	V	Fr
151. Pc	O	C
152. Pc	Ri	Fr
153. Pc	Ra	Fr

Species	Anatomical part	State
154. Pc	Ri	Fr
155. Sp	Fe	Fr
156. Pc	Ri	Fr
157. Sp	Ti	Fr
158. Pc	Ri	Fr
159. Pc	Cr	Fr
160. Pc	Ri	Fr
161. Pc	Cr	Fr
162. Pc	P	Fr
163. Pc	H	Fr
164. Pc	Ri	Fr
165. Pc	Ri	Fr
166. Pc	M	Fr
167. Pc	Ti	Fr
168. Pc	V	C
169. Sp	V	C
170. Sp	V	C
171. Pc	V	C
172. Pc	V	C
173. Pc	P	Fr
174. Pc	V	Fr
175. Pc	Ri	Fr
176. Pc	Cr	Fr
177. Pc	Fe	Fr
178. Sp	Fi	C
179. Pc	Ri	Fr
180. Pc	Ri	Fr
181. Pc	Ri	Fr
182. Sp	M	Fr
183. Sp	M	Fr
184. Pc	V	Fr
185. Pc	V	C
186. Pc	Fe	Fr
187. Sp	M	Fr
188. Sp	Hp	Fr
189. Sp	Cr	Fr
190. Sp	P	Fr
191. Sp	Fi	C
192. Pc	V	Fr
193. Sp	M	Fr
194. Sp	Ri	Fr
195. Sp	Cr	Fr
196. Pc	Cr	Fr
197. Pc	Ri	Fr
198. Pc	Ri	Fr
199. Sp	Ra	Fr
200. Pc	V	Fr
201. Pc	Ri	Fr
202. Uf	Uf	Fr

Species	Anatomical part	State
203. Pc	Cr	Fr
204. Pc	Cr	Fr
205. Pc	M	Fr
206. Pc	M	Fr
207. Pc	V	Fr
208. Pc	Sc	C
209. Pc	M	Fr
210. Pc	Cr	Fr
211. Pc	Fe	Fr
212. Pc	Fe	Fr
213. Pc	V	C
214. Pc	O	C
215. Pc	Sc	Fr
216. Pc	V	C
217. Pc	V	C
218. Sp	Hp	Fr
219. Pc	H	Fr
220. Pc	H	Fr
221. Pc	V	Fr
222. Sp	V	Fr
223. Pc	Ri	Fr
224. Sp	V	C
225. Pc	V	C
226. Pc	V	C
227. Pc	V	C
228. Pc	Ri	Fr
229. Pc	V	C
230. Sp	Cr	Fr
231. Pc	V	C
232. Pc	Sc	Fr
233. Pc	Ri	Fr
234. Pc	Ri	Fr
235. Pc	Cr	Fr
236. Uf	Uf	Fr
237. Pc	Ri	Fr

Second Occupation

Species	Anatomical part	State
5′. Pc	P	Fr
6′. Wh	Cr	Fr
7′. Pc	M	C
8′. Pc	Cr	Fr
9′. Pc	Ra & Ul	C
10′. Pc	V	Fr
11′. Sp	Cr	Fr
12′. Wh	H	Fr
13′. Wh	H	Fr
14′. Pc	Fe	Fr
15′. Wh	H	Fr

Species	Anatomical part	State
16'. Pc	V	C
17'. Pc	Fe	Fr
18'. Wh	M	Fr
19'. Wh	Ri	Fr
20'. Pc	Ri	Fr
21'. Pc	V	C
22'. Pc	V	C
23'. Pc	V	C
24'. Pc	Ri	Fr
25'. Pc	P	Fr
26'. Wh	Ri	Fr
27'. Sp	V	C
28'. Pc	Cr	Fr
29'. Pc	Sc	C
30'. Pc	Cr	Fr
31'. Wh	Ri	Fr
32'. Wh	Ri	Fr
33'. Pc	Ri	Fr
34'. Pc	Ri	Fr
35'. Pc	Ri	Fr
36'. Wh	Ra	Fr
37'. Pc	V	C
38'. Wh	M	Fr
39'. Wh	Ul	Fr
40'. Wh	Sc	Fr
41'. Pc	P	Fr
42'. Pc	Fe	Fr
43'. Pc	Ri	Fr
44'. Pc	Cr	Fr
45'. Wh	Cr	Fr
46'. Pc	Fe	Fr
47'. Pc	Fe	Fr
48'. Pc	H	Fr
49'. Wh	Cr	Fr
50'. Wh	Ri	Fr
51'. Wh	Ri	Fr
52'. Pc	V	C
53'. Pc	V	C
54'. Pc	Cr	Fr
55'. Pc	P	Fr
56'. Pc	Ti	Fr
57'. Pc	Cr	Fr
58'. Pc	V	Fr
59'. Sp	Fe	Fr
60'. Sp	Ri	Fr
61'. Sp	Cr	Fr
62'. Sp	P	Fr
63'. Wh	Fe	Fr

Species	Anatomical part	State
64'. Sp	H	C
65'. Pc	Ri	Fr
66'. Sp	V	C
67'. Pc	Sc	Fr
68'. Sp	Cr	Fr
69'. Wh	Ri	Fr
70'. Pc	Cr	Fr
71'. Sp	V	C
72'. Wh	Cr	Fr
73'. Sp	V	C
74'. Pc	Ri	Fr
75'. Pc	Cr	Fr
76'. Wh	Ri	Fr
77'. Wh	H	Fr
78'. Wh	Ri	Fr
79'. Pc	Ri	Fr
80'. Wh	Ri	Fr
81'. Pc	Ti & Fi	C
82'. Pc	Ri	Fr
83'. Pc	Ra	Fr
84'. Pc	V	C
85'. Wh	Cr	Fr
86'. Sp	Fe	Fr
87'. Pc	V	C
88'. Sp	Fe	Fr
89'. Sp	Ti	Fr
90'. Wh	Ri	Fr
91'. Wh	Ul	Fr
92'. Pc	Ri	Fr
93'. Wh	H	Fr
94'. Pc	V	C
95'. Pc	Te	C
96'. Sp	Fe	Fr
97'. Wh	H	Fr
98'. Pc	Ri	Fr
99'. Pc	Cr	Fr
100'. Sp	Ul	Fr
101'. Pc	Cr	Fr
102'. Pc	H	Fr
103'. Wh	O	C
104'. Pc	H	Fr
105'. Pc	P	Fr
106'. Pc	O	Fr
107'. Pc	Ri	Fr
108'. Sp	Ri	Fr
109'. Wh	Ri	Fr
111'. Wh	H	Fr
112'. Pc	Cr	Fr

Species		Anatomical part	State
113'.	Sp	Cr	Fr
114'.	Wh	O	Fr
115'.	Pc	Cr	Fr
116'.	Pc	H	Fr
117'.	Wh	Ri	Fr
118'.	Pc	Ri	Fr
119'.	Wh	M	Fr
120'.	Pc	Cr	Fr
121'.	Pc	Cr	Fr
122'.	Sp	Sc	Fr
123'.	Sp	Ti	Fr
124'.	Pc	P	Fr
125'.	Wh	Te	C
126'.	Pc	H	Fr
127'.	Wh	V	C

OTHER REMAINS

Hardpan nut cracking stones (2 are present after the first occupation, and a total of 4 are observed after the second occupation).
80.   Fragment of ostrich egg shell.
241.   A butcher's knife (of the store-bought variety). This was left at the site by accident. It belongs to n!aishe; his children had used it and left it lying away from the hut. N!aishe forgot to take it with him and was upset when I found it and returned it to him.

FEATURES

A, B.   These scatters of charcoal are on the surface with no associated raising or depression. These are both remains of hearths from very old camps.

C.   A small, very irregular, semicircular enclosure formed of dead branches about 1.3 m in height placed upright in the ground. This "hut" was made by children at play.

G.   Hearth associated with Hut 2. Ash and charcoal form a well-raised mound above the ground level.

H.   Hearth associated with Hut 1. It is large and well defined, with a depression in the center surrounded by a raised ridge. The depression is primarily ash and most of the charcoal is on the ridge.

I.   Hearth associated with Hut 3. It is smaller than Feature H and level with the ground.

J.   Shallow depression with a slightly raised area surrounding it and with concentrations of charcoal on two areas along the rim.

B'.*   Hearth associated with Hut 4. The central area is level with the ground but has large ash mound around one side of it.

* The following derive from the second occupation and were not present at the first mapping.

C'. Scatter of burned mongongo shells.
D'. Scatter of wild sisal fiber. This is a byproduct of twine manufacture.
E'. Stalks of thick grass. They are incomplete arrow shafts abandoned during manufacture.
F'. Scatter of burned mongongo shells.
G'. Scatter of whole, unpeeled, and uncracked mongongo nuts.
H'. Scatter of burned mongongo shells.
J'. Hearth associated with Hut 5. It has no pronounced depression in the center but a slightly raised lip.
K'. Scatter of charcoal and burned mongongo shells.

Hut 1. N!aishe's hut. A very substantial hut, fully roofed over the very heavy thatch.
Hut 2. ≠gau's hut. Similar in size and plan to Hut 1.
Hut 3. ≠toma's hut. Similar in size and plan to Hut 1.
Hut 4. Kã//ka (1)'s hut. Built during the second occupation after the rains are over. Thus is less substantial; it is unroofed and has no thatch.
Hut 5. /"xashe n!a and wives' hut. An addition to the children's "hut" (Feature C), it was built during the second occupation and is similar in construction to Hut 4.

CAMP 8 !GWI DUM (Mapped April 30, 1968)

Summary

Occupation Approximately 1 month (late March–late April, 1968) by five nuclear families and one unmarried male.

Water Available in a small pan approximately 1 km from the camp. This pan gradually dried during the occupation and Camp 8 was abandoned when the water completely disappeared.

Vegetable foods Tsin beans provided the single most important source, supplemented by roots and a variety of fruits and berries. No mongongo nuts are available in the region.

Animal foods Gemsbok.
Duiker.
Steenbok.
Steenbok.
Porcupine.

Notes on Occupation

!gwi dum is a *molapo* about 60 km to the south of Dobe, and Camp 8 is the only mapped site not occupied by the Dobe group. Although the information about both it and its occupants is slim, it has been included to provide a basis of comparison to the other camps. The camp was occupied by a group of five nuclear families and one unmarried male. It is located on the crest of a sand dune, with the water source in the adjacent *molapo*. The group had moved northward to trade with the Herero villagers at /kai /kai, a pan located about 20 km to the northeast. They camped at !gwi dum because the hunting and gathering was good and then moved on to /kai / kai after Camp 8 was abandoned. A second group was also camped at !gwi dum about 100 m from Camp 8 at this time. Some meat passed back and forth between these two camps.

Notes on Site Plan

FLORAL REMAINS

Water root:	complete root
Spiny melon:	shell fragments only
Tsin bean:	seed pods and bean skins

FAUNAL REMAINS

	Species	*Anatomical part*	*State*
1.	Gb	Ri	Fr
2.	St	V	C
3.	St	Sc	C
4.	St	V	C
5.	Pc	Cr	Fr
6.	Dk	F	Fr
7.	St	Cr	Fr
8.	Pc	Cr	Fr
9.	Dk	F	Fr
10.	Dk	F	Fr
11.	Dk	F	Fr
12.	Dk	F	Fr
13.	Dk	V	Fr
14.	Dk	Ti	Fr
15.	St	Ri	Fr
16.	Uf	Uf	Fr
17.	Dk	Ri	Fr
18.	St	Ri	Fr
19.	St	Ri	Fr
20.	St	F	Fr
21.	St	Ca	Fr
22.	Uf	Uf	Fr
23.	Dk	Ca	Fr

Species	Anatomical part	State
24. Pc	Te	Fr
25. St	Sc	C
26. Pc	M	Fr
27. Pc	M	Fr
28. Pc	Cr	Fr
29. Dk	Cr	Fr
30. Gb	V	Fr
31. Dk	P	Fr
32. Pc	Ri	C
33. St	Ti	Fr
34. Gb	V	C
35. Du	Ca	Fr
36. Pc	Ri	C
37. Uf	Uf	Fr
38. Uf	Uf	Fr
39. Pc	Ri	C
40. Pc	Ri	C
41. Pc	Cr	Fr
42. Dk	P	Fr
43. Dk	M	Fr
44. St	Cr	Fr
45. Dk	M	Fr
46. Dk	Cr	Fr
47. St	Ti	Fr
48. Pc	Sc	C
49. St	M	Fr
50. St	F	Fr
51. Uf	Uf	Fr
52. St	Ri	Fr
53. Uf	Uf	Fr
54. Pc	Ri	C
55. Pc	Ri	C
60. Gb	V	Fr
61. St	F	Fr
62. St	P	Fr
63. Gb	P	Fr
64. Pc	H	Fr
68. St	Ul	Fr
69. St	H	Fr
70. Uf	Uf	Fr
71. Pc	F	Fr
72. Gb	P	Fr
73. Gb	P	Fr
74. Gb	P	Fr
75. Gb	Ri	Fr
76. Gb	Ri	Fr
77. Gb	Uf	Fr

Species	Anatomical part	State
78. Gb	P	Fr
80. Gb	V	Fr
81. Gb	Ti	Fr
82. Gb	V	Fr
83. Gb	P	Fr
84. Gb	V	Fr
85. Pc	Ti	Fr
86. Gb	V	Fr
87. Gb	P	Fr
88. Gb	P	Fr
89. Gb	Ri	Fr
90. Gb	Ri	Fr
91. Uf	Uf	Fr
92. Gb	Ri	Fr
93. Gb	Ri	Fr
94. Pc	F	Fr
95. Pc	F	Fr
96. Pc	Ti & Fi	Fr
99. Gb	Ri	Fr
106. Gb	V	Fr
107. Pc	P	Fr
108. Dk	Ca & O	Fr
109. Pc	Ul	Fr
110. St	Ra	Fr
111. St	H	Fr
112. St	Ra	Fr
113. Pc	Ul	C
114. Dk	Ul	Fr
115. Gb	Ri	Fr
116. Gb	Ri	Fr
117. Gb	Ri	Fr
118. Gb	St	Fr
120. Gb	Ri	Fr
122. Gb	Ca	Fr
123. Pc	Sc	C
124. Uf	Uf	Fr
125. St	Ca	Fr
126. Pc	P	Fr
127. Gb	Ca	Fr
128. Uf	Uf	Fr
129. Dk	Ri	Fr
130. St	P	Fr
137. St	Cr	Fr
138. Gb	Ri	Fr
139. Uf	O	Fr
142. St	M	Fr

OTHER REMAINS

79.   Digging stick. (This was taken and saved by informants after the camp had been plotted.)
97.   Stick about 0.4 m in length, rounded and charred at both ends. Used for stirring tsin beans in hot ashes and for cracking them.
98.   A broken section of springhare pole, about 1.3 m in length.
121.   Fragment of ostrich egg shell.
133–136.   Four stalks of grass of the kind used for making arrow shafts.
140.   Two segments of springhare pole.
141.   A bundle of grass bound with bark twine to form a semicircle about 0.7 m in diameter. Used by children in building a play house.

FEATURES

B.   Fire associated with Hut 1. Mostly ash with a small amount of charcoal. Marked by a very slight depression only.
C.   Raised area of mixed ash and sand surrounding Feature B. Includes scattered charcoal fragments and roasted tsin shells.
D, E.   Rough mats of branches. Used for skinning animals.
F.   A small heap of ash and charcoal. This is ash carted away from fire and dumped.
G.   Small pile of tsin shells.
H.   Fire associated with Hut 2. It is slightly raised with no central depression.
I.   Slightly raised area of ash, charcoal, and burned tsin pods, which are widely but sparsely scattered.
J.   Area of charcoal, thinly scattered, with high concentration of tsin pods.
L.   Small heap of ash and charcoal. Same as Feature F.
M.   Scatter of tsin pods and ash.
N.   Scatter of tsin pods only.
O.   Small fire with neither a raised nor a depressed area.
P.   Sparse scatter of gemsbok hair.
R.   Hearth associated with Hut 3. It is raised in the center with level ground surrounding it.
S.   Slightly raised area of soil mixed with ash and charcoal.
T.   Scatter of charcoal and ash, slightly raised.
U.   A small heap of ash and charcoal. Same as Feature F.
V.   Irregular, thin, but wide scatter of burned tsin pods.
X.   Fire associated with Hut 4. It is small and level with the surface, lacking a surrounding ridge.
Y.   Matting of grass with duiker hair on top of it. The duiker skin was pegged out to dry here.

A'.   A very ill-defined fire associated with Hut 5. It is very slightly depressed and surrounded by a slight rise.

B'.   Scatter of ash and charcoal. Level with ground surface.

C'.   Thin scatter of burned tsin pods.

E'.   A sunshade constructed of grass piled on top of a clump of living brush, with only a few upright branches added. It has a small depression toward the front which contains grass matting.

F'.   Grass matting with about 50 pegs in the immediate area as well as traces of gemsbok hair. Here the gemsbok skin was pegged.

G'.   Slightly raised fire associated with Hut 6.

H'.   Scatter of ash and charcoal.

I'.   Shallow pit filled with sand and charcoal. Was used to roast the gemsbok's head.

J'–L'.   Piles of roasted tsin bean skins.

Huts 1–5.   All five huts are built on the same plan. They are domed over to give a complete roof, and all are well thatched.

CAMP 9 SHUM !KAU 1 (Mapped May 5, 1968)

Summary

Occupation   2 days (March 14, 15, 1968) by n!aishe, ≠toma, and families, and ≠gau (5 adults, 7 children).

Water   Water is plentiful in a small pan in the shum !kau *molapo*, about 0.5 km from camp.

Vegetable foods   The vegetable foods, which do not include mongongo nuts, are varied—mostly several species of roots and the tsin bean.

Animal foods   Porcupine. Adult male ⎫
                Porcupine. Adult female ⎬ all killed by the men on March 14 in a single hole.
                Porcupine. Immature
                Porcupine. Immature ⎭
                Springhare. Nursing female, killed by n!aishe and ≠gau, March 15.
                Springhare. Nursing female, killed by n!aishe and ≠gau, March 15.

Notes on Occupation

Camp 9 represents a more or less fortuitous stop on the way from Camp 7, n!abesha, to n/on/oni ≠toa in the north. Because the men kill four porcupines soon after leaving Camp 7 and do not wish to carry them further than necessary, and also because it starts to rain, they decide to break their trip near a small pan in the shum !kau *molapo*. They remain there a second day to hunt and eat roots and other assorted vegetable foods; they then continue their trip north. Their two days at Camp 9 were spent as follows:

MARCH 14

The group leaves Camp 7 because they say that "there is no more food there." On the way north they detour to a porcupine burrow which the women had seen the previous day while gathering. The men crawl part of the way down the burrow to determine where the nest is located and then dig down to it from above. Their first hole misses the nest and they must dig another one. The second time they succeed and kill all four porcupines in the burrow. As the group continues north, it starts to rain and they decide to camp in the shum !kau *molapo*.

MARCH 15

N!aishe and ≠gau hunt, killing two springhare. The women gather a variety of vegetable foods, and the porcupines and springhare are all completely eaten. The group decides to continue north the following day.

Notes on Site Plan

FLORAL REMAINS

Tsin bean: A very few bean pods are widely and sparsely scattered across the camp and are not included in the site map

FAUNAL REMAINS

	Species	Anatomical part	State
1.	Sp	Cr	Fr
2.	Pc	Cr	Fr
3.	Pc	F	Fr
4.	Pc	M	Fr
5.	Pc	Cr	Fr
6.	Pc	Cr	Fr
7.	Sp	Uf	Fr
8.	Sp	Uf	Fr
9.	Pc	H	Fr
10.	Sp	Cr	Fr
11.	Pc	Cr	Fr

Species		Anatomical part	State
12.	Pc	M	Fr
13.	Pc	Sc	Fr
14.	Pc	V	Fr
15.	Pc	Cr	Fr
16.	Pc	P	Fr
17.	Pc	Ul	Fr
18.	Sp	M	C
19.	Sp	Cr	Fr
20.	Pc	Ri	Fr
21.	Sp	V	Fr
22.	Sp	Cr	Fr
23.	Pc	Cr	Fr
24.	Sp	Cr	Fr
25.	Sp	Cr	Fr
26.	Sp	Uf	Fr
27.	Sp	Te	C
28.	Sp	Cr	Fr
29.	Pc	O	C
30.	Pc	O	C
31.	Uf	Uf	Fr
32.	Sp	Cr	Fr
33.	Sp	Ul	C
34.	Pc	Ri	Fr
35.	Sp	O	C
36.	Pc	V	C
37.	Pc	Ra & Ul	C
38.	Pc	P	Fr
39.	Pc	Sc	C
40.	Sp	Uf	Fr
41.	Pc	H	Fr
42.	Pc	H	Fr
43.	Pc	Ri	Fr
44.	Sp	Uf	Fr
45.	Sp	P	Fr
46.	Pc	F	Fr
47.	Pc	Ri	Fr
48.	Pc	Cr	Fr
49.	Pc	Ri	Fr
50.	Sp	V	Fr
51.	Sp	P	Fr
52.	Sp	F	Fr
53.	Pc	V	C
54.	Pc	H	Fr
55.	Pc	F	Fr
56.	Sp	V	Fr
57.	Pc	Ra	Fr
58.	Pc	M	C
59.	Pc	Ri	Fr

Species	Anatomical part	State
60. Sp	Uf	Fr
61. Pc	Sc	C
62. Pc	Cr	Fr
63. Pc	Cr	Fr
64. Pc	V	C
65. Pc	V	C
66. Pc	V	C
67. Pc	V	C
68. Pc	V	C
69. Pc	Ra & Ul	Fr
70. Pc	P	Fr
71. Sp	Uf	Fr
72. Pc	F	Fr
73. Pc	Ri	C
74. Sp	Ri	Fr
75. Pc	Ri	Fr
76. Sp	Ti	Fr
77. Pc	F	Fr
78. Pc	O	C
79. Pc	Cr	Fr
80. Pc	Cr	Fr
81. Pc	Cr	Fr
82. Pc	Cr	Fr
83. Pc	H	Fr
84. Pc	H	Fr
85. Pc	Cr	Fr
86. Pc	Cr	Fr
87. Sp	V	Fr
88. Sp	Sc	C
89. Pc	V	C
90. Pc	V	C
91. Pc	Sc	C
92. Pc	O	C
93. Pc	V	C
94. Pc	Cr	Fr
95. Sp	Cr	Fr
96. Pc	Cr	Fr
97. Pc	Ri	Fr
98. Pc	Ri	Fr

OTHER REMAINS

Hardpan mongongo nut cracking stones (4 total).
Small digging stick made for a child.

FEATURES

A. Remains of a small playhouse built by the children. Consists of two pairs of forked sticks set in the ground to form a rough rectangle. A horizontal stick is placed across each of the pairs and similar straight, unforked sticks are scattered around the area.

D. Hearth associated with Hut 1. It is level with the ground in the center with a pronounced surrounding ridge.

E. Hearth associated with Hut 2. Similar to Feature D.

Hut 1. N!aishe's hut. This is a large hut, about 1.7 m high, domed and well thatched. It has grass matting on the floor.

Hut 2. ≠toma's hut. Similar in size and construction to Hut 1.

Hut 3. ≠gau's hut. On the same plan as Huts 1 and 2, but smaller and much less carefully thatched.

CAMP 10 //GAKWE ≠DWA (Mapped May 10, 1968)

Summary

Occupation   12 days (April 15–26, 1968) by n!aishe, ≠toma, dam, kã//ka n!a, and families; kumsa n!a, ≠gau, and /"xashe n!a and his two wives (13 adults, 11 children).

Water   The //gakwe ≠dwa pan, holding abundant water, is located about 0.5 km from this camp. Thus water is plentiful during the entire stay.

Vegetable foods   At time of occupation the new mongongo nuts are just starting to fall. The camp is adjacent to a grove which also contains nuts from the previous season. Thus nuts are relatively plentiful and are supplemented by other vegetable foods.

Animal foods

Gemsbok. Young male, shot by ≠toma April 14.
Young male, shot by ≠toma between April 16 and 24.

Notes on Occupation

Camp 10 is occupied at an ideal time of year, since both mongongo nuts and water are plentiful. The new crop of nuts is just starting to fall, and water is still plentiful in the temporary pans. //gakwe ≠dwa is such a pan, located close to the edge of a mongongo grove. It is also within easy hunting distance of hwanasi, where gemsbok concentrate at this time of year. The purpose of this trip is primarily to eat mongongo nuts. While camped at Camp 11, in ≠tum ≠toa, ≠toma shoots the first gemsbok at chu!ko n!a, and the following day the entire group establishes Camp 10, which is only several kilometers from that point.

On April 15, the first day of occupation, all the men go after the gemsbok that ≠toma had wounded the day before. They find it dead and butcher it, eating all the marrow from cannon bones, some ribs, the liver, and the head. The rest of the animal is carried back to camp and consumed there. Later during their stay, ≠toma wounds another young male gemsbok at !kau !kasi. The men go after it the next day and find it alive but unable to run, and they kill it with a spear. At the kill site, the men eat the marrow from the cannon bones, some ribs, and part of the liver. The skin and horns are left at the kill, and the remainder of the animal is carried back to camp. On April 27 the entire group leaves //gakwe ≠dwa to start a move back to Dobe.

Through an unfortunate oversight on may part, day-by-day records for this camp are not available.

Notes on Site Plan

FLORAL REMAINS

Spiny melon:	one whole, five shell fragments
Water root:	one complete root—probably collected by children to carve into a toy
Mongongo nut:	cracked shells only

FAUNAL REMAINS

Sixteen bone fragments (numbers 146–161) were found at Camp 10 after mapping had been completed. Although included here, their position is not marked in the site plot.

Series	Anatomical part	State
1. Gb	P	Fr
2. Gb	V	Fr
3. Gb	V	Fr
4. Gb	P	Fr
5. Gb	P	Fr
6. Gb	P	Fr
7. Gb	P	Fr
8. Gb	H	Fr
9. Gb	V	Fr
10. Gb	H	Fr
11. Gb	Cr	Fr

Series		Anatomical part	State
12.	Gb	V	Fr
13.	Gb	P	Fr
14.	Gb	St	Fr
15.	Gb	P	Fr
16.	Gb	Ri	Fr
21.	Gb	Ul	Fr
22.	Gb	Ri	Fr
23.	Gb	Ri	Fr
24.	Gb	Ri	Fr
25.	Gb	Ri	Fr
26.	Gb	Ri	Fr
27.	Gb	Fe	Fr
28.	Gb	Sc	Fr
29.	Gb	Sc	Fr
30.	Gb	P	Fr
31.	Gb	Sc	Fr
32.	Gb	Sc	Fr
33.	Gb	P	Fr
34.	Gb	P	Fr
35.	Gb	V	Fr
36.	Gb	P	Fr
37.	Gb	Ra	Fr
38.	Gb	Ra	Fr
39.	Gb	Ul	Fr
40.	Gb	V	Fr
41.	Gb	V	Fr
42.	Gb	V	Fr
43.	Gb	Ri	Fr
44.	Gb	Ri	Fr
45.	Gb	Ri	Fr
46.	Gb	Fe	Fr
47.	Gb	P	Fr
54.	Gb	O	Fr
55.	Gb	Ri	Fr
56.	Gb	Fe	Fr
57.	Gb	Fe	Fr
58.	Gb	Fe	Fr
59.	Gb	Ri	Fr
60.	Gb	Sc	Fr
61.	Gb	Ri	Fr
62.	Gb	Ri	Fr
63.	Gb	Ri	Fr
64.	Gb	V	Fr
65.	Gb	V	Fr
66.	Gb	Ri	Fr
67.	Gb	V	Fr
68.	Gb	V	Fr
69.	Gb	V	Fr
70.	Gb	Sc	Fr

Series	Anatomical part	State
71. Gb	Sc	Fr
72. Gb	Fe	Fr
73. Gb	Fe	Fr
74. Gb	V	Fr
75. Gb	V	Fr
76. Gb	Sc	Fr
77. Gb	V	Fr
78. Gb	H	Fr
79. Gb	H	Fr
80. Gb	Ri	Fr
81. Gb	Fe	Fr
82. Gb	V	Fr
83. Gb	V	Fr
84. Gb	V	Fr
85. Gb	V	Fr
86. Gb	P	Fr
87. Gb	V	Fr
88. Gb	Ri	Fr
89. Gb	H	Fr
90. Gb	V	Fr
91. Gb	V	Fr
92. Gb	Ri	Fr
93. Gb	Ri	Fr
100. Gb	Uf	Fr
101. Gb	V	Fr
102. Gb	Ri	Fr
103. Gb	V	Fr
104. Gb	Ri	Fr
105. Gb	V	Fr
106. Gb	V	Fr
107. Gb	V	Fr
108. Gb	V	Fr
109. Gb	Sc	Fr
110. Gb	Sc	Fr
111. Gb	Ri	Fr
112. Gb	V	Fr
113. Gb	Ri	Fr
114. Gb	Ri	Fr
115. Gb	V	Fr
116. Gb	V	Fr
117. Gb	V	Fr
118. Gb	V	Fr
119. Gb	V	Fr
120. Gb	Sc	Fr
121. Gb	Sc	Fr
122. Gb	Sc	Fr
123. Gb	V	Fr
128. Gb	Hp	C
129. Gb	Ri	Fr

Series	Anatomical part	State
130. Gb	Hp	C
131. Gb	V	Fr
132. Gb	V	Fr
133. Gb	Ri	Fr
134. Gb	P	Fr
135. Gb	Sc	Fr
136. Gb	H	Fr
137. Gb	Ri	Fr
138. Gb	Sc	Fr
139. Gb	Sc	Fr
140. Gb	Cr	Fr
141. Gb	V	Fr
142. Gb	Ri	Fr
143. Gb	Ri	Fr
146. Gb	Ri	Fr
147. Gb	H	Fr
148. Gb	Ul	Fr
149. Gb	V	Fr
150. Gb	Cr	Fr
151. Gb	O	C
152. Gb	V	Fr
153. Gb	Cr	Fr
154. Gb	V	Fr
155. Gb	V	Fr
156. Gb	O	C
157. Gb	Ti	Fr
158. Gb	P	Fr
159. Gb	Ri	Fr
160. Gb	O	C
161. Gb	Sc	Fr

OTHER REMAINS

Hardpan mongongo nut cracking stones (8 hammers, 4 anvils total). When Camp 10 was plotted, many of the same individuals were living nearby at Camp 14. They had collected some of the hammers and anvils from Camp 10 and carried them to the new site.

Unfinished quivers. Two unfinished quivers were abandoned at the site.

FEATURES

B.   Fire associated with Hut 1. Marked by a depression in the center with a pronounced ridge around it.

C.   Scatter of cracked mongongo shells.

D.	Rough mat of branches and leaves (probably for sitting on) with interspersed cracked mongongo shells.
F.	Fire associated with Hut 2. Marked by a slight depression in the center and a raised rim.
G, J.	Scatters of cracked mongongo shells.
I.	A small sunshade. Made of five leafy branches stuck vertically into the ground.
K–M.	Scatter of outer mongongo shell coverings.
N.	Scatter of cracked mongongo shells.
P.	Fire associated with Hut 3. Pronounced raised area surrounding depression in center.
R.	Fire associated with Hut 4. No noticeable depression, but ridging around the sides is noticeable.
S, T.	Scatters of cracked mongongo shells.
U.	A meat-drying rack consisting of a horizontal branch, about 2 m long, set 1.7 m above the ground. One end rests in the fork of a tree and the other in a forked branch set into the ground. It is used for drying strips of gemsbok meat.
W.	Fire associated with Hut 7. Exhibits no noticeable ridge or depression.
X.	Sunshade of five widely spaced leafy branches pointed slightly inward.
Y, Z.	Scatters of cracked mongongo shells.
BB.	Fire associated with Hut 6. Shows neither noticeable ridging nor depression.
DD.	Fire associated with Hut 5. Similar to Feature BB.
EE, FF.	Scatters of outer mongongo shell coverings.
GG–II.	Scatters of cracked mongongo shells.
JJ.	Sunshade associated with Hut 4.
KK.	Fire associated with Feature JJ. Marked by a slight depression with a raised area around it. Cracked mongongo shells are mixed with the charcoal.
LL.	A meat-drying rack. Similar to Feature U.
Hut 1.	/″xashe n!a's hut. Shared with his two wives. It is small, about 1.5 m high, fairly well thatched, and shallow enough so that it slightly resembles a windbreak.
Hut 2.	≠gau's hut. Similar to Hut 1 but smaller.
Hut 3.	≠toma's hut. On the same plan as Huts 1 and 2 but larger and well thatched.
Hut 4.	N!aishe's hut. Similar to Hut 3.
Hut 5.	Kumsa n!a's hut. This is different from all the others and was made by him. It is a rough lean-to with a horizontal branch supported by two forked sticks. Additional sticks are placed on the horizontal, each perpendicular to it with one end on the ground. Some rough thatching is placed on top. Kumsa n!a is a very old man, his wife is dead and his do-in-law is lazy.
Hut 6.	Dam's hut. Similar in plan to the others but very open in front. Almost as much a windbreak or sunshade as a hut.
Hut 7.	Kã//ka n!a's hut. This is large, more nearly a full circular shape, domed rather than pointed, and heavily thatched.

CAMP 11 ≠ TUM ≠ TOA 4 (Mapped July 6, 1968)

Summary

Occupation	3 days (April 12–14, 1968) by n!aishe, ≠toma, dam, kã//ka n!a, and families, kumsa n!a, ≠gau, and /″xashe n!a and his two wives (13 adults, 11 children).
Water	From hollows in the roots and trunks of mongongo trees. The rains are just ending, and water is still plentiful.
Vegetable foods	The new crop of mongongo nuts is just starting to fall in the ≠tum ≠toa grove and the nuts, which until now have been quite scarce, are the main source of vegetable food.
Animal foods	Porcupine. Adult male Porcupine. Adult female Porcupine. Immature Porcupine. Immature } all killed by ≠toma and /″xashe n!a on either April 12 or 13.

Notes on Occupation

The group arrives at Camp 11 almost directly from Dobe, with only a one night stopover at Dobe ≠toa along the way. Water, mongongo nuts, which have just started to fall, and game are all plentiful at this time of year. ≠tum ≠toa is a good place to camp, since nuts are plentiful there and hwanasi, a game rich area to the north, is within a day's hunting distance. The three brothers who form the core of this group often follow this pattern: They camp at ≠tum ≠toa, hunt primarily to the north and, if they wound a large animal, move camp in that direction.

On April 12, the group reaches ≠tum ≠toa from Dobe ≠toa and eat a large number of mongongo nuts. On either that or the following day ≠toma and /″xashe n!a kill four porcupines, all in the same hole. They skin the porcupines at the kill site and take the bodies back to camp. During this period, dam wounds a steenbok but the rain washes the tracks away and he does not recover the animal. N!aishe also shoots at a gemsbok and misses it. On April 14, ≠toma shoots a gemsbok at chu!ko n!a to the north and the following day the entire group moves northward to //gakwe ≠dwa, Camp 10, to be closer to the eventual kill.

Notes on Site Plan

FLORAL REMAINS

Spiny melon:	shell fragments only
Mongongo nut:	whole nuts, and cracked shells
Water root:	one complete root—probably for carving into a child's toy

FAUNAL REMAINS

Species	Anatomical part	State
1. Pc	Sc	Fr
2. Pc	F	Fr
3. Pc	Sc	Fr
6. Pc	P	Fr
7. Pc	Sc	Fr
19. Pc	F	Fr
20. Pc	Ra & Ul	C
21. Pc	F	Fr
25. Pc	M	Fr
26. Pc	M	Fr
27. Pc	P	Fr
28. Pc	Ra	Fr
29. Pc	Cr	Fr
30. Pc	Te	Fr
31. Pc	Ri	Fr
32. Pc	Ri	Fr
33. Pc	F	Fr
34. Pc	Cr	Fr
35. Pc	V	C
36. Pc	Cr	Fr
37. Pc	Te	C
38. Pc	Cr	Fr
39. Pc	Te	C
40. Pc	Cr	Fr
41. Pc	Te	C
42. Pc	Ri	Fr
50. Pc	Cr	Fr
51. Pc	Cr	Fr
52. Pc	Ti	Fr
53. Pc	Ti	Fr
54. Pc	M	Fr

OTHER REMAINS

Hardpan hammers and anvils for cracking mongongo nuts (6 hammers, 4 anvils).
55. Unfinished ostrich egg shell bead. The piece is roughly rounded, has a hole in the center but is not smoothed.
56. Incomplete quiver. Abandoned in process of manufacture.
57. Adze handle. Old and broken.

FEATURES

B. Fire associated with Hut 1. It has a very slight depression in the center with a slight raised lip around it.

C.	Scatter of kudu hair. The kudu skin was scraped here, but the animal was killed elsewhere some time earlier.
D.	Scatter of cracked mongongo shells and charcoal.
E, F.	Scatters of cracked mongongo shells, and charcoal.
G.	Scatter of mongongo shells.
I.	Fire associated with Hut 2. Marked by a slight depression and outer ridging.
J–L.	Scatters of cracked mongongo shells and charcoal.
N.	Fire associated with Hut 3. It is small, marked only by a bit of ash, charcoal and one log.
O.	Scatter of a few mongongo shells and charcoal.
P.	A small pile of cracked mongongo shells.
R.	Fire associated with Hut 4. Not at all well defined, and marked only by ash, charcoal scatter, and one log.
S, T.	Very thin scatters of charcoal and cracked mongongo shells.
V.	Fire associated with Hut 6. It has neither depression nor raised lip.
W, X.	Scatters of charcoal and cracked mongongo shells.
Z.	Small pile of unopened mongongo nuts.
BB.	Fire associated with Hut 7. It has a slight central depression and a raised rim.
CC.	Scatter of charcoal and cracked mongongo shells.
DD.	Scatter of cracked mongongo shells.
EE, FF.	Scatters of outer mongongo shells.
HH.	Fire associated with Hut 5. Exhibits depressed centre and raised rim.
II.	Scatter of charcoal and cracked mongongo shells.
JJ.	Scatter of outer mongongo shells.
KK.	Scatter of charcoal and cracked mongongo shells.
LL, MM.	Small piles of unopened mongongo nuts.

Hut 1.	Kã//ka n!a's hut. A rainy season hut, about 2 m high, with good thatch.
Hut 2.	Dam's hut. Built on same plan as Hut 1 but more substantial, neater, and with more thatch.
Hut 3.	Kumsa n!a's hut. A small, poorly constructed lean-to, built by him. (See note on kumsa n!a's hut at Camp 10.)
Hut 4.	≠toma's hut. Built on same plan as Hut 1.
Hut 5.	/''xashe n!a and two wives' hut. Built on same general plan as the others but much more open on the sides; actually more a combination windbreak and sunshade.
Hut 6.	≠gau's hut. Built on same plan as Hut 1 but much smaller.
Hut 7.	N!aishe's hut. Large, spacious, and well built; on the same plan as Hut 1.

CAMP 12 ≠ TUM ≠ TOA 5 (Mapped July 7 and 8, 1968)

Summary

Occupation	3 days (June 4–6, 1968) by kã//ka (1), ≠toma, n!aishe, and families; /"xashe n!a and his two wives, and ≠gau (10 adults, 7 children).
Water	Drinking water from hollows in mongongo trees. Water is scarce, since the rains are over and the supply is not being replenished.
Vegetable Foods	The mongongo nut, which is newly fallen and plentiful provides the main source of vegetable food.
Animal Foods	Steenbok. Killed by a caracal (a small feline) and recovered by /"xashe n!a, June 4.
	Porcupine. Killed by kã//ka (1), ≠gau, and n!aishe, June 6.
	Porcupine. Killed by kã//ka (1), ≠gau, and n!aishe, June 6.

Notes on Occupation

Camp 12 is a way station on the way back to Dobe. It is chosen in part because n!aishe is becoming ill (he was diagnosed with pneumonia several days later) and the eastern end of ≠tum ≠toa grove provides a good resting point on the route. The nuts, which have just fallen, are plentiful, but water is scarce, since the rains are over; the only water sources in the area, hollows in mongongo trees, are drying up and not being replenished. The three days at Camp 12 were spent as follows:

JUNE 4

The group leaves Camp 13, because of n!aishe's illness and establishes Camp 12, which is nearer to Dobe. After camp is established, /"xashe n!a and n!aishe's son go to !kau !kasi and find a steenbok which had been killed by a caracal. They bring it back to camp. ≠gau and ≠toma hunt north to //gakwe ≠dwa but see nothing and return to camp. The women gather mongongo nuts. N!aishe remains in camp.

JUNE 5

≠toma and kã//ka (1) go to hwanasi where they see fresh kudu tracks and then a gemsbok which runs from them. Kã//ka (1) goes to !kau !kasi to dig sha (a root food) and sees neither tracks nor animals. N!aishe stays in camp with the children. /″xashe n!a hunts in the n/on/oni ≠toa–≠tum ≠toa *molapo*. Just before dark he sees very fresh roan tracks but does not follow them because it is almost dark. He neglects to tell the others about the tracks on his return to camp. The women gather mongongo nuts.

JUNE 6

Only three men—kã//ka (1), ≠toma, and ≠gau—leave camp. They go to a porcupine burrow that /″xashe n!a had seen the day before in the n/on/oni ≠toa–≠tum ≠toa *molapo*. The three men dig down directly above it and kill two porcupines, bringing them directly back to camp. They learn about the roan later in the day but it is too late to follow them. They eat most of the porcupine at Camp 12, but carry some away with them when camp is abandoned the following day.

Notes on Site Plan

FLORAL REMAINS

Monkey orange:	shell fragments and whole, unripe fruit
Mongongo nut:	cracked shells only

FAUNAL REMAINS

	Species	Anatomical part	State
6.	Pc	Cr	Fr
7.	Pc	Cr	Fr
8.	Pc	Cr	Fr
9.	Pc	Cr	Fr
10.	Pc	Ti & Fi	C
11.	Pc	Sc	C
12.	Pc	P	Fr
13.	St	Ri	Fr
14.	St	Fi	Fr
15.	Pc	Ul	Fr
16.	St	Ri	Fr
17.	St	H	Fr
18.	St	Ri	Fr
19.	St	Cr	Fr
20.	Pc	V	Fr
21.	St	Fe	Fr
22.	St	Fe	Fr
24.	St	Sc	C
25.	St	P	Fr
26.	Pc	H	Fr

Series	Anatomical part	State
27. St	Ca	Fr
28. Pc	Ra & Ul	C
29. St	Ul	Fr
32. St	H	C
33. St	Cr	Fr
34. Pc	P	Fr
35. St	P	Fr
36. Pc	O	C
37. St	Ca	Fr
38. St	Ca	Fr
39. St	O	C
40. St	Uf	Fr
41. St	Ca	Fr
42. St	Ca	Fr
43. St	Uf	Fr
47. Pc	Ti & Fi	C
48. Pc	Ti & Fi	Ti:C, Fi:Fr
50. Pc	V	C
51. Pc	Cr	Fr
52. Uf	Uf	Fr
53. Pc	Sc	Fr
54. Pc	M	Fr
55. Pc	Ri	Fr
56. Pc	M	Fr
57. St	Cr	Fr
58. St	Sc	Fr
59. Pc	P	Fr
60. Pc	F	Fr

OTHER REMAINS

Mongongo nut cracking stones (8 total).
30. Small piece of wood partially shaped into bowl for a pipe. The wood cracked during manufacture and was discarded.

FEATURES

B.   Scatter of charcoal and mongongo shells.
C, D.   Neat stacks of mongongo shells.
E.   Fire associated with Hut 1. The entire area is raised and consists of a mixture of charcoal and sand.
G.   Fire associated with Hut 2. Slightly raised with a low depression around it.
H.   Scatter of mongongo shells.
I.   Thin scatter of charcoal.
J, K.   Mongongo shells.
L.   Unused firewood.

N.   Fire associated with Hut 5. The entire area is slightly raised.
O.   Mongongo shells and charcoal.
P.   Mongongo shells and thin scatter of charcoal and ash.
Q.   Small pile of mongongo shells.
S.   Fire associated with Hut 4. The entire area is slightly raised.
U.   Fire associated with Hut 3. The central area is slightly raised.
V.   Small area of ash, charcoal, and mongongo shells.
W.   Thin scatter of charcoal.
X, Y.   Charcoal and a pile of mongongo shells.
Z.   Very small fire, slightly raised.

Hut 1.   ╪toma's hut. This is a dry-season hut, composed only of leafy branches set into the ground. The branches are about 1.5 m high and are placed vertically in the ground; they do not meet in the center to form a roof, and lack grass thatching on the sides. Some living bushes are incorporated into the hut wall.

Hut 2.   Kã//ka (1)'s hut. Built along the same lines as Hut 1, but has a small amount of thatch placed vertically along the lower portion of the outside.

Hut 3.   N!aishe's hut. Consists only of two vertical side walls incorporating, in large part, living bushes. Has no back, roof, or thatch.

Hut 4.   ╪gau's hut. Similar to Hut 3, but smaller.

Hut 5.   /"xashe n!a and his two wives' hut. Built on the same lines as Hut 2.

CAMP 13 N/ON/ONI ╪TOA 2 (Mapped July 10, 1968)

Summary

Occupation   5 days (May 30–June 3, 1968) by kã//ka (1), ╪toma, and n!aishe, and families; /"xashe n!a and his two wives, and ╪gau (10 adults, 7 children).

Water   All water is obtained from the hollows in mongongo trees. This becomes increasingly scarce, as the rains are over and the water is not being replenished.

Vegetable foods   The mongongo nut provides the main source of food. The nuts are newly fallen, plentiful, and readily available in the immediate environs of the camp.

Animal foods   Gemsbok. Immature, shot by kã//ka (1) June 1 and recovered the following day.

Notes on Occupation

During this occupation of n/on/oni ╪toa, water is fast disappearing, but the newly fallen mongongo nuts are plentiful, and the group occupies Camp 13 to eat the nuts while some water is still available. They arrive there from Camp 15, to the south, having planned, after the water had been depleted, to move further north to eat the ≠tum ≠toa nuts. During the Camp 13 occupation however, n!aishe becomes ill with pneumonia; this drastically changes the course of the trip, since the group leaves n/on/oni ≠toa sooner than they had expected and moves to the eastern end of the ≠tum ≠toa grove (Camp 12) as a way station on their way to seek medical aid at the anthropologists' Dobe camp. Day-by-day records for the Camp 13 occupation are as follows:

MAY 30

The group leaves Camp 15 and arrives at n/on/oni ≠toa by midmorning. N!aishe, his son, and ≠gau then hunt north to da shum, where they see fresh elephant tracks; they are afraid of elephants and turn back to camp, digging sha roots along the way. During this time, ≠toma, and kã//ka (1) hunt to cha/to, where they separate. Kã//ka (1) sees the tracks of a female gemsbok and her young, and follows them. He sees the young one, shoots at it and misses, and the animals run. Kã//ka (1) goes to find ≠toma, and together they follow the mother but do not see her. On their way back to camp they see some warthogs which they shoot at and miss.

MAY 31

All the men go west to Mokoro to look for honey. ≠toma has seen a nest during a previous visit there, and he leads the group back to it. They empty it as well as a second hive, and they find a third, in which the honey is not yet ripe. This one they leave for a future visit. The group returns to camp just before sunset. On the way back to camp kã//ka (1) separates from the group and returns to cha/to to look for the gemsbok, but sees nothing.

JUNE 1

N!aishe begins to feel ill, and he remains in camp with his father and all the children. The women go gathering, while all the remaining men go together to cha/to to hunt. They see the tracks of the young gemsbok of several days before and follow them. ≠toma sees and follows fresh wildebeest tracks, but the animals sight him and run. Kã//ka (1) and ≠gau see hartebeest tracks, which they follow. While doing so, they see the tracks of the mother gemsbok and turn off to follow them. They see the animal and stalk it, but the gemsbok smells them and runs. The men start back to camp, slightly separated, and kã//ka (1) sees the young gemsbok running by him. Both men follow, and kã//ka (1) spots it lying in the shade. He stalks it, shoots two arrows, missing both times, then hits it in the head on his third try. The men then return to camp.

JUNE 2

While n!aishe and his father remain in camp, the other men go after the wounded gemsbok. They do not go straight for it, but circle around looking for the mother's tracks. They see nothing so they follow the wounded animal. Although it covers a lot of distance, it does not leave the area in which it was wounded but does a good deal of circling around. The men find it alive but very weak, and kã//ka (1) kills it by hitting it near the ear with a stick. The men eat nothing at the kill site because the animal is quite small, and they carry it back to camp.

JUNE 3

≠toma, kã//ka (1), their wives, and ≠gau go to //kain!oa ≠toa to look for honey. They go to a tree that ≠toma had seen some time before, collect the honey from it, and then return to camp in the late afternoon. In the evening, the group finishes the gemsbok meat, and they decide to start back to Dobe the following day because of n!aishe's illness.

Notes on Site Plan

When this camp was mapped, the informants present commented on the lack of faunal remains and the numerous porcupine tracks that criss-crossed the site. They told me that the porcupines had taken and eaten the bones.

FLORAL REMAINS

Mongongo nut:	cracked shells only
Spiny melon:	shell fragments only

FAUNAL REMAINS

Species	Anatomical part	State
6. Gb	Ul	Fr
7. Gb	H	Fr
12. Gb	Cr	Fr

OTHER REMAINS

Mongongo nut cracking stones (11 total).

19.   Twenty unfinished wooden mortars, abandoned in process of manufacture.

FEATURES

B.   Hearth associated with Hut 1. The entire area of ash, sand, and charcoal is slightly raised.

C–E.   Scatters of cracked mongongo shells and charcoal.

F.   Scatter of charcoal and ash.

H.   Hearth associated with Hut 2. It is similar in form to Feature B.

I.   Scatter of cracked mongongo shells and charcoal.

J.   Scatter of cracked mongongo shells.

K.   Mat of grass with 20 sharpened sticks about 15 cm long piled in the center. This is where kã//ka (1) dried the gemsbok skin.

M.   Hearth associated with Hut 3. It is similar in form to Feature B.

N.   Hearth associated with Hut 4. The central area only is slightly raised with ash, sand, and large pieces of charcoal.

O.   Area of ash, sand, and charcoal surrounding Feature N.

P, Q.   Scatters of cracked mongongo shells and charcoal.

T.   Hearth associated with Hut 5. It is similar to Feature B.

U.   Markedly raised area of sand, charcoal, and ash.

V.   Scatter of charcoal and cracked mongongo shells.

Hut 1.   Kã//ka (1)'s hut. This is a post–rainy-season hut, formed primarily of leafy branches set in a semicircle in the ground. It is approximately 1.4 m high and lacks a roof. A small amount of thatch is placed along the northeast side.

Hut 2.   N!aishe's hut. It has two sides only and lacks both a roof and a back. The sides are composed of leafy branches with no thatch added. A small amount of grass is placed on the ground inside as a matting.

Hut 3.   ≠gau's hut. Built in the same style as Hut 2 but smaller. The west wall is formed by two living shrubs only.

Hut 4.   ≠toma's hut. Built in the same style as Hut 2. The south wall is composed primarily of living shrubs.

Hut 5.   /"xashe n!a's hut. Built in the same style as Hut 2. It incorporates a good deal of living shrub into its construction.

CAMP 14 //GAKWE ≠DWA 2
(Mapped July 23–25, 1968)

Summary

Occupation   7 days (July 4–10, 1968) by ≠toma, n!aishe, kã//ka (1), kã//ka (2), debe, and families; /"xashe n!a and his two wives, ≠gau, /tasa, J. Yellen, P. Draper, and field assistant (18 adults, 8 children).

Water	A small amount of water is available in the hollows of mongongo trees. The major source is water in the 44-gallon drums in Yellen's truck, which is located about 9 km from the site.
Vegetable foods	Mongongo nuts are plentiful in the immediate region of the camp. They are newly fallen.
Animal foods	Aardwolf Guinea fowl Duiker Porcupine Porcupine Porcupine

Notes on Occupation

This is the last camp away from the Dobe waterhole occupied by the Dobe group, since, by mid-July, all temporary water sources will be dry. ≠toma, n!aishe, kã//ka (1), and kã//ka (2), with their families, and /"xashe n!a and his wives agreed beforehand to meet Yellen at //gakwe ≠dwa on July 4 or 5. They had camped at the shum !kau well (Camp 16), then spent 2 days at Mokoro and a single night at n/on/oni ≠toa before arriving at //gakwe ≠dwa on July 4. The following day, Yellen, Draper, and one assistant, together with debe and his family and /tasa, drove from Dobe to within 9 km of Camp 14 and walked the rest of the way there. The group had planned to camp there, and Yellen, for the most part was coordinating his movements with theirs. During his stay however, Yellen supplied most of the drinking water, and each day men made the 18 km round trip to his truck to obtain it. The men also took Yellen to some of their old camps and served as informants while these camps were mapped. For these reasons, day-by-day activity records are of little value. On July 10 the entire party walked to Yellen's truck and were driven back to Dobe. During the occupation, the primary emphasis was on honey gathering; hunting was of secondary importance.

Notes on Site Plan

Floral Remains

Water root:	complete root
Monkey orange:	complete fruits
Mongongo nut:	whole nuts and cracked shells

FAUNAL REMAINS

	Species	Anatomical part	State
10.	Pc	Cr	Fr
11.	Gf	St	C
12.	Gf	St	C
13.	Gf	P	Fr
18.	Pc	Sc	C
19.	Pc	Ti & Fi	C
25.	Pc	H	Fr
26.	Aw	Fe	Fr
27.	Pc	Ri	Fr
28.	Pc	H	Fr
29.	Pc	Cr	Fr
30.	Pc	P	Fr
31.	Pc	V	C
32.	Pc	V	C
33.	Pc	Ri	Fr
34.	Pc	Ri	Fr
35.	Pc	Ri	Fr
36.	Pc	Ri	Fr
37.	Pc	Fe	Fr
38.	Pc	P	Fr
39.	Pc	V	Fr
40.	Pc	V	C
41.	Pc	Ri	Fr
42.	Pc	Ri	Fr
43.	Pc	Ra & Ul	C
44.	Pc	V	C
45.	Pc	Ma	Fr
46.	Aw	Ti	Fr
47.	Pc	V	Fr
48.	Pc	V	C
49.	Pc	H	Fr
50.	Pc	Cr	Fr
51.	Pc	Ul	Fr
52.	Pc	Cr	Fr
53.	Pc	V	Fr
54.	Pc	Ri	Fr
55.	Pc	Cr	Fr
56.	Pc	Fe	Fr
57.	Gf	H	Fr
58.	Pc	Ri	Fr
59.	Pc	Ri	Fr
66.	Pc	Cr	Fr
67.	Pc	Cr	Fr
68.	Pc	Cr	Fr
69.	Pc	Cr	Fr

	Species	Anatomical part	State
70.	Pc	Cr	Fr
71.	Pc	Cr	Fr
72.	Pc	Cr	Fr
73.	Pc	Cr	Fr
74.	Pc	Cr	Fr
75.	Pc	V	C
76.	Pc	V	C
77.	Pc	Fe	Fr
78.	Pc	M	C
79.	Pc	P	Fr
80.	Pc	Ri	Fr
81.	Pc	Ri	Fr
82.	Pc	V	C
83.	Pc	Ri	Fr
84.	Pc	Ri	Fr
85.	Pc	P	Fr
86.	Pc	Ri	Fr
87.	Pc	Ri	Fr
88.	Pc	Ri	Fr
89.	Pc	Ri	Fr
90.	Pc	V	C
98.	Pc	Cr	Fr
99.	Pc	Cr	Fr
100.	Pc	Cr	Fr
101.	Pc	Ri	Fr
102.	Pc	Ri	Fr
103.	Pc	Ri	Fr
104.	Pc	Ri	Fr
105.	Pc	Ra	C
106.	Pc	Ri	Fr
107.	Pc	Ri	Fr
108.	Gi	O	Fr
109.	Pc	Ti & O	C
110.	Pc	Ti & Ri	C
111.	Pc	Sc	C
112.	Pc	V	C
113.	Pc	M	C
114.	Pc	Cr	Fr
115.	Pc	Ul	Fr
116.	Aw	Ul	Fr
117.	Pc	V	C
118.	Pc	V	C
119.	Pc	Ri	Fr
120.	Pc	Ul	Fr
121.	Aw	Sc	C
122.	Pc	Fe	Fr
123.	Pc	Sc	C
124.	Pc	Fe	Fr

Species	Anatomical part	State
125. Pc	P	Fr
127. Pc	Cr	Fr
128. Pc	Ra & Ul	C
129. Pc	Fe	Fr
130. Pc	V	Fr
131. Pc	Ul	C
132. Pc	H	Fr
133. Pc	Ra	C
134. Gi	O	Fr
135. Gi	O	Fr
136. Gi	O	Fr
137. Gi	O	Fr
138. Pc	M	Fr
139. Pc	Cr	Fr
140. Pc	Cr	Fr
141. Dk	Cr	Fr
142. Dk	Cr	Fr
143. Pc	Ti & Fi	Fr & C
144. Pc	V	C
145. Aw	Ti	Fr
146. Pc	Fe	Fr
147. Pc	P	Fr
148. Pc	Fi	Fr
149. Aw	Ti	Fr
150. Pc	P	Fr
151. Pc	Sc	C
152. Pc	Sc	C
153. Dk	O	Fr
154. Dk	O	Fr
155. Dk	Fe	Fr
156. Pc	Ri	Fr
157. Pc	Ri	C
161. Pc	Ul	Fr
162. Pc	Fe	Fr
163. Pc	Sc	C
164. Pc	P	Fr
165. Pc	Ti	C
166. Pc	P	Fr
167. Dk	P	Fr
168. Pc	Fi	C
170. Pc	Fe	Fr
171. Aw	H	Fr
172. Pc	V	C
173. Pc	H	Fr
174. Pc	H	Fr
175. Pc	H	Fr
176. Aw	St & Ri	St:C Ri:Fr
177. Pc	Ri	Fr

	Species	Anatomical part	State
178.	Pc	Ri	Fr
179.	Pc	Ri	Fr
180.	Pc	Ri	Fr
181.	Pc	V	Fr
182.	Aw	Ra & Ul	C
183.	Gf	Ti & Fi	Fr
184.	Pc	H	Fr
185.	Pc	H	Fr
186.	Pc	Ri	Fr
187.	Aw	Ri	C
188.	Pc	Fe	Fr
189.	Pc	V	C
190.	Pc	O	C
191.	Dk	Ra & Ul	C
192.	Pc	Fi	Fr
193.	Pc	Fe	Fr
194.	Pc	Ri	Fr
195.	Pc	Ri	Fr
196.	Pc	Ri	Fr
197.	Pc	Ra & Ul	Fr
198.	Pc	Cr	Fr
199.	Pc	Ri	Fr
201.	Pc	Ri	Fr
202.	Pc	Ri	Fr
203.	Aw	V	C
204.	Pc	Hp	Fr
205.	Pc	Cr	Fr
206.	Aw	P	Fr
207.	Pc	H	Fr
208.	Dk	Sc	C
209.	Aw	Ri	Fr
210.	Gf	Cr	Fr
211.	Aw	V	C
212.	Pc	Cr	Fr
213.	Dk	M	Fr
214.	Gf	Ti & Fi	Fr
215.	Gf	P	Fr
216.	Pc	Cr	Fr
217.	Pc	Cr	Fr
218.	Pc	Cr	Fr
219.	Pc	O	C
220.	Dk	H	Fr
221.	Dk	H	Fr
222.	Dk	P	Fr
223.	Pc	Ri	Fr
224.	Pc	Cr	Fr
225.	Dk	Ti	Fr

Species	Anatomical part	State
226. Pc	Ri	Fr
227. Pc	Ri	Fr
228. Pc	Ri	Fr
229. Pc	Ra & Ul	C
230. Pc	Ra & Ul	C
231. Pc	Fe	Fr

OTHER REMAINS

Mongongo nut cracking stones (14 total).

1–9.	Empty tin cans.
14, 15.	Tin can lids.
16.	Small digging stick.
24.	Broken wooden sheath for a knife.
64.	Empty tin cans.
65.	Broken digging stick.
96, 97.	Empty tin cans.
169.	Inner portion of root from which a quiver was made.
200.	Fragment of arrow linkshaft made of giraffe bone.

FEATURES

A.	Large fire marked by raised mound of ash and charcoal. Was used by Draper, Yellen, and assistant. They did not build huts.
B, C.	Piles of guinea fowl feathers.
D.	Small pit with charcoal and ash in it.
E.	Hearth associated with Hut 6. Marked only by a slight mound of ash and charcoal.
F.	Area of ash, charcoal, and cracked mongongo shells.
G.	Pile of cracked mongongo shells.
I.	A second fire associated with Hut 6. It is marked by a slight mound of ash and charcoal.
J.	Surface scatter of charcoal.
K.	Scatter of cracked mongongo shells.
M.	Hearth associated with Hut 7. Marked by a raised pile of ash and charcoal.
N.	Hearth associated with Hut 1. Marked by a raised mound of ash, sand, and charcoal.
O, P.	Piles of cracked mongongo shells and charcoal.
S.	Scatter of charcoal.
T.	Scatter of cracked mongongo shells.

V.   Hearth associated with Hut 2. Marked by a small depression in the center surrounded by a ridge of sand, ash, and charcoal.
W.   Scatter of cracked mongongo shells and charcoal.
X.   Scatter of charcoal with a few cracked mongongo shells.
Z.   Hearth associated with Hut 4. Marked by a raised mound of ash, sand, and charcoal.
BB.   Hearth associated with Hut 5. Marked only by a raised mound of ash.
CC–EE.   Piles of cracked mongongo shells.
FF.   Scatter of charcoal with a very small pit in the center. /tasa slept near this fire.
HH.   Hearth associated with Hut 3. Marked by a raised mound of ash, sand, and charcoal.
II.   Scatter of cracked mongongo shells and charcoal.
JJ.   Small pile of whole mongongo nuts.
KK.   Scatter of cracked mongongo shells and charcoal.
LL.   Scatter of charcoal.
MM.   Scatter of cracked mongongo shells and charcoal.

Hut 1.   N!aishe's hut. Composed of branches stuck vertically in the ground to form a semicircle. It has neither thatch nor a roof. A small amount of grass matting is placed on the floor.
Hut 2.   ≠toma's hut. It is built on the same plan as Hut 1 and incorporates some living shrubs into its walls.
Hut 3.   Kã//ka (1)'s hut. It is built on the same plan as Hut 2.
Hut 4.   Kã//ka (2)'s hut. It is formed of cut branches placed vertically in the ground and has neither roof nor back. It lacks thatching, but has some grass placed on its floor.
Hut 5.   Debe's hut. Built on the same plan as Hut 2.
Hut 6.   /"xashe n!a's hut. Built on the same plan as Hut 4.
Hut 7.   ≠gau's hut. Built on the same plan as Hut 4.

CAMP 15 SHUM !KAU 2 (Mapped September 17, 1968)

Summary

Occupation	1 day (May 29, 1968) by n!aishe, ≠toma, kã//ka (1), and families; /"xashe n!a and his two wives, and ≠gau (10 adults, 7 children).
Water	During this brief stay the group drinks only water that has been brought with them in ostrich egg shells.
Vegetable foods	Mongongo nuts from the nearby shum !kau ≠toa nut grove.
Animal foods	Porcupine. Killed by n!aishe and ≠gau. Porcupine. Killed by n!aishe and ≠gau.

Notes on Occupation

On their move from Camp 7 at n!abesha to n/on/oni ≠toa (where Camp 13 was established the following day) the group had not planned to stop at shum !kau. They leave Camp 7 later in the day than they had planned and, on the march, kã//ka (1)'s wife sees two porcupines and shouts to the men. N!aishe and ≠gau run over and spear both the animals. As it is already getting late, the group decides to spend the night in the shum !kau *molapo,* near a small pan, close to the place where the animals were killed. thus they make a very temporary camp, completely consume the porcupines there, and gather some mongongo nuts. The next morning they move north again.

Notes on Site Plan

FLORAL REMAINS

Spiny melon:	shell fragments only
Mongongo nut:	cracked shells only
Wild sisal:	fibers from the outer covering

FAUNAL REMAINS

Species	Anatomical part	State
1. Pc	Cr	Fr
2. Pc	Cr	Fr
3. Pc	Cr	Fr
4. Pc	Cr	Fr
5. Pc	Cr	Fr
6. Pc	Ri	Fr
9. Pc	Sc	Fr
10. Pc	Cr	Fr

OTHER REMAINS

Mongongo nut cracking stones (2 of hardpan and 1 of flint).

FEATURES

A. Confined surface scatter of charcoal. This is a small fire built by kã//ka (1) to roast the skin of one porcupine.

C.   Fire associated with Hut 1. Level with only a small amount of ash and char-coal.

D.   Scatter of cracked mongongo shells.

E.   Scatter of the outer strands of a type of wild sisal plant. This is a byproduct of twine making.

F.   Small level fire marked by charcoal and ash. /"xashe n!a and his wives slept around it, not bothering to build a hut.

G.   Scatter of cracked mongongo shells.

I.   Fire associated with Hut 2. Level and marked only by scattered charcoal and a small amount of ash.

J.   Scatter of cracked mongongo shells.

L.   Fire associated with Hut 3. Similar to Feature I.

M.   Scatter of wild sisal fiber.

N.   Scatter of wild sisal fiber.

O.   Fire associated with Hut 4. Similar to Feature I.

P.   Scatter of cracked mongongo shells.

Q.   Scatter of charcoal and ash which forms a slightly raised mound. The second porcupine skin was roasted here.

Hut 1.   Kã//ka (1)'s "hut," marked by a matting of grass and a single branch stuck into the ground.

Hut 2.   N!aishe's hut. Marked by four branches stuck into the ground showing the outlines of a hut, and by a patch of grass matting on the ground.

Hut 3.   ≠gau's "hut." Marked by a single large branch stuck into the ground. Really a symbolic hut.

Hut 4.   ≠toma's hut. Four branches stuck into the ground only.

CAMP 16 SHUM !KAU 3
(Mapped September 18, 19, 1968)

Summary

Occupation   6 days (June 25–30, 1968) by ≠toma, n!aishe, kã//ka (1), kã//ka (2) and families; /"xashe n!a and his two wives, and ≠gau. (12 adults, 7 children).

Water   Available at a small well dug by Bushmen in the shum !kau pan. When the well becomes dry, the camp is abandoned.

Vegetable foods   Mongongo nuts are very plentiful in the shum !kau grove as they have recently fallen.

Animal foods Porcupine. Killed by ≠gau and kã//ka (1), June 28.
Guinea fowl. Trapped by kã//ka (1), June 28.
Guinea fowl. Trapped by kã//ka (2), June 28.
Guinea fowl. Trapped by n!aishe and eaten by a small carni-
vore, June 29.
Porcupine. Killed by kã//ka (1), June 29.

Notes on Occupation

Camp 16 was occupied by the Dobe group during the last trip possible for them before the start of the next rainy season in late 1968 or early 1969. Water, now quite scarce, places extreme limitations on group movement, since the mongongo trees and small pans are now dry. Members of the group leave Dobe at different times and agree to meet at the shum !kau well. /''xashe n!a and his wives, and kã//ka (1) and kã//ka (2) with their families leave Dobe on June 23 and reach shum !kau 2 days later, with brief stopovers just north of Dobe and at n!abesha. On June 25, n!aishe, his family, and ≠gau leave Dobe, spend that night at n!abesha, and arrive at the shum !kau camp the following day. On June 30, ≠toma and family go directly from Dobe to Camp 16, driving part of the way there with Yellen who is on his way to n!abesha.

The purpose of this trip, the group says, is to get honey and to eat the mongongo nuts, which are plentiful, but will soon be unavailable because of the lack of water. Hunting is of secondary importance and relatively little effort is expended on it. The group goes to the largest pan in the shum !kau *molapo* because of a well, approximately 5 m deep which had been dug by Bushmen sometime in the past. It holds water after the pan itself is dry and is the only remaining water source in that region. They remain there until the well is dry and then move west to another pan at Mokoro. This one, they find, is dry, and their stay at Mokoro is a brief one. The day-by-day activities at Camp 16 are given below.

JUNE 25

Kã//ka (1), kã//ka (2) and their families and /''xashe n!a and his wives leave n!abesha early in morning and reach shum !kau about noon. They camp near the large shum !kau pan in the *molapo*. The pan itself is dry but the well still holds water. /''xashe n!a then goes east down the *molapo* to two smaller dry pans and sees nothing. Kã//ka (1) and kã//ka (2) dig loose dirt out of the well and spend the rest of the day in camp. The women all gather mongongo nuts from the nearby shum !kau =toa nut grove. On this day, n!aishe and family and ≠gau leave Dobe at mid-morning and go straight to n!abesha, arriving in the later afternoon; they see nothing along the way. After their arrival, n!aishe hunts but sees neither fresh tracks nor animals.

JUNE 26

Kã//ka (1) and kã//ka (2) go out in the morning and chop honey from a tree near the well. They return to camp and meet n!aishe and ≠gau who had set out from n!abesha early that morning. /"xashe n!a, kã//ka (1), and kã//ka (2) then head west along the shum !kau *molapo* to Mokoro, a forested area which contains a pan. They are looking primarily for honey but see none. They do, however, see day-old kudu and giraffe tracks, and kudu tracks from that morning as well. They decide not to follow, and return to camp. N!aishe and ≠gau go with the women and children to the next *molapo* north to a bee tree they had seen the previous year. They collect a great deal of honey but see no game.

JUNE 27

N!aishe and ≠gau again go north with the women and collect more honey. Kã//ka (1) and kã//ka (2) remain in camp doing nothing, while /"xashe n!a hunts alone and sees no game.

JUNE 28

The entire group, with the exception of /"xashe n!a and his wives, go to Mokoro to trap guinea fowl and to look for honey. On arrival in the area, n!aishe sets 4 snares for guinea fowl, ≠gau, kã//ka (1) and kã//ka (2) set about 10 each, and n!aishe's son sets 2. The group then goes on to a honey tree that kã//ka (2) had previously located and remove honey from it. On the way, ≠gau and kã//ka (1) see a porcupine burrow; ≠gau goes down it, widening it as he goes, and is finally able to spear the porcupine. The men see no other game. On the way back to camp, the group checks the bird snares. Kã//ka (1) and kã//ka (2) have each trapped one bird. /"xashe n!a hunts alone and sees nothing.

JUNE 29

Again the entire group with the exception of /"xashe n!a and his wives return to Mokoro. They first check the snares set the day before and find only one guinea fowl. It has been eaten by some small carnivore. The group then divides, and kã//ka (2) and ≠gau set off in one direction to hunt. They see some kudu, which run from them, and also gemsbok tracks from the previous day. The rest of the group remain in Mokoro searching for honey and find hives in two different trees. They also go to a porcupine burrow that kã//ka (1) had seen some time before. Kã//ka (1) digs down on the porcupine from above and kills it with a spear. Each group returns to shum !kau separately.

JUNE 30

In the morning, Yellen drives ≠toma and family more than half the way to shum !kau, and the family continues to Camp 16 on foot, arriving about midafternoon.

Although ≠toma sees fresh gemsbok tracks on his walk he does not follow them; he spends the remainder of the day in camp. In the morning, n!aishe and kã//ka (2) hunt to the west and see fresh gemsbok tracks. They soon realize, however, that the animals are heading to an area of hard ground where tracking is difficult and they give up the chase. On the way back to camp, they see some warthogs, but the animals spot them and run. Kã//ka (1), his wife, ≠gau, and n!aishe's son go to Mokoro to check the bird traps; they are empty. The group has forgotten to take an ax with them and although they find two hives, they cannot take the honey from them. They return to camp. /"xashe n!a hunts alone and sees nothing. The group decides to move to Mokoro the following day.

Notes on Site Plan

FLORAL REMAINS

Mongongo nut:	whole nuts and cracked shells
Wild sisal:	fibers from the outer covering
Spiny melon:	shell fragment only

FAUNAL REMAINS

	Species	Anatomical part	State
5.	Gf	Ti	Fr
6.	Gf	P	C
7.	Gf	H	Fr
8.	Gf	Ul	Fr
9.	Gf	Ul	Fr
10.	Pc	M	Fr
11.	Pc	M	Fr
12.	Pc	V	C
13.	Pc	Sc	Fr
14.	Gf	Cr	Fr
15.	Pc	Ri	C
16.	Pc	Ri	C
17.	Pc	H	Fr
18.	Gf	Ul	Fr
19.	Gf	St	Fr
21.	Gf	St	Fr
22.	Gf	Ti	Fr
23.	Gf	Sc	C
24.	Gf	Ul	Fr
25.	Li	V	C
26.	Gf	St	Fr
27.	Gf	Ri	C
28.	Gf	Ri	C

Species	Anatomical part	State
29. Gf	Ri	C
30. Gf	Ri	C
31. Li	Cr	Fr
32. Gf	St	C
33. Pc	O	Fr
34. Pc	Ti	Fr
35. Pc	Ti	Fr
36. Gf	H	C
37. Pc	P	Fr
41. Pc	P	Fr
42. Pc	P	Fr
43. Pc	P	Fr
44. Pc	Sc	C
45. Pc	Fe	Fr
46a. Pc	Ul	Fr
46b. Pc	Ra	Fr
47. Gf	Ul & Ra	Fr
48. Pc	Cr	Fr
49. Gf	Ti	Fr
50. Pc	Sc	C
51. Pc	V	C
52. Pc	Sc	C
53. Pc	Ri	Fr
54. Pc	Ri	C
55. Gf	H	C
56. Li	V	C
57. Pc	H	Fr
58. Uf	Uf	Fr
59. Hb	H, Ul, & Ra	H & Ul:C; Ra:Fr
60. Pc	O	C
61. Pc	Fe	Fr
62. Pc	Ul	Fr
63. Pc	P	Fr
64. Pc	Ri	C
67. Gf	St	Fr
68. Pc	P	Fr
69. Pc	Cr	Fr
70.* Gi	Ri	Fr
71. Pc	Fe	Fr
72. Gi	Ri	Fr
74. Pc	Ri	Fr
75. Gi	Ri	Fr
76. Gi	Ri	Fr
77. Gi	Ri	Fr
78. Gi	Ri	Fr
79. Gi	Ri	Fr
80. Pc	Cr	Fr

* All giraffe bones are rejected arrow linkshaft blanks.

Species	Anatomical part	State
81. Gi	Ri	Fr
82. Gi	Ri	Fr
83. Gi	Ri	Fr
84. Pc	M	Fr
85. Pc	H	Fr
86. Pc	Cr	Fr
87. Pc	Cr	Fr
88. Pc	Cr	Fr
89. Pc	M	Fr
90. Pc	Cr	Fr
91. Gf	St	Fr
92. Gf	St	Fr
93. Pc	H	Fr
94. Pc	Uf	Fr
95. Pc	Ul	Fr
96. Pc	V	Fr
97. Gf	St	Fr
98. Gf	H	Fr
99. Li	V	Fr
100. Pc	P	Fr
101. Pc	H	Fr
102. Pc	P	Fr
103. Gf	Ul	Fr
104. Pc	Ri	C
105. Gf	Ra	C
106. Gf	Ul	Fr
107. Gf	Ul	Fr
108. Pc	Cr	Fr

OTHER REMAINS

Hardpan mongongo cracking stones (6 total).
4. Bushman pipe: a hollow, short segment of bone, with a wad of grass stuffed into one end.
20. A small nodule of flint with several irregularly placed removal scars.
38. Fragment of digging stick.
66. One half of an ostrich egg shell.

FEATURES

B. Hearth associated with Hut 1. Marked by a raised area of ash and charcoal.
C. Scatter of wild sisal fiber.
D. Very small scatter of a few cracked mongongo shells.
F. Hearth associated with Hut 6. Marked by a raised area of ash and charcoal.
G. Low mound of ash and charcoal.

H.   Small pile of unopened mongongo nuts.
I.   Small fire marked only by a scatter of charcoal.
J.   Scatter of cracked mongongo shells.
L.   Fire associated with Hut 2. Marked by a slightly raised area of ash and charcoal.
M.   Slightly raised area of ash, charcoal, and sand.
N.   Small fire marked by surface scatter of charcoal.
O.   Scatter of cracked mongongo shells.
P.   Scatter of guinea fowl feathers.
Q.   Hearth associated with Hut 4. Marked by raised mound of ash and charcoal.
R.   Pile of wild sisal fibers.
S.   Scatter of cracked mongongo shells.
U.   Hearth associated with Hut 3. Marked by a slightly raised mound of ash and charcoal.
V.   Slightly raised area of ash, sand, and charcoal.
W.   Scatter of cracked mongongo shells.
X.   Hearth associated with Hut 5. Marked by a pronounced heap of sand, ash, and charcoal.
AA.   Fan-shaped, slightly raised area of ash, sand, and charcoal.
BB.   Scatter of cracked mongongo shells.
CC.   Scatter of wild sisal fibers.
DD.   Scatter of wild sisal fibers.
EE.   Small pile of unopened mongongo nuts.

Hut 1.   ≠toma's hut. A very crude shelter, typical of those built after the rains. Consists of three bare, upright branches stuck vertically into the ground; two of these mark the entrance, and the third is on one side of the circle just behind the entrance. One side of the hut consists of several small leafy branches placed irregularly and roughly on the ground. The entire inside of the hut is marked by a shallow depression in the sand, which was created when the surface debris was removed.

Hut 2.   /"xashe n!a's hut. Composed of a series of leafy branches placed vertically in the ground to form an unroofed semicircle. A small amount of grass thatch is piled around the lower part of the hut's exterior.

Hut 3.   N!aishe's hut. Similar to Hut 2 but lacks thatch.

Hut 4.   ≠gau's hut. This "hut" utilizes only living shrubs and is fitted among them. It is marked only by its slightly concave floor.

Hut 5.   Kã//ka (2)'s hut. Similar in form to Hut 3.

Hut 6.   Kã//ka (1)'s hut. Similar in form to Hut 2. It has a thin matting of grass.

APPENDIX C

GROUPED DATA FROM SIXTEEN
!KUNG CAMPS[1]

TABLE C-1. Key to Grouped Data

ALS	Absolute limit of scatter
LMS	Limit of most scatter
LNAT	Limit of nuclear area, total
LNAS	Limit of nuclear area, scatter
LNA_1 (*etc.*)	Limited nuclear area
LS_1 (*etc.*)	Limited scatter
m^2	Area in square meters
H'	Richness coefficient
$H'(C)$	Richness coefficient with correction
NA	Nuclear area
SA	Special activity area

Greatest diameter indicates the greatest diameter of scatter area.

Distances from hut to hut are measured in meters from the center of each hut entrance. Top line of numbers indicates hut number from camp plans.

Distances from hearth to hearth are measured in meters from the center of each hearth. Top line of numbers indicates the hut association of each hearth. Note: for some huts, hearths are lacking.

See Chapter 6 for full explanation.

[1] The data in Appendix C are keyed to the scatter distributions contained in the packet.

CAMP 1   ≠ TUM   ≠ TOA 1

Length total occupation: 9 days
Reoccupations: 1
Total number occupants: 10
    Adult: 4
    Young: 6
Total number social units: 2
    Nuclear family: 2
    Other: 0

	Greatest diameter	m^2	H'	$H'(C)$	Occupant
ALS	17.0	149.46	2.32	2.44	
LMS	15.7	105.21	2.30	2.42	
LNAT	10.0	55.88	2.27	2.49	
LNAS	10.0	38.50	2.26	2.55	
LNA₁	6.5	23.62			bo
2	7.2	26.36			/n!au

	Greatest diameter	m^2	H'	$H'(C)$	Type	Occupant or purpose
LS₁	6.5	20.64	2.05	2.42	NA	bo
2	5.8	17.50	2.40	2.46	NA	/n!au
3	1.4	1.07	0.69	0.69	SA	shade
4	1.8	1.91	0.89	1.03	SA	shade
5	2.8	3.87	0.69	0.69	SA	shade
6	1.9	1.31	1.34	1.18	SA	shade
7	1.1	0.62	0.00	0.00	SA	shade

Distance hut to hut: 3.3 m
Distance hearth to hearth: 3.2 m

CAMP 2   ≠ TUM ≠ TOA 2

Length total occupation: 9 days
Reoccupations: 0
Total number occupants: 11
  Adult: 4
  Young: 7
Total number social units: 2
  Nuclear family: 2
  Other: 0

	Greatest diameter	m^2	H'	$H'(C)$	Occupant
ALS	13.7	127.22	1.14	1.53	
LMS	13.5	88.84	1.16	1.46	
LNAT	10.0	39.14	0.95	1.11	
LNAS	10.0	29.72	0.95	1.11	
LNA$_1$	4.3	12.11			n!aishe
2	6.5	25.52			≠toma

Greatest diameter	m^2	H'	$H'(C)$	Type	Occupant or purpose
4.0	9.10	0.71	1.09	NA	n!aishe
6.5	18.87	1.00	1.05	NA	≠toma
1.00	0.36	0.00	0.00	SA	skin pegging
0.40	0.09	0.00	0.00	SA	skin pegging
1.80	1.23	0.10	0.42	SA	shade
2.90	3.26	0.68	1.04	SA	shade
2.20	2.74	0.87	0.69	SA	shade

Distance hut to hut: 4.9 m
Distance hearth to hearth: 4.2 m

CAMP 3 $\neq$ TUM $\neq$ TOA 3

Length total occupation: 11 days
Reoccupations: 1
Total number occupants: 22
  Adult: 9
  Young: 13
Total number social units: 5
  Nuclear family: 4
  Other: 1

	Greatest diameter	m^2	H'	$H'(C)$	Occupant
ALS	30.20	345.00	1.76	1.88	
LMS	24.50	239.00	1.70	1.90	
LNAT	24.50	239.00	1.74	1.88	
LNAS	22.30	216.00	1.87	1.84	
LNA$_1$	8.20	35.87			n!aishe
2	5.90	21.97			$\neq$ toma
3	6.10	25.48			/n!au
4	5.60	15.79			bo
5	3.20	5.89			$\neq$ gau

	Greatest diameter	m^2	H'	$H'(C)$	Type	Occupant or purpose
LS$_1$	7.20	30.26	1.71	1.94	NA	n!aishe
2	5.30	14.32	1.67	1.71	NA	$\neq$ toma
3	6.00	19.98	1.32	1.61	NA	/n!au
4	5.30	10.48	1.50	1.29	NA	bo
5	2.30	1.77	1.33	1.33	NA	$\neq$ gau
6	1.50	1.31	0.63	0.63	SA	skin preparation

Distance hut to hut: 3 $\longrightarrow$ 4 $\longrightarrow$ 2 $\longrightarrow$ 5 $\longrightarrow$ 1 $\longrightarrow$ 3
                        11.0 m   12.0 m   4.5 m   3.0 m   15.3 m

Distance hearth to hearth: 3 $\longrightarrow$ 4 $\longrightarrow$ 2 $\longrightarrow$ 1 $\longrightarrow$ 3
                        6.3 m   11.2 m   3.2 m   15.3 m

(Hut 5 has no hearth)

CAMP 4   N/ON/ONI ≠TOA 1

Length total occupation: 20 days
Reoccupations: 5
Total number occupants: 14
  Adult: 7
  Young: 7
Total number social units: 4
  Nuclear family: 3
  Other: 1

	Greatest diameter	m^2	H'	$H'(C)$	Occupant
ALS	23.90	310.00	2.04	1.70	
LMS	17.90	182.00	2.11	1.72	
LNAT	10.60	79.00	2.10	1.75	
LNAS	10.60	79.00	2.10	1.75	
LNA$_1$	5.40	15.96			/"xashe n!a + 1 wife
2	2.20	3.24			≠gau
3	7.00	19.72			≠toma
4	6.10	19.88			n!aishe

	Greatest diameter	m^2	H'	$H'(C)$	Type	Occupant or purpose
LS$_1$	5.40	15.18	2.37	1.77	NA	/"xashe n!a + 1 wife
2	1.90	1.29	1.39	1.43	NA	≠gau
3	5.50	16.41	1.94	1.70	NA	≠toma
4	5.20	18.52	2.05	2.06	NA	n!aishe
5	1.40	1.33	1.10	0.85	SA	shade
6	3.90	11.00	1.76	1.80	SA	shade
7	1.00	0.73	0.00	0.00	SA	shade
8	2.20	2.94	0.80	1.00	SA	shade
9	6.40	13.3	1.56	1.15	SA	shade
10	2.40	3.45	0.91	0.91	SA	skinning
11	3.30	3.14	0.88	1.13	SA	skinning

Distance hut to hut: 1 ⟶ 2 ⟶ 3 ⟶ 4 ⟶ 1
                          2.0 m   2.0 m   5.3 m   6.5 m

Distance hearth to hearth: 1 ⟶ 3 ⟶ 4 ⟶ 1
                             3.6 m   5.4 m   5.8 m

(Hut 2 has no hearth)

CAMP 5 /TANAGABA

Length total occupation: 2 days
Reoccupations: 0
Total number occupants: 11
  Adult: 4
  Young: 7
Total number social units: 2
  Nuclear family: 2
  Other: 0

	Greatest diameter	m^2	H'	$H'(C)$	Occupant
ALS	15.30	59.00	0.85	0.91	
LMS	7.00	38.00	0.81	1.05	
LNAT	7.00	26.00	0.72	1.01	
LNAS	6.60	14.00	0.55	0.92	
LNA₁	4.30	11.08			n!aishe
2	4.20	8.55			≠toma

	Greatest diameter	m^2	H'	$H'(C)$	Type	Occupant or purpose
LS₁	3.60	7.38	0.43	0.83	NA	n!aishe
2	3.10	5.62	0.68	0.98	NA	≠toma
3	0.60	0.21	0.00	0.00	SA	fire for quiver making

Distance hut to hut: 3.60 m
Distance hearth to hearth: 3.00 m

CAMP 6   HWANASI

Length total occupation: 3 days
Reoccupations: 0
Total number occupants: 12
  Adult: 5
  Young: 7
Total number of social units: 3
  Nuclear family: 2
  Other: 1

	Greatest diameter	m^2	H'	$H'(C)$	Occupant
ALS	20.80	165.00	0.95	1.47	
LMS	14.20	96.00	0.95	1.47	
LNAT	8.50	34.00	0.86	1.12	
LNAS	8.50	32.00	0.86	1.12	
LNA$_1$	5.90	11.98			≠toma
2	2.20	2.36			≠gau
3	4.00	9.58			n!aishe

	Greatest diameter	m^2	H'	$H'(C)$	Type	Occupant or purpose
LS$_1$	5.90	11.98	0.86	1.09	NA	≠toma
2	0.00	0.00	0.00	0.00	NA	≠gau
3	3.30	7.31	0.65	0.92	NA	n!aishe
4	1.30	0.94	0.69	0.69	SA	shade
5	2.20	2.80	0.69	0.69	SA	skin drying
6	2.40	2.86	0.46	0.72	SA	fire pit for head roasting
7	1.10	0.79	0.32	0.69	SA	quiver making

Distance hut to hut: 1 ⟶ 2 ⟶ 3 ⟶ 1
                                           3.7 m   2.6 m   4.9 m

Distance hearth to hearth: 1 ⟶ 3
                                              3.4 m

(Hut 2 has no hearth)

CAMP 7   N!ABESHA

Length total occupation: 10 days
Reoccupations: 1
Total number occupants: 17
  Adult: 10
  Young: 7
Total number social units: 5
  Nuclear family: 4
  Other: 1

	Greatest diameter	m^2	H'	$H'(C)$	Occupant
ALS	16.1	151.00	1.06	1.40	
LMS	12.5	88.50	1.01	1.35	
LNAT	12.5	88.50	1.01	1.35	
LNAS	11.0	71.00	1.01	1.35	
LNA$_1$	5.2	15.73			n!aishe
2	4.9	10.00			≠gau
3	5.6	16.89			≠toma
4	2.9	5.37			kã//ka (1)
5	3.2	5.08			/''xashe n!a + 2 wives

	Greatest diameter	m^2	H'	$H'(C)$		Occupant Type or purpose
LS$_1$	5.5	12.95	1.04	1.37	NA	n!aishe
2	3.6	6.26	0.83	1.20	NA	≠gau
3	4.3	11.44	0.86	1.07	NA	≠toma
4	2.7	3.27	1.51	1.49	NA	kã//ka (1)
5	2.3	3.46	1.54	1.60	NA	/''xashe n!a + 2 wives
6	1.6	1.03	0.00	0.00	SA	old fire—purpose?
7	1.9	1.16	0.00	0.00	SA	old fire—purpose?

Distance hut to hut: 1 ⟶ 2 ⟶ 3 ⟶ 4 ⟶ 5 ⟶ 1
                              2.5 m 4.4 m 5.9 m 10.4 m 4.5 m

Distance hearth to hearth: 1 ⟶ 2 ⟶ 3 ⟶ 4 ⟶ 5 ⟶ 1
                              2.5 m 3.9 m 5.3 m 9.3 m 3.5 m

CAMP 8 !GWI DUM

Length total occupation: About 30 days
Reoccupations: 0
Total number occupants: ?
  Adult: ?
  Young: ?
Total Number Social Units: 6
  Nuclear family: 5
  Other: 1

	Greatest diameter	m^2	H'	$H'(C)$	Occupant
ALS	34.8	581.00	2.38	2.07	
LMS	29.4	378.00	2.43	2.05	
LNAT	25.2	307.00	2.20	1.82	
LNAS	23.3	278.00	2.20	1.82	
LNA$_1$	5.7	20.26			?
2	7.3	29.02			?
3	6.6	22.47			?
4	3.9	7.67			?
5	4.9	12.75			?
6	7.0	16.19			?

	Greatest diameter	m^2	H'	$H'(C)$	Type	Occupant or purpose
LS$_1$	5.7	15.56	1.65	1.88	NA	?
2	7.3	24.40	1.92	1.29	NA	?
3	6.6	21.82	1.88	1.59	NA	?
4	3.8	5.13	1.36	1.50	NA	?
5	4.5	11.42	2.08	1.88	NA	?
6	3.2	6.10	0.94	0.42	NA	?
7	2.6	3.21	0.95	0.32	SA	shade
8	2.2	1.98	0.00	0.00	SA	shade
9	0.7	0.47	0.00	0.00	SA	shade
10	3.5	2.81	1.25	1.04	SA	shade
11	1.1	0.54	0.25	0.67	SA	shade
12	0.4	0.22	0.00	0.00	SA	shade
13	0.4	0.29	0.00	0.00	SA	shade
14	2.6	3.39	1.10	1.10	SA	skin pegging area
15	1.2	1.13	0.00	0.00	SA	roasting pit
16	0.9	0.44	0.00	0.00	SA	shade
17	0.9	0.59	0.00	0.00	SA	ash pile
18	2.6	2.64	0.83	1.06	SA	shade
19	0.6	0.29	0.00	0.00	SA	ash pile

Distance hut to hut: 1 $\longrightarrow$ 2 $\longrightarrow$ 4 $\longrightarrow$ 5 $\longrightarrow$ 6 $\longrightarrow$ 3 $\longrightarrow$ 1
                        10.6 m   10.2 m   5.3 m   5.6 m   8.0 m   11.3 m

Distance hearth to hearth: 1 $\longrightarrow$ 2 $\longrightarrow$ 4 $\longrightarrow$ 5 $\longrightarrow$ 6 $\longrightarrow$ 3 $\longrightarrow$ 1
                        10.4 m   8.5 m   5.9 m   4.7 m   9.3 m   11.8 m

CAMP 9   SHUM !KAU 1

Length total occupation: 2
Reoccupations: 0
Total number occupants: 12
   Adult: 5
   Young: 7
Total number social units: 3
   Nuclear family: 2
   Other: 1

	Greatest diameter	m^2	H'	$H'(C)$	Occupant
ALS	13.2	83.50	1.13	1.40	
LMS	13.2	74.00	1.13	1.39	
LNAT	9.7	47.00	1.01	1.27	
LNAS	9.7	40.50	1.01	1.27	
LNA₁	4.2	10.44			n!aishe
2	4.8	14.16			≠toma
3	4.3	6.26			≠gau

	Greatest diameter	m^2	H'	$H'(C)$		Occupant or purpose
LS₁	3.4	7.08	1.19	1.31	NA	n!aishe
2	4.8	9.50	0.94	1.22	NA	≠toma
3	4.3	6.26	0.56	0.56	NA	≠gau
4	4.2	8.89	1.00	1.00	SA	large children's play area

Distance hut to hut: 1 ⟶ 2 ⟶ 3 ⟶ 1
                  4.8 m   4.3 m   3.8 m

Distance hearth to hearth: 1 ⟶ 2
                    4.9 m

(Hut 3 has no hearth)

CAMP 10   //GAKWE ≠DWA 1

Length total occupation: 12 days
Reoccupations: 0
Total number occupants: 24
  Adult: 13
  Young: 11
Total number social units: 7
  Nuclear family: 5
  Other: 2

	Greatest diameter	m^2	H'	$H'(C)$	Occupant
ALS	24.60	348.50	0.99	1.51	
LMS	24.60	330.50	0.99	1.51	
LNAT	24.60	325.50	1.01	1.49	
LNAS	24.60	325.50	1.01	1.49	
LNA₁	5.00	16.47			/''xashe n!a + 2 wives
2	5.90	16.85			≠gau
3	6.00	16.68			≠toma
4	6.00	19.35			n!aishe
5	5.60	13.33			kumsa n!a
6	6.20	21.68			dam
7	5.40	22.14			kã//ka n!a

	Greatest diameter	m^2	H'	$H'(C)$	Type	Occupant or purpose
LS₁	4.50	12.80	1.35	1.59	NA	/''xashe n!a + 2 wives
2	5.90	16.85	0.50	1.04	NA	≠gau
3	6.00	15.09	0.85	1.35	NA	≠toma
4	5.60	13.78	0.46	1.23	NA	n!aishe
5	5.60	12.66	0.50	1.04	NA	kumsa n!a
6	6.10	16.86	0.68	1.03	NA	dam
7	5.50	15.32	1.01	1.37	NA	kã//ka n!a
8	1.10	0.52	0.00	0.00	SA	shade
9	1.30	0.75	0.00	0.00	SA	shade
10	2.00	1.43	0.00	0.00	SA	meat hanging rack
11	6.70	18.16	0.88	1.40	SA	shade (sunshade + fire)

Distance hut to hut: 1 ⟶ 2 ⟶ 3 ⟶ 4 ⟶ 5 ⟶ 6 ⟶ 7 ⟶ 1
                         4.2 m 5.9 m 8.7 m 12.2 m 4.0 m 6.5 m 14.3 m

Distance hearth to hearth: 1 ⟶ 2 ⟶ 3 ⟶ 4 ⟶ 5 ⟶ 6 ⟶ 7 ⟶ 1
                         5.0 m 5.0 m 8.5 m 9.8 m 4.8 m 6.1 m 14.0

CAMP 11 ≠ TUM ≠ TOA 4

Length total occupation: 3 days
Reoccupations: 0
Total number occupants: 24
   Adult: 13
   Young: 11
Total number social units: 7
   Nuclear family: 5
   Other: 2

	Greatest diameter	m^2	H'	$H'(C)$	Occupant
ALS	19.60	187.50	1.66	1.43	
LMS	19.00	158.00	1.65	1.41	
LNAT	19.00	158.00	1.65	1.41	
LNAS	19.00	158.00	1.65	1.41	
LNA$_1$	5.40	13.08			kã//ka n!a
2	3.00	7.29			dam
3	3.10	4.51			kumsa n!a
4	3.30	7.29			≠toma
5	4.30	9.69			/"xashe n!a + 2 wives
6	3.10	5.59			≠gau
7	4.20	9.28			n!aishe

	Greatest diameter	m^2	H'	$H'(C)$	Type	Occupant or purpose
LS$_1$	3.80	9.55	1.57	1.04	NA	kã//ka n!a
2	2.90	3.36	1.62	1.66	NA	dam
3	3.10	4.51	1.12	1.25	NA	kumsa n!a
4	3.30	5.89	0.84	1.28	NA	≠toma
5	4.30	9.69	1.45	1.11	NA	/"xashe n!a + 2 wives
6	2.30	2.89	0.96	0.80	NA	≠gau
7	4.20	3.63	1.39	1.10	NA	n!aishe
8		0.77	0.00	0.00	SA	skin preparation

Distance hut to hut: 1 ⟶ 2 ⟶ 3 ⟶ 4 ⟶ 5 ⟶ 6 ⟶ 1 / 6 ⟶ 7
                 4.0 m 4.3 m 6.9 m 6.6 m 5.1 m 8.7 m   3.5 m

Distance hearth to hearth: 1 ⟶ 2 ⟶ 3 ⟶ 4 ⟶ 5 ⟶ 6 ⟶ 1 / 6 ⟶ 7
                 5.7 m 5.0 m 7.0 m 7.2 m 3.5 m 9.3 m   2.6 m

CAMP 12   ≠ TUM   ≠ TOA 5

Length total occupation: 3 days
Reoccupations: 0
Total number occupants: 17
   Adult: 10
   Young: 7
Total number social units: 5
   Nuclear family: 4
   Other: 1

	Greatest diameter	m^2	H'	$H'(C)$	Occupant
ALS	16.80	174.50	1.59	1.84	
LMS	16.80	146.50	1.61	1.81	
LNAT	16.80	146.50	1.61	1.81	
LNAS	16.80	146.50	1.61	1.81	
LNA$_1$	4.80	12.08			≠toma
2	4.90	10.43			kã//ka (1)
3	5.80	16.43			n!aishe
4	3.00	5.68			≠gau
5	5.00	14.29			/"xashe n!a + 2 wives

	Greatest diameter	m^2	H'	$H'(C)$	Type	Occupant or purpose
LS$_1$	4.80	12.08	1.40	1.70	NA	≠toma
2	4.90	10.43	0.95	1.49	NA	kã//ka (1)
3	5.80	16.43	1.50	1.30	NA	n!aishe
4	2.70	4.18	0.87	0.99	NA	≠gau
5	5.00	14.29	1.30	1.67	NA	/"xashe n!a + 2 wives

Distance hut to hut: 1 ⟶ 2 ⟶ 5 ⟶ 4 ⟶ 3 ⟶ 1
                         8.8 m   7.1 m   4.3 m   3.0 m   6.0 m

Distance hearth to hearth: 1 ⟶ 2 ⟶ 5 ⟶ 4 ⟶ 3 ⟶ 1
                         8.0 m   6.0 m   5.1 m   3.4 m   5.3 m

CAMP 13 N/ON/ONI ≠TOA 2

Length total occupation: 5 days
Reoccupations: 0
Total number occupants: 17
    Adult: 10
    Young: 7
Total number social units: 5
    Nuclear family: 4
    Other: 1

	Greatest diameter	m^2	H'	$H'(C)$	Occupant
ALS	18.6	157.50	1.90	1.79	
LMS	16.3	144.50	1.84	1.76	
LNAT	13.7	115.50	1.69	1.54	
LNAS	13.7	111.50	1.69	1.54	
LNA₁	4.30	8.88			kã//ka (1)
2	4.60	11.03			n!aishe
3	3.20	4.23			≠gau
4	4.40	11.51			≠toma
5	5.10	9.23			/"xashe n!a + 2 wives

	Greatest diameter	m^2	H'	$H'(C)$	Type	Occupant or purpose
LS₁	3.10	4.77	0.95	0.95	NA	kã//ka (1)
2	4.60	11.03	1.10	1.39	NA	n!aishe
3	1.80	2.09	0.00	0.00	NA	≠gau
4	3.80	8.88	1.25	1.37	NA	≠toma
5	3.80	6.51	1.66	1.42	NA	/"xashe n!a + 2 wives
6	1.30	0.81	0.61	0.61	SA	shade
7	1.80	2.21	0.44	0.44	SA	skin pegging

Distance hut to hut: 1 ⟶ 2 ⟶ 3 ⟶ 4 ⟶ 5 ⟶ 1
                               4.4 m   3.5 m   3.5 m   7.2 m   8.1 m

Distance hearth to hearth: 1 ⟶ 2 ⟶ 3 ⟶ 4 ⟶ 5 ⟶ 1
                               5.0 m   3.7 m   3.5 m   6.8 m   8.0 m

CAMP 14   //GAKWE ≠DWA 2

Length total occupation: 7 days
Reoccupations: 0
Total number occupants: 23
  Adult: 15
  Young: 8
Total number social units: 8
  Nuclear family: 6
  Other: 2

	Greatest diameter	m^2	H'	$H'(C)$	Occupant
ALS	23.80	329.00	1.19	1.70	
LMS	22.6	261.00	1.19	1.70	
LNAT	22.0	199.50	1.27	1.73	
LNAS	22.0	199.50	1.27	1.73	
LNA₁	6.10	23.31			n!aishe
2	6.00	20.9			≠toma
3	5.50	17.98			kã//ka (1)
4	5.00	12.59			kã//ka (2)
5	5.80	14.55			debe
6	7.30	22.24			/"xashe n!a + 2 wives
7	5.00	8.90			⩜gau

	Greatest diameter	m^2	H'	$H'(C)$	Type	Occupant or purpose
LS₁	6.10	23.31	0.64	1.15	NA	n!aishe
2	5.0	14.50	1.28	1.66	NA	≠toma
3	5.50	17.98	1.06	1.55	NA	kã//ka (1)
4	5.00	12.59	1.25	1.42	NA	kã//ka (2)
5	5.80	14.55	1.33	1.61	NA	debe
6	7.30	22.24	1.45	1.79	NA	/"xashe n!a + 2 wives
7	5.00	8.90	0.20	0.61	NA	≠gau
8	3.90	9.03	0.75	1.18	SA	shade
9	1.60	1.58	0.58	0.58	SA	sleeping fire for /tasa
10	1.00	0.81	0.00	0.00	SA	fire pit for quivers
11	1.70	1.52	1.25	1.04	SA	shade

Distance hut to hut: 1 ⟶ 2 ⟶ 4 ⟶ 5 ⟶ 6 ⟶ 7 ⟶ 1/2 ⟶ 3
                  9.0 m   5.4 m   4.2 m   4.8 m   3.9 m   3.2 m   5.5 m

Distance hearth to hearth: 1 ⟶ 2 ⟶ 4 ⟶ 5 ⟶ 6 ⟶ 7/ ⟶ 1/2 ⟶ 3
                  8.4 m   5.0 m   4.0 m   4.8 m   2.8 m   3.0 m   5.1 m

CAMP 15   SHUM !KAU 2

Length total occupation: 1 day
Reoccupations: 0
Total number occupants: 17
  Adult: 10
  Young: 7
Total number social units: 5
  Nuclear family: 4
  Other: 1

	Greatest diameter	m^2	H'	$H'(C)$	Occupant
ALS	17.9	151.50	1.55	1.47	
LMS	16.0	121.00	1.52	1.60	
LNAT	16.0	121.00	1.52	1.60	
LNAS	16.0	121.00	1.52	1.60	
LNA$_1$	3.60	8.99			kã//ka (1)
2	4.90	8.19			n!aishe
3	4.20	9.61			≠gau
4	5.00	14.29			≠toma
5	3.50	7.30			/xashe n!a + 2 wives

	Greatest diameter	m^2	H'	$H'(C)$	Type	Occupant or purpose
LS$_1$	3.20	4.29	0.58	1.28	NA	kã//ka (1)
2	3.30	3.88	1.34	1.16	NA	n!aishe
3	3.80	8.07	0.63	0.63	NA	≠gau
4	3.50	7.54	0.67	0.67	NA	≠toma
5	2.70	3.54	1.08	1.36	NA	/"xashe n!a + 2 wives
6	1.00	0.65	0.00	0.00	SA	fire for porcupine skin roasting
7	1.20	0.80	0.00	0.00	SA	fire for porcupine skin roasting

Distance hut to hut: not measured because no true huts constructed

Distance hearth to hearth: 1 ⟶ 2 ⟶ 3 ⟶ 4 ⟶ g ⟶ 1
  6.8 m   4.0 m   7.2 m   7.4 m   5.5 m

fire of /"xashe n!a + wives

CAMP 16   SHUM !KAU 3

Length total occupation: 6 days
Reoccupations: 0
Total number occupants: 19
  Adult: 12
  Young: 7
Total number social units: 6
  Nuclear family: 5
  Other: 1

	Greatest diameter	m^2	H'	$H'(C)$	Occupant
ALS	21.90	238.00	1.81	2.05	
LMS	18.80	177.50	1.80	2.12	
LNAT	18.80	159.00	1.85	2.15	
LNAS	18.80	159.00	1.85	2.15	
LNA$_1$	4.80	8.84			≠toma
2	5.90	14.94			/''xashe n!a + 2 wives
3	4.80	14.71			n!aishe
4	4.70	9.95			≠gau
5	4.10	9.14			kã//ka (2)
6	5.70	14.38			kã//ka (1)

	Greatest diameter	m^2	H'	$H'(C)$	Type	Occupant or Purpose
LS$_1$	4.80	8.84	1.33	1.72	NA	≠toma
2	5.90	14.94	1.37	1.84	NA	/''xashe n!a + 2 wives
3	4.80	8.69	1.55	2.01	NA	n!aishe
4	4.70	9.95	1.13	1.58	NA	≠gau
5	3.30	6.03	1.68	1.66	NA	kã//ka (2)
6	5.70	14.38	1.32	1.74	NA	kã//ka (1)

Distance hut to hut: 1 ⟶ 2 ⟶ 3 ⟶ 5 ⟶ 6 / 2 ⟶ 4 ⟶ 5
                           5.5 m   7.1 m   7.4 m   9.0 m   3.5 m   4.6 m

Distance hearth to hearth: 1 ⟶ 2 ⟶ 3 ⟶ 5 ⟶ 6 / 2 ⟶ 4 ⟶ 5
                           5.7 m   7.7 m   7.5 m   7.8 m   3.1 m   4.0 m

REFERENCES

Allen, W.L., and J.B. Richardson III
  1971   The reconstruction of kinship from archaeological data: The concepts, the methods, and the feasibility. *American Antiquity* **36**(1):41–53.
Ascher, R.
  1961   Analogy in archaeological interpretation. *Southwestern Journal of Anthropology* **17**:317–325.
Binford, L.R.
  1966   A preliminary analysis of functional variability in the Mousterian of Levallois facies. *American Anthropologist* **68**(2, Part 2):238–295.
  1967   Smudge pits and hide smoking: The use of analogy in archaeological reasoning. *American Antiquity* **32**(1):1–12.
  1968   Post-pleistocene adaptations. In *New perspectives in archaeology,* edited by S.R. Binford and L.R. Binford. Pp. 313–341. Chicago: Aldine.
  n.d. (ca. 1973)   *Forty-seven trips: A case study in the character of some formation processes of the archaeological record.* (Mimeograph)
Binford, S.R., and L.R. Binford
  1968   *New perspectives in archeology.* Chicago: Aldine.
Brain, C.K.
  1967   Bone weathering and the problem of bone pseudo-tools. *South African Journal of Science* **63**(3):97–99.
  1969   The contribution of Namib Desert Hottentots to an understanding of Australopithecine bone accumulations. *Scientific Papers of the Namib Desert Research Station* **39**:13–22.
Bronte-Stewart, B., Budtz-Olsen, J. Hickley, and J. Brock
  1960   The health and nutritional status of the !Kung Bushmen of South West Africa. *South African Journal of Clinical and Laboratory Medicine* **6**:187–216.

254

Buzas, M.A.
   n.d. (ca. 1972)   *The measurement of species diversity.* (Mimeograph)
Cavalli-Sforza, L., and W. Bodmer
   1971   *The genetics of human populations.* San Francisco: Freeman.
Chang, K.C.
   1967a   Major aspects of the interrelationship of archaeology and ethnology. *Current Anthropology* **8**(3):227–243.
   1967b   *Rethinking archaeology.* New York: Random House.
Christy, H., and E. Lartet
   1865   *Reliquae aquitanica,* edited by T.R. Jones. London: Williams and Norgate (1875).
Clark, J.D.
   1960   Human ecology during Pleistocene and later times in Africa south of the Sahara. *Current Anthropology* **1**(4):307–324.
   1970   *The prehistory of Africa.* New York: Praeger.
Cook, S.F., and R.F. Heizer
   1968   Relationships among houses, settlement areas, and population in aboriginal California. In *Settlement archaeology,* edited by K.C. Chang. Palo Alto: National Press.
Cooke, H.B.S.
   1964   The Pleistocene environment of Southern Africa. In *Ecological studies in Southern Africa,* edited by D.H.S. Davis. Monographiae Biologicae **14**:1–23.
Daly, P.
   1969   Approaches to faunal analysis in archaeology. *American Antiquity* **34**(2):146–153.
Dart, R.A.
   1957a   The Makapansgat Australopithecine Osteodontokeratic culture. *Proceedings of the Third Pan-African Congress of Prehistory,* 161–171.
   1957b   The Osteodontokeratic culture of Australopithecus prometheus. *Transvaal Museum Memoir* No. 10.
Deetz, J.
   1965   The dynamics of stylistic change in Arikara ceramics. *Univeristy of Illinois Series in Anthropology* **4**.
   1968a   The inference of residence and descent rules from archaeological data. In *New perspectives in archaeology,* edited by S.R. Binford and L.R. Binford. Pp. 41–48. Chicago: Aldine.
   1968b   Discussions (Part VI, 31a): Hunters in archaeological perspective. In *Man the hunter,* edited by R.B. Lee, and I. DeVore. Pp. 281–285. Chicago: Aldine.
Evans, J.
   1860   Reigate flints. *Proceedings of the Society of Antiquities.* January 1860.
Evans-Pritchard, E.E.
   1940   *The Nuer.* Oxford: Oxford University Press.
Flannery, K.V.
   1967   Review of *Introduction to American Archaeology* **5**(1): North and Middle America by Gordon R. Willey. *Scientific American* **217**:119–121.
Flannery, K.V., and M.D. Coe
   1968   Social and economic systems in formative mesoamerica. In *New perspectives in archaeology,* edited by S.R. Binford and L.R. Binford. Pp. 267–284. Chicago: Aldine.
Freeman, L.G., Jr.
   1968   A theoretical framework for interpreting archeological materials. In *Man the hunter,* edited by R.B. Lee and I. DeVore. Pp. 262–267. Chicago: Aldine.
   1973   The analysis of some occupation floor distributions from earlier and middle

Paleolithic sites in Spain. Paper presented at the Ninth International Congress of Anthropological and Ethnological Sciences, Chicago. (Mimeograph)

Gould, R.A.
  1969   Subsistence behavior among the Western Desert Aborigines of Australia. *Oceania* **39**(4):253–274.
  1971   The lithic assemblage of the Western Desert Aborigines of Australia. *American Antiquity* **36**(2):149–169.

Grove, A.T.
  1969   Landforms and climatic change in the Kalahari and Ngamiland. *Geographical Journal* **135**:191–212.

Gulliver, P.H.
  1964   The Arusha family. In *The family estate in Africa,* edited by P.H. Gulliver and R.F. Gray. Boston: Boston University Press.

Harpending, H.
  n.d. (ca. 1972)   *Genetic and demographic variation in Zu/wasi populations.* (Mimeograph)

Harpending, H., and T. Jenkins
  1971   *!Kung Population Structure.* (in press)

Higgs, E.S., C. Vita-Finzi, D. Harris, and A. Fagg
  1967   The climate, environment, and industries of Stone Age Greece. Part III. *Proceedings of the Prehistoric Society* **33**(1):1–29.

Hill, J.N.
  1968   Broken K Pueblo: Patterns of form and function. In *New perspectives in archaeology,* edited by S.R. Binford and L.R. Binford. Pp. 103–142. Chicago: Aldine.

Hole, F.
  1968   Evidence of social organization from Western Iran, 8000–4000 B.C. in *New perspectives in archaeology,* edited by S.R. Binford and L.R. Binford. Pp. 245–266. Chicago: Aldine.

Howell, F.C.
  1968   Discussions (Part VI, 31a): Hunters in archaeological perspective. In *Man the hunter,* edited by R.B. Lee and I. DeVore. Pp. 287–288, Chicago: Aldine.

Isaac, G.L.
  1967   Towards the interpretation of occupation debris: Some experiments and observations. *The Kroeber Anthropological Society Papers* **37**.

Jarman, M.E., C. Vita-Finzi, and E.S. Higgs
  1972   Site catchment analysis in archaeology. In *Man, Settlement and Urbanism,* edited by P.J. Ucko, R. Tringham, and G.W. Dimbleby. Pp. 61–66, Cambridge, Mass.: Schenkman.

Keay, R.W.J.
  1959   *Vegetation map of Africa south of the Tropic of Cancer.* London: Oxford University Press.

Kitching, J.W.
  1963   *Bone, tooth and horn tools of Paleolithic man.* Manchester: Manchester University Press.

Kokernot, R., E. Szlamp, J. Levill, and B. McIntosh
  1965   Survey for antibodies against arthropod-borne viruses in the sera of indigenous residents of the Caprivi Strip and Bechuanaland Protectorate. *Transactions of the Royal Society of Tropical Medicine and Hygine* **59**:553–562.

Leach, E.R.
  1961   *Rethinking anthropology.* London: Athlone Press.

Lee, R.B.
  1965 *Subsistence ecology of !Kung Bushmen.* Doctoral dissertation in anthropology. University of California, Berkeley.
  1968 What hunters do for a living, or, how to make out on scarce resources. In *Man the hunter,* edited by R.B. Lee and I. DeVore. Pp. 30–48. Chicago: Aldine.
  1972a !Kung spatial organization: An ecological and historical perspective. *Human Ecology* 1(2):125–147.
  1972b The !Kung bushmen of Botswana. In *Hunters and gatherers today,* edited by M.G. Bicchieri. Pp. 327–368. New York: Holt, Rinehart and Winston.
  1973 Mongongo: The ethnography of a major wild food resource. *Ecology of food and nutrition* 0:1–15.
Lee, R.B., and I. DeVore
  1968 *Man the hunter.* Chicago: Aldine.
  1976 *Kalahari hunter-gatherers.* Cambridge, Mass.: Harvard University Press.
Levi-Strauss, C.
  1968 The concept of primitiveness. In *Man the hunter,* edited by R.B. Lee and I. DeVore. Pp. 349–352. Chicago: Aldine.
Longacre, W.
  1964 Archaeology as anthropology. *Science* 144(3625):1454–1455.
  1968 Some aspects of prehistoric society in east-central Arizona. In *New perspectives in archaeology,* edited by S.R. Binford and L.R. Binford. Pp. 89–103. Chicago: Aldine.
Longacre, W.A. and J.E. Ayres
  1968 Archaeological lessons from an Apache wickiup. In *New perspectives in archaeology,* edited by S.R. Binford and L.R. Binford. Pp. 151–160. Chicago: Aldine.
MacArthur, R.H., and J.W. MacArthur
  1961 On bird species diversity. *Ecology* 42(3):594–598.
Maguire, B.
  n.d. (ca. 1954) A report on the food plants (*veldkos*) of the !Kung bushmen of the Gautsha Pan and Cigarette areas of northeastern South West Africa, based on collections and observations made from mid-December 1952, until February 1953, in collaboration with the Harvard–Peabody Anthropological Expedition to South West Africa. (Ms.)
Marshall, J.
  1957 Ecology of the !Kung Bushmen of the Kalahari. Harvard senior honors thesis. (Ms.)
Marshall, L.
  1957 The kin terminology system of the !Kung Bushmen. *Africa* 27:1–25.
  1960 !Kung Bushman bands. *Africa* 30:325–355.
  1961 Sharing, talking and giving: Relief of social tensions among !Kung Bushmen. *Africa* 31:231–249.
  1965 The !Kung Bushmen of the Kalahari Desert. In *The peoples of Africa,* edited by J.L. Gibbs. Pp. 241–278. New York: Holt, Rinehart and Winston.
Michel, P.
  1967 Les Grandes étapes de la morphogenese dans les bassins des fleuves Senegal et Gambie pendant le Quaternaire. Paper presented at the Sixth Pan-African Congress on Prehistory. Dakar. (Mimeograph)
Monod, T.
  1958 Majaôat/al/Koubra. *Contribution a l'etude de l'Empty Quarter ouest-Saharien. Notes Aricaines:* 52.
Naroll, R.
  1962 Floor area and settlement population. *American Antiquity* 27(4):587–589.

Orme, B.
1973   Archaeology and ethnography. In *The explanation of culture change,* edited by C. Renfrew. Pp. 481–492. Pittsburgh: University of Pittsburgh Press.

Ortner, D.J., D.W. VonEndt, and M.S. Robinson
1972   The effect of temperature on protein decay in bone: Its significance in nitrogen dating of archaeological specimens. *American Antiquity* 37(4):514–520.

Perkins, D. Jr., and P. Daly
1968   A hunters' village in Neolithic Turkey. *Scientific American* 219(5):96–106.

Pielou, E.C.
1966   The measurement of diversity in different types of biological collections. *Journal of Theoretical Biology* 13:131–144.

Radcliffe-Brown, A.R.
1930   The social organization of Australian tribes: Part I. *Oceania* 1:34–63.

Sabloff, J.A., T.W. Beale, and A.M. Kurland, Jr.
1973   Recent developments in archaeology. *Annals of the American Academy of Political and Social Science* 408:103–118.

Sadek-Kooros, H.
1972   Primitive bone fracturing: A method of research. *American Antiquity* 37(3):369–382.

Sampson, C.G.
1974   *The Stone Age archaeology of Southern Africa.* New York: Academic Press.

Semenov, S.A.
1964   *Prehistoric technology.* Translated by M.W. Thompson. London: Cort, Adams and MacKay.

Service, E.R.
1962   *Primitive social organization: An evolutionary perspective.* New York: Random House.
1966   *The hunters.* Englewood Cliffs, N.J.: Prentice-Hall.

Silberbauer, G.B.
1965   *Report to the government of Bechuanaland on the Bushman survey.* Gaberones.

Simpson, E.H.
1949   Measurement of diversity. *Nature* 163:688.

Smith, C.A.B.
1969   Local fluctuations in gene frequencies. *Annals of Human Genetics* 32:251–260.

Steward, J.M., and F.M. Setzler
1938   Function and configuration in archaeology. *American Antiquity* 4(1):4–10.

Story, R.
1958   Some plants used by the Bushmen in obtaining food and water. Department of Agriculture, Division of Botany, *Memoirs Botanical Survey South Africa,* 30.

Tallgren, A.
1937   The method of prehistoric archaeology. *Antiquity* 11:152–161.

Tanaka, J.
1969   The ecology and social structure of Central Kalahari Bushmen: A preliminary report. *Kyoto University African Studies* 3.

Thomas, E.M.
1958   *The harmless people.* New York: Knopf.

Thompson, D.F.
1939   The seasonal factor in human culture. *Proceedings of the Prehistoric Society* (n.s.) 10:209–221.

Tinley, K.L.
1966   *An ecological reconnaissance of the Moremi Wildlife Reserve—Botswana.* Okavango Wildlife Society, Johannesburg.

Watson, P.J., S.A. LeBlanc, and C.L. Redman
   1971   *Explanation in archaeology.* New York: Columbia University Press.
Weare, P., and A. Yalala
   1971   Provisional vegetation map of Botswana (first revision). *Botswana Notes and Records* **3:**131–147.
Wellington, J.
   1955   *Southern Africa,* Volume I. Cambridge: The University Press.
   1964   *South West Africa and its human issues.* London: Oxford University Press.
Whallon, R., Jr.
   1973   Spatial analysis of occupation floors I: Application of dimensional analysis of variance. *American Antiquity* **38**(3):266–278.
White, C.
   1971   Man and environment in Northwest Arnhem Land. In *Aboriginal man and environment in Australia,* edited by D.J. Mulvaney and J. Golson. Pp. 141–157. Canberra: Australian National University Press.
Wiessner, P.
   1974   A functional estimator of population from floor area. *American Antiquity* **39**(2, Part 1):343–350.
Williams, B.J.
   1968   Establishing cultural heterogeneities in settlement patterns: An ethnographic example. In *New perspectives in archaeology,* edited by S.R. Binford and L.R. Binford. Pp. 161–170. Chicago: Aldine.
   1974   "A model of Band Society." *American Antiquity* **39**(4 Part 2):Memoir 29.
Wilmsen, E.
   1968   Lithic analysis in paleoanthropology. *Science* **191:**982–987.
   1972   *Interaction, spacing behavior and the organization of hunting bands.* (Ms.)
Wilson, D.
   1851   *Archaeology and the prehistoric annals of Scotland.* Edinburgh:
Yellen, J.E.
   1972a   *Honey and plant foods.* Cambridge, Mass.: Social Studies Program, Educational Development Center, Inc.
   1972b   *Animals.* Cambridge, Mass.: Social Studies Program, Educational Development Center, Inc.
   1974   *The !Kung settlement pattern: An archaeological perspective.* Doctoral dissertation, Harvard University, Cambridge, Mass.
   1976   Settlement pattern of the !Kung Bushmen: An archaeological perspective. In *Kalahari hunter gatherers,* edited by R.B. Lee and I. DeVore. Cambridge, Mass.: Harvard University Press. 47–72.
   in press a   Cultural patterning in faunal remains: Evidence from the !Kung Bushmen. In *Experimental archaeology,* edited by D.W. Ingersoll and J.E. Yellen. New York: Columbia University Press.
Yellen, J.E., and H. Harpending
   1972   Hunter gatherer populations and archaeological inference. *World Archaeology* **4**(2):244–253.
Yellen, J.E., and R.B. Lee
   1976   The Dobe-/du/da environment: Considerations for a hunting and gathering way of life. In *Kalahari hunter-gatherers,* edited by R.B. Lee and I. DeVore. Cambridge, Mass.: Harvard University Press. 27–46.

A
B   7
C   8
D   9
E   0
F   1
G   2
H   3
I   4
J   5